SHOTGUN SHOOTING FACTS

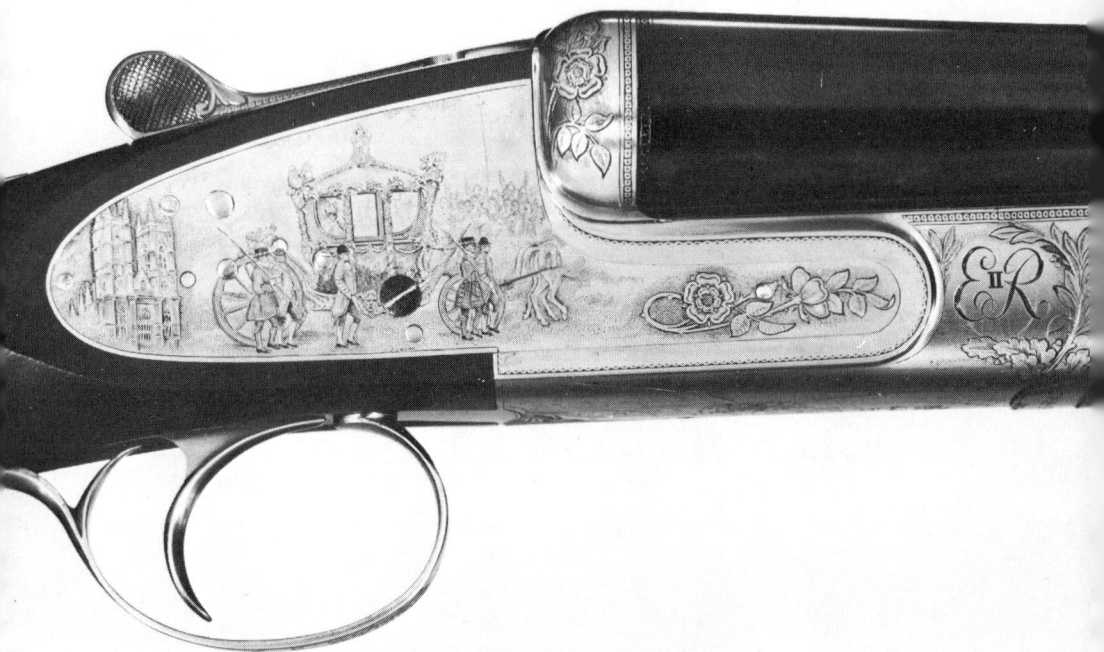

One of the Holland & Holland 'Jubilee' guns. This gun is one of a set of four (two 12-bores and two 20s) made by these celebrated gunmakers to commemorate the Silver Jubilee of Queen Elizabeth II in 1977. All four guns have been engraved by K. C. Hunt with scenes of outstanding occasions in Her Majesty's reign, and they have been assembled in a luxurious silver-mounted cabinet of Macassar ebony specially designed by Algernon Asprey.

SHOTGUN SHOOTING FACTS

Gough Thomas
(G. T. Garwood)

WINCHESTER PRESS

Library of Congress Cataloging in Publication Data

Garwood, Gough Thomas.
    Shotgun shooting facts.

    Published in 1978 under title:
Shooting facts & fancies.
    Includes index.
    1. Shotguns. I. Title.
SK274.5.G37   1979   799.2'02834   78-25639
ISBN 0-87691-283-8

All Rights Reserved
Published by Winchester Press
205 East 42nd Street
New York, N.Y. 10017
First Published in Great Britain by A & C Black Limited

Winchester is a Trademark of Olin Corporation used by Winchester Press, Inc. under
authority and control of the Trademark Proprietor

Printed in the United States of America

Portions of this book first appeared in GOUGH THOMAS'S SECOND GUN BOOK

Contents

List of illustrations

Preface

The previous printings of my *Second Gun Book* having been exhausted by sustained demand, I agreed with the publishers that it should be reissued in this new and much enlarged edition, and under a fresh title to accord with the change in its size and scope. The title of *Shotgun Shooting Facts* was chosen as being more indicative of its content, as well as serving to avoid the confusion often hitherto observed between the two *Gun Books* from my pen.

The object of the book remains the same—that of endeavouring to promote 'a better understanding of the sporting gun and of the things that conduce to its most successful and enjoyable employment in the field'; and I feel I may hope that that object is more fully attained in the present volume than in its predecessor.

I remain gratefully indebted as heretofore to the Editors, proprietors and readers of the *Shooting Times* and to Joan Clifford for her invaluable services as amanuensis and critic.

Acknowledgments

The author and publishers are gratefully indebted to the following firms and parties for permission to use their illustrations in this book:

Messrs. Holland & Holland Ltd., Parker-Hale Ltd. and Luigi Franchi, s.p.a.; the proprietors of *Punch*, Miss Ursula Perry and Mr. Roger Barlow.

To Mildred, my Wife

SHOOTERS, GENERAL

'The first requirement is undoubtedly a deeply-rooted set of gun-safety habits. There is no standard of marksmanship that will atone for any shortcomings in this department.'

1 A Word to Beginners

Given normal physique, eyesight and powers of co-ordination, anyone can become at least an average shot. Beginners who have run into difficulty – and more especially those who are no longer young – may sometimes come to doubt this; but it is true for all that, and they should lay it to heart.

To shoot well, confidence is indispensable, and if, in the course of his early experience, a beginner has lost confidence, or has never acquired it, he can make little progress until it has been restored or built up. He will hardly need to be reminded of the inhibitory effect of loss of confidence on any kind of skilled performance, and of how, in extreme cases, it can bring about something approaching paralysis. And if he still distrusts his ability to learn to shoot as well as the next man, he would do well to consider the essential naturalness of the process.

Thus, the best shooting at winged game is done by the instinctive use of natural faculties that are part of our common heritage. They are the ability to judge the distance and speed of external objects and to co-ordinate our actions therewith. Shooting makes no greater demand on these faculties than catching a ball or throwing a stone; and if, given sufficient practice, we can do such things satisfactorily, then we can shoot equally well, subject only to certain points that I will come to in a moment.

It may be objected that the introduction of the gun removes shooting from all possible comparison with natural actions such as throwing a stone; that the speed of the shot alone makes shooting entirely unnatural, and that the mounting and pointing of the gun and the pulling of the trigger are actions for which our instincts have in no way prepared us.

I would not agree. The high speed of the shot requires only an adjustment of timing, and is entirely advantageous inasmuch as it greatly reduces the distance travelled by the object in the vital interval of the missile's flight. It is partly for this reason that a man can shoot an arrow more accurately than he can throw a spear at a running target – or so I take it.

As for the mounting and pointing of the gun, if it is a reasonably good fit it will conform to the shooter's natural energetic pointing attitude, so that it is very nearly as natural for him to point it correctly as it is to point a finger with an extended arm. The pulling of a well-adjusted trigger is nothing – a mere reflex of the mind's decision to fire.

Yet the fundamental difference between throwing a stone and shooting must be recognised. In the act of throwing, a man makes use of nothing beyond the facilities provided by nature, whereas in shooting he has to use an agent or intermediary in the shape of a gun. And if this intermediary does not conform entirely to his intentions – if it does not shoot just where or when he intends it to shoot, it may more or less completely frustrate him. So it may if

3

it imposes difficulties not inherent in the situation, which it can do – for example, by being too heavy and giving rise to fatigue errors, or by recoiling painfully and causing him to flinch, or by throwing its shot in too tight a cluster, and thus making insufficient allowance for his normal inaccuracy.

Basic needs

So, successful shooting needs not only an adequate physical endowment, a liberal measure of confidence, a sound technique and plenty of practice, but also a gun that is reasonably well adapted both to the shooter and to the kind of sport in which he chiefly engages. Yet many guns are not so adapted, and if the beginner is in persistent difficulty, he should not be too ready to blame himself, or to accept any facile reassurance concerning his gun. It may indeed be gravely at fault, and I have known many cases in which performance has been transformed overnight, so to speak, by a different gun, or by the appropriate modification of one that has previously given unsatisfactory results.

No shooter, therefore, who aspires to improve his performance can afford to ignore those aspects of shotgun lore that may enable him to appraise his gun and ammunition more critically, and to form a closer judgment of their suitability for the tasks they are called upon to perform.

2   Making a Start

It is related of Graf Moritz Sandor, that legendary horseman of the Napoleonic period, that he never even mounted a horse until after his 21st birthday. The story goes that his father, a member of the lesser Hungarian nobility, had, like many before and since, contrived to ruin himself, or at least to involve himself in serious embarrassment, through his excessive devotion to the noblest of beasts, and had determined that his son should not follow his example. The young Sandor accepted the parental prohibition until after he had attained his majority, whereupon he appears to have leapt instantly into the saddle, and in no time at all to have become the nearest thing to a centaur that has ever galloped across the pages of history.

I write from memory and subject to correction, but the case of Sandor certainly represents one of the extreme principles in introducing a beginner to any kind of sport involving personal skill. It is the principle of keeping a boy away from all participation until he is old enough and intelligent enough to benefit from the best instruction available. The opposite principle is, of course, to encourage him to start going through the basic motions as soon as he is physically capable of doing so.

Both schools of thought have their supporting arguments. The delayed-introduction school says that their method is the only one that avoids the formation of what may be undesirable habits at the impressionable age when they may become rooted beyond any possibility of later eradication. The catch-'em-early school, on the other hand, are usually practical people who consider that the total familiarity brought about by early participation is worth the risk.

In shooting, these alternative paths are not so clearly marked, for whereas a boy cannot learn much about horsemanship without getting into the saddle, he can learn and practice much that is important for shooting without actually firing a gun. I myself, when at the Christopher Robin stage, had a very relevant experience. My mother, having had my flaxen curls shorn at a tenderer age than was customary among my early Edwardian contemporaries, agreed that I might be allowed to have a gun. It was one that I had already marked down at a local toyshop, and on an auspicious morning I was taken out by my nurse to buy it. This splendid and unforgettable weapon probably cost all of a couple of shillings, and its strict classification was that of a spring-actuated pop-gun, cocked by a ramrod, and firing a captive cork and a paper percussion cap simultaneously, with superb and astonishing effect.

My first act on arriving home was to free the cork from its degrading ligature, and then to convey to my mother the fact of my new acquisition, and my appreciation of it, in what I thought, in my innocence, was the most appropriate way. In short, I ambushed her, and shot her very successfully; whereat, to my utmost dismay, she descended on me like a ton of bricks, and impressed on me in unforgettable terms that guns must never, never, NEVER be pointed at people. I have learned and forgotten much in the succeeding years, but I have never forgotten that.

This single incident points to what is undoubtedly a fact – that the best way of introducing a boy to the sport of shooting is to let him accompany his father, guardian or other supervising elder on shooting days, and at the earliest stage at which he can be relied on not to get in the way. There should be no suggestion of his carrying even an unloaded gun at this stage – indeed, he should be free to help the proceedings in any appropriate way, and should be called on to do so. He may reinforce the beaters occasionally, or act as a stop, or help with a young dog, or carry spare cartridges.

This treatment will very quickly reveal if the boy is keen. In that case, he will ask questions – all sorts of questions – when he gets home. 'What was that funny bird . . . ?' 'Why didn't you shoot at that single partridge . . . ?' 'Why did you grip my arm when Mr A. stepped over that barbed wire . . . ?' All the while he will be learning fast. The funny bird was a so-and-so. You didn't shoot at the single partridge because the beaters were getting too close. And you gripped his arm because you wanted him to notice that Mr A. had not unloaded his gun, which he should have done.

But if the questions are not forthcoming, and especially if he does not ask when you are going out again, and whether he may go with you, you should contemplate the possibility that his interests may lie elsewhere.

If, on the other hand, there is no doubt about the boy's keenness, the question will soon arise as to when he is going to be allowed to have a gun. Much here will depend on the sort of boy; but I am a great believer in letting one of the right kind have a gun at the earliest reasonable age, and allowing him to carry it unloaded on regular occasions out with his elders. It should be made clear to him that he will be allowed to start shooting when he has fully demonstrated his mastery of the safety rules, in which he should have been suitably instructed. It is a good idea to provide him with a copy of the *Gun Code*, and to check his knowledge of it, and to require him to go through the appropriate motions in the field with his unloaded gun, as an essential qualifying course, before being allowed to have live ammunition.

At this stage a normal, healthy boy's preoccupation will be to get into action as soon as possible, and given half an opportunity, he will do so on his own. This, then, is the time to see that he absorbs some sound shooting doctrine – on the responsibility that goes with the power of a gun; on the ethics of taking life and the avoidance of all wantonness in killing; and on the rôle of the sportsman as a conservator. Soon he will be fully grown, and should be equipped at all points to defend his sport against those who would abolish it.

Choice of gun

There are others far more competent than I am to offer instruction on the art of shooting, as such, and all I want to add on behalf of the young beginner are some thoughts on guns and cartridges.

Some people think that a boy should be started on a ·410 as a matter of course. Others will start him straightaway on a 12-bore. I have known of a 17-year-old hesitantly speculating whether he might take to something a bit more adult than his 28-bore; and conversely, in *Gough Thomas's Gun Book*, I have shown a photograph of a little squidge of an 11½-year-old girl (now, I am sure, grown into a beautiful young lady) who at that age was regularly and successfully shooting skeet with an F.N. 2-shot 12-bore, weighing probably over 7 lbs and firing full trap loads.

Middle-of-the-road opinion inclines to the 20-bore as the ideal gun on which to start a boy. Much again depends on the boy: but it needs recognising that it is more important to protect him from painful recoil than it is from rather too much weight. Weight may tire him but undue recoil, *such as that of a fully-loaded, light 20-bore*, can cause him to develop the fatal habit of flinching. For my own part, I would give a boy a light 12-bore as soon as he can carry and swing it; and I would start him with $\frac{7}{8}$ oz 'Trainer' cartridges, loaded with No. 7 shot.

At the same time, I would do everything I could to disabuse his mind of some of the typical delusions of young shooters. They are delusions respecting the merit of heavy or magnum loads; of heavily choked barrels; and of certain types of modern guns. But since these delusions are not infrequently shared by beginners of more mature years, I will deal with them later.

All I would add for the young beginner is the advice to broaden his knowledge by reading good shooting and natural history books, and to recognise that a gun is only a passport. It is in the subsequent travel that most of the enduring delights of shooting are to be found.

The late beginner

The beginner of mature years presents a whole range of special problems. The age bracket is much wider than that we have been considering. There are men still young who have been too busy with their education and training, and mounting the first rungs of some professional ladder, to have had much time to think of shooting, but in whom an early predisposition revives as the pressure eases. There are men in middle age, but still vigorous, who may take to it for social, or even business reasons, and who get firmly hooked. And there are those who have retired and taken to a country life, and who wish to take part in country pursuits.

That, I think, is a fairly typical spectrum of the late beginners. They will share a progressively reduced physical adaptability, which may be compensated in part by an increased readiness to submit to instruction and advice. They should accordingly put themselves under the best man they can for preliminary coaching, and for getting fitted out with a suitable gun.

There is, however, a danger here. I find that the older beginners are especially prone to what I have called gun–fit hypochondria, and to attribute any preliminary lack of proficiency to their guns. I have known them to go from expert to expert and to become thoroughly frazzled by the different advice they have received, both on shooting technique and on the kind of stock they require for a perfect fit.

To say this is not to impugn the experts: there is more than one established and successful technique, and their leading exponents may reasonably prescribe something different in the way of stock dimensions for a given man. For example, the majority of shooters undoubtedly use the Stanbury or natural stance, with the feet at 1 and 3 o'clock. But according to the Churchill school, this is wrong: the forward stance which they advocate requires that the feet should be at 11 and 1 o'clock, and this usually involves a larger cast-off for a perfect fit.

A – The Churchill or forward stance.

B – The Stanbury or natural stance. The photographs show how, in (A), the shooter has to lean his head more over to the left than in (B) in order to align his gun. This explains why instructors who favour the Churchill style often prescribe conspicuously more cast-off than do others.

The position of a beginner who allows himself to oscillate between these rivals schools is not to be envied. He needs to make up his mind once and for all in the light of his personal reactions and experience. The fact of the matter is probably that the Churchill method is best suited to men who resemble Churchill's physical type – short-necked men, that is to say, of sturdy build, and rather stiff in the middle piece. As I have said before, a man is a flexible, adjustable and educable form of gun carriage, and is unlikely to be dependent for success on the adoption of a particular technique or a particular form of stock. One thing is certain – that so long as he is introspectively preoccupied with these things he will not shoot well. It is not until the mind and the attention are directed fully outwards that he will realise his natural potential.

Guns and ammunition

Some special considerations arise on the choice of a gun for late beginners. Left to themselves, these men incline to conservative decisions, and wisely so in the present instance. One who is unconscious of any decline of strength and stamina, and is free from any abnormality of physique or vision, would be well advised to adopt a conventional gun for mixed shooting in this country. By that I mean a regular English game gun – a 12-bore side-by-side with double triggers and 28-in. barrels, weighing not more than $6\frac{1}{2}$ lbs. The right barrel should be bored improved cylinder, proved by test at the gunmaker's plate to give a well-distributed pattern of about 50 per cent with a standard load of No. 6 shot, and the left bored half to three quarters choke.

Older beginners, conscious of declining powers, may well be advised to go in for a lighter gun, more especially a 25-in. barrelled 12-bore weighing about 6 lbs. The lightness, balance and fast-handling quality of these guns makes them outstandingly attractive to elderly shooters, many of whom indeed have found them admirably adapted to their needs. But not all: some need more forward inertia to keep their swing going, and are better served by somewhat longer barrels. For such as these, 27 inches can be a most satisfactory length.

False gods

Beginners, and more especially young beginners, are prone to certain familiar delusions. Broadly, they arise from a conception that our ordinary English double-barrelled guns, and the standard cartridges and loads with which they are associated, are out of date, and that better results are obtainable with repeaters, over-and-unders, small-bore magnums, magnum loads and so on. In individual cases, and to meet special needs, all these things may have merit, but broadly their advantages are delusory. It must be remembered that our conventional guns were evolved under intense competition, and by a trade so loosely organised that improvements could be and were introduced almost as soon as they were conceived. Their present static character is thus a measure of their nearness to perfection. The repeaters were introduced as an outlet for the American arms industry after the Civil War and in response to the needs of the American market gunner, now dead along with the heca-tombs of game he slaughtered.

The over-and-under, though sharing so many of the virtues of the side-by-side gun, is the older form of double-barrelled weapon. It was reintroduced as a novelty, but is marginally disadvantageous as a sporting gun on most points of appraisal. Small-bore magnums are largely a commercial cult.

As for magnum loads, it must be recognised that our standard loads, and the gauges to which they were assigned, were freely evolved out of considera-tion of their fitness for purpose. Heavier loads add very little range indeed in return for the heavier and less responsive guns they demand, or the greater recoil they inflict on the active shooter.

3 *The Complete Shooter*

In the circles in which I spent my youth, my contemporaries and I seemed to be chronically hard-up. Different family circumstances did not seem to modify the prevalence of this condition to any marked extent, probably be-cause it was held by most parents and guardians of our day to be a good thing to keep the rising generation on a short financial tether. There was much to be said for it, for it gave us a sense of value for money, and made us resource-ful, as well as fostering our appreciation of the simpler and more enduring pleasures.

One of the consequences of this state of affairs is that those of us who were keen on shooting, and who found ourselves in due season in possession of a thoroughly presentable sporting gun, were to be counted as the lucky ones. Not for the likes of us were the pairs of Purdeys subscribed for by a grateful tenantry to mark our coming of age. Rather were we fortunate to acquire a parental cast-off in sound condition, or, by heroic saving or stroke of good fortune, to be in a position to buy ourselves a good second-hand gun. Such guns were plentiful then; and if of a slightly out-of-date character, such as non-ejectors or hammer guns, were amazingly cheap by modern standards.

In these circumstances, some of us came to be the delighted owners of undeniable old thoroughbreds, which, without our realising it, not only established in our minds certain standards of what a sporting gun should be and do, but provided us with a worthy object for that curious atavistic affection which a gun is capable of inspiring in the heart of a civilised man. 'We've only one virginity to lose,' said Kipling, 'and where we lose it there our heart shall be'; and many a man in the circumstances I have imagined will find some echo of that truth in his memory of his first real gun and the sport he had with it.

With this background to my thoughts, I am occasionally disconcerted by the appearance of what is to me a relatively new phenomenon – that of a young man, with no special facilities for shooting, or even family traditions of shooting, who has already surrounded himself with a seraglio of guns, almost invariably of the wrong kind. I suppose he is the British representative of a class long known by the Americans as 'gun-bugs' – men who have a compulsive urge to acquire guns simply as guns, and not for specific use, or as objects of technical study, or as investments, or with the taxonomical discipline of a genuine collector. The comparatively recent emergence of these young, homegrown gun-bugs is obviously one of the results of changing social conditions whereby the younger generation have far more money to spend than we ever dreamt of, and at a time of their lives when impulse suffers least constraint from prudence and judgment.

The origin of this particular impulse is not far to seek: we have only to scratch the thin veneer of our civilisation to lay it bare. Our primitive ancestors – so very near to us on the anthropological time-scale – had no built-in weapons, as had so many of their fellow-members of the animal kingdom, and those they learned to contrive greatly improved their ability to defend themselves from their enemies, and to procure nourishing food. What, perhaps, is more significant in the present context is that they did much to redress the physical balance between one man and another, and to remove the sense of inferiority likely to afflict young, immature males as they regarded their fully-developed, powerful and maybe oppressive elders.

We need look no farther, then, for the origins of the instinct that causes young boys to find delight in toy weapons, and young men in real ones. It is an instinct that, in a mature and civilised man, may be sublimated and led off into several channels, where it may fertilise a whole field of rewarding activities. The consideration brings me sharply to my point.

It is not for me to suggest how anyone else should spend his money or seek his pleasure, but I may be allowed to point out how extensive and delightful is the field to which the sporting gun provides the passport, and the pity of not passing beyond the gate. Inside it, may be found a range of absorbing interests to which guns are merely incidental. Yet so absorbing are these interests that they are capable of bringing about a complete reorientation of a man's life from a town-centred to a country-centred existence, whereby he may gain great relief from the physical and mental stresses of our over-urbanised civilisation.

I have a good instance in mind. It is that of a successful young business man of the pre-war days, who had a dormant fondness for guns – probably a mere hangover from his boyhood. But something made him think that he would like to take up shooting, and as the idea developed in his mind, he realised that, lacking a country background, he could never become a regular sportsman until he had made good his deficiencies. So he started, not by buying a gun, but, if you please, by studying farming. It was a very intelligent proceeding, for originally he would probably have been unable to distinguish between oats and barley, or between a swede and a mangold. He also studied bird books and, in due course, shooting books, and later, when I met him partridge shooting, now many years ago, he impressed me as a thoroughly competent sportsman, knowledgeable beyond the average, and rich in his mental acquisitions and the splendid dividends they had brought him. When I last knew him, he had become very keen on working spaniels, of which he was a successful breeder. All that, and his invariably good field manners, had made him a good specimen of a complete shooter.

Ptarmigan shooting in Wester Ross. An aspect of the 'extensive and delightful field to which the sporting gun provides the passport'.

4 Be Natural

I remember a case of a young shooter who had been entered to the sport in what might well appear to have been the best possible way. He had been sent to a shooting school, where he probably received good and competent instruction, and had been duly provided with a correctly fitted gun. Contrary to expectations, things had not gone well with him. The fit of the gun had come under suspicion; there had been a return visit to the shooting school; and in the upshot he found himself to be thoroughly frazzled and shooting worse than ever.

This case led me to speculate whether it is altogether a good thing to start a young beginner in this way. Cases are common in which boys – perhaps I should say confident and extrovert boys – are given a gun, or manage to lay hands on one, which they then proceed to use with little or no formal instruction, but with a surprising degree of competence at the simpler kinds of shots. Shooting, after all, is an entirely natural process, as natural as throwing a stone. True, guns were only invented yesterday, when viewed against the time-scale of human development, but they introduced no problem with which our natural powers of co-ordination were not fully competent to deal. Even some of the apes throw stones and make good play with them, according to travellers' accounts; and to adapt this faculty – highly developed, no doubt, in primitive man – to shooting with a gun, the only essential thing needed was an adjustment of timing.

The secret of success

If we watch a really first-class performer at work, we are likely to be impressed most of all by the unhurried naturalness of his shooting. Percy Stanbury was outstanding for this, and I suspect that it was the foundation on which he built his remarkable success. But if a young beginner is placed under professional instruction from the start and duly impressed with all the things that he must not do, as well as all those that he must try to remember, he may well acquire a degree of stiffness that will impair his performance until he can learn to get rid of it.

Of course, much depends on the instructor, as well as on the pupil. Most of us can remember schoolmasters who had the unfortunate capacity to freeze us into a dumb stupor, whilst others were able to stimulate such intelligence as we possessed into happy activity. I hope that there are no shooting school instructors in the first category: if there are, they must do a lot of harm. The best instructor, other things being equal, is the man who can impart knowledge without imparting inhibitions. The late and truly lamented

Norman Clark was, I feel, outstandingly good at this. No one could watch him instructing some tiny squidge of a boy without appreciating the essential gentleness of the man, and its calming and encouraging effect on his small pupil.

An old friend of mine, a very good and experienced shot, when asked what was his secret, replied in short order, 'A Purdey gun, Schultze powder and a big dose of applied psychology.' We can pass over the gun and the powder, but I am not sure what he meant by a big dose of applied psychology. From the style and competence of his performance, however, I am inclined to think that he was referring to the importance of approaching shooting with the right mental attitude – relaxed, and with a clear recognition that no great issue hangs on whether a bird is hit or missed. He was quick, but never jerky, and his shooting had a notable air of spontaneity, like an instinctive physical reaction, and equally natural.

Spontaneity, indeed, is a key word in this context, and I shall have occasion to repeat it several times in these pages. When I first tried to shoot the ZZ birds at Monte Carlo, the thing that crippled my style was the lack of spontaneity imposed by the formal preparations involved before taking the shot – gun to shoulder, 'Apprêtez!' and then 'Tirez!' – probably not the right words, but the trapper seemed to understand them. I recall that when I returned home, I performed a practical experiment designed to compare the speed and accuracy of performing a simple physical motion or exercise, first spontaneously, and then deliberately. The results, I thought, were striking. Not only was the spontaneous performance more nearly perfect than the deliberate one, but it took only one-tenth of the time. (See page 57).

Stance and fit

There is more than general style involved in this subject of naturalness in shooting. It extends to footwork, stance and fitting.

A West Country shooter has remarked that our two leading instructional books on shooting, by Churchill and Stanbury & Carlisle respectively, lay down totally different rules for the basic stance when preparing to take a shot, as explained in the preceding chapter, and I am asked to say which of these attitudes is the better.

I am afraid that I am not qualified to adjudicate. In most shooting, apart from trapshooting and driving, the question is largely an academic one, the position of the shooter's feet being determined to a large extent by the tussocks, stones, mud, brambles, swedes, turnips, mangolds, kale-stems, clay, plough-furrows and other features of the terrain in or among which they happen to be placed at the critical moment.

Still, on the formal question, my ideas are based on what is natural. Thus, it is generally agreed that the best work with the shotgun at flying targets is done by instinctive pointing, rather than by aiming and calculation; and the best shooting posture is therefore the one that most nearly corresponds to a natural, energetic pointing attitude, such as one would adopt without a gun. This leads straight to the second or Stanbury stance, as already described.

From this it follows that the best way of fitting a gun is to mould it, so to speak, to the natural pointing attitude, as described. A shooter thus fitted is called on to the least possible extent to adapt himself to his gun and to the act of shooting. He does not have to remember to do this, that or the other with his head or limbs or body, or even to acquire any corresponding habits. Such habits, however well grounded, are liable to break down under the stress of excitement, with the result that the gun is incorrectly mounted, and a miss is almost certain to follow.

This principle of deriving the shooting posture from the natural energetic pointing attitude, and then moulding the gun to that attitude, is one in which I have great confidence. I call it the principle of 'minimum adaptation', and have described it more fully in the third edition of *Shotguns and Cartridges*. As already mentioned, Churchill's preference for the forward stance is, I believe, traceable to the fact of his having been a stocky man, with a stiff middle-piece, which made it difficult for him to cope with birds swinging to his left unless he was already half turned round to meet them. I have tried it in the past, but, with me, it involves a marked stiffness, and a bad departure from what is natural.

5   Shoot With Your Mind

One does not have to dip very deeply into shooting literature before coming across advice to concentrate as being indispensable to success. Yet I believe that advice to be largely misconceived.

It used to be, and probably still is, one of the tenets of psychology that it is impossible to concentrate for more than a brief interval on anything that does not change. It is more than ever difficult to do so if the thing concerned is not a material object, but only an abstract idea. And when there is not even an idea to concentrate on, the difficulty becomes insurmountable. In such circumstances, the only response a willing student can make to the command to concentrate is to go rigid in expectation of the next move. But rigidity and good shooting do not mix.

Consider a driven game shooter standing in his place at the beginning of a drive. If you ask him to concentrate, what has he to concentrate on? The blank sky before him? Or the idea of a bird appearing in that blank sky? If it is the first, I would say that he simply cannot do that for long. And if it is the second,

The veteran shooter can often out-shoot his juniors despite some inevitable decline in his physical powers. The chief reason is likely to be the more relaxed and philosophical state of mind in which he approaches his task.

I would submit that concentration on an imaginary bird is a poor preparation for dealing with a real one which, when it appears, may appear in a different place or follow a different course.

The rough shooter, working a spaniel or other hunting dog, is better situated to concentrate, for he can concentrate on his dog, and should undoubtedly do so. Indeed, it is easy, for in that case he has something that is on the move, and of intrinsic interest, to concentrate on. But that is not concentrating on shooting. All he can do in that respect is to be prepared; and being prepared is a very different thing from concentrating. Preparedness is in fact the key to the point I am trying to make.

My cat once gave me a valuable lesson in the difference between concentration and preparedness. He had caught a mouse, and while it was still undamaged as a runner, put it on the ground, as if inviting it to run away. But the poor mouse knew that there was no hole or cover near enough at hand for him to stand a chance of reaching it before the cat could catch him again. The cat knew it too. So well did he know it that he lay down and relaxed and pretended to go to sleep. The relaxation was genuine enough, but there was nothing genuine about the appearance of sleep. If that mouse had stirred a whisker, the cat would have been in action before you could say 'knife'. Poor mousey knew that as well as I did.

So if the studious shooter would strike out all references to 'concentration' from his shooting books and substitute 'relaxed preparedness', I think the change would be for the better.

But although I believe this to be the right formula for the shooter waiting to take a shot, it offers little guidance to the state of mind in which he can best go into action. Then indeed he needs to concentrate – but on what? On the bird, unmistakably, if he is using the follow-through technique, or on the appropriate spot ahead of it if he is practising lead-and-swing.

For success, the concentration in this case must be total: there must be no partial diversion of it towards the gun barrels, and no internal reflection of it. By that I mean that the shooter must not indulge in any introspection – he must not say to himself, 'Now I must remember to do so-and-so, and not to do something else.' Until any such admonitions, which he may have derived from a coach or from his own experience, have sunk below the level of conscious thought, they may actually hinder performance, as when an instrumentalist deliberately changes his technique. For a time he may have to go into purdah, until the new technique has seeped invisibly into his brain, nerves, and muscles.

Spontaneity plus

Given a relaxed preparedness before the shot, and a total concentration on the right thing while it is being taken, there still remains something necessary if the shooter is to realise his full potential. It was a factor that emerged when I was discussing with an American friend the curious and distressing lapses from which most shooters occasionally suffer, and more particularly one of my own. My friend quoted a similar case in which one of the guns at a field trial, and a very competent performer in the ordinary way, fired no less than twelve shots in succession without touching a bird. Until a recent experience, I cannot remember ever doing as badly as that.

In my case, the trouble was clearly due to concentrating on the wrong thing – to trying to remember, in short, that I was shooting with a single-triggered gun. All went well until I missed a good second-barrel chance, and then another, through fumbling for a second trigger that was not there. Then, my concentration on trigger-pulling rather than on the birds caused my shooting to go really to pieces, until I struck an all-time low.

My friend, lumping cases of this sort together, diagnoses them as being caused in the first instance by 'trying too hard'. But then he goes on to couple that with what he calls a total loss of *élan vital*; and there, I think, he put his finger right on the missing ingredient. No doubt he used that French expression for lack of a ready English equivalent. I should say that he meant what I have previously tried to convey by the word spontaneity, and perhaps something more. *Elan*, according to my dictionary, implies 'ardour inspired by . . . enthusiasm,' and it is a quality that has been conspicuous in some of the best shots I have seen in action. It mixes with my idea of spontaneity as brandy does with soda. How many times, I wonder, have you been stung by a right-barrel miss into swinging with an access of energy and determination – or *élan*, if you like – on to the same bird with your second barrel, and killing it stone dead at greater range? Perhaps as often as I have, and that is quite a few times.

When I was a lot younger than I am now, I used to try to protect myself from loss of self-esteem, and consequent loss of confidence, by pitching my pretensions unduly low. True, if you take the line that you are but an indifferent shot, you are insured against disappointing your friends. But the mental attitude is inconsistent with the cultivation of spontaneity and *élan vital*. Better to keep a faithful record of kills to cartridges for a season or two, and thus establish irrefutable evidence that, far from being an indifferent shot, you are fully up to the average – perhaps well beyond the average – laid down by game-shooting authorities of undeniable reputation. Armed and fortified with this, and perhaps with the more philosophical attitude that comes with age and experience, and you can ride with ease the buffets of temporary adversity.

6 *The Importance of Style*

One of the words which reflect current outlooks by the frequency or infrequency with which they are used is undoubtedly 'style'. We hear much less about style in anything now than we did in the days of my youth – which suggests a line of thought that I must resolutely avoid following. After all, I am writing here about guns and shooting.

My dictionary has a great deal to say about style, but the definition best in line with my theme is this one: 'Manner or method of acting or performing, especially a distinctive manner or method; as the Italian style of singing, or a cricketer's style of play.'

Unless my memory has betrayed me, several of the old shooting classics stress the importance of cultivating a good style, which transcends mere technique, and is scarcely less important. Someone once said that he would rather see a bird missed in good style than killed in a bad one – a remark justified by the consideration that the possessor of a good style is in every way likely to do better on the whole than one of opposite case.

I would endorse that; and, in so doing, must face the need to say just what I mean by a good style in shooting. It is not easy, because there are several things that contribute to a good style. Separately regarded, they are posture, timing and motion; but it is only in the synthesis, and not in the analysis, that style can be seen.

Marked contrasts

Perhaps the outstanding thing about a good style is that it makes shooting look easy. My friend A. makes the point. He never seems to be taken by surprise by the appearance of game; and although he can move like lightning when required he never flusters, and always seems to have more time than my other friend, B. When something gets up unexpectedly in front of B., he gives the impression of having had an electric shock, and I am sure that a high-speed camera would show him to make some superfluous, spasmodic motions of limbs and body before he settles into his shooting posture. These preliminary and superfluous movements take time, of which there may be extremely little to spare. The result is that when he fires, he does so more hurriedly than does A., and with less prospect of success.

Of course, we have to recognise that there is something in a good style that cannot be cultivated, and something in a bad one that cannot be rectified. There are innate qualities involved, such as those that make one person habitually graceful and another one clumsy. Yet there is a mental element concerned on which the man who studies to improve his style can operate. I am sure that the impression I get of B's having had an electric shock is caused by the discharge – I could almost call it the disruptive discharge – of a preliminary mental tension, which he has to get rid of before he can settle down to doing what is necessary for taking his shot. A study of shooting photographs will occasionally reveal a man caught in this electric shock phase. I have been so caught myself, and the result is not flattering.

But a man should not, and need not, approach field shooting in a state of mental tension. There is nothing significant at stake, and the mind can be tranquillised by a deliberate recognition of the fact. Only thus can that condition of relaxed preparedness be achieved, whereby the shot can be taken with complete spontaneity. And in that word lies much of what goes to make a good style and good shooting. Elsewhere in this book there is a description of an experiment in the performance of a simple physical exercise, first spontaneously and then deliberately. The result was striking: not only was the required exercise carried out more fluently and accurately when done spontaneously, but it took only one-tenth of the time required for its deliberate performance. The significance of this in relation to shooting hardly needs stressing.

If I had not previously realised the value of spontaneity in shooting, it would have been brought to my notice by an experience I had this morning on which I write. I was walking alone over some of my ground, nominally in pursuit of partridges, for which I was prepared. But there was nothing tense about my preparedness, for my mind was turning sadly on the recent loss of my little springer bitch, Shelagh, until her death my only dog. I was just thinking what a barren exercise shooting would be to me if it depended solely on the gun, when a covey of partridges got up rather wild and swung off to my left. But even as they took off, I saw to my astonishment the leading bird collapse in the air. Heart failure? Not a bit of it: I had shot it! But the remarkable thing is that the fact did not penetrate to my conscious mind until after I had seen the bird fall, and had just had enough time to start registering astonishment. My action in shooting, therefore, must have been absolutely spontaneous, and very quick. There could have been nothing corresponding to B's disruptive discharge of mental tension, and in the circumstances I am prepared to believe that, for once, I shot in good style.

I would say, therefore, that so far as good style does not depend on innate qualities – so far as it can be cultivated – it is largely a matter of cultivating the right mentality. This requires a balanced view of the issue of hit or miss, and something that is not concentration, for that produces tension, but rather a relaxed preparedness and a free spontaneity of action.

'Better a bird missed in good style than hit in bad.'

7　A Whiff of Atavism

I was looking through some old photographs in the hope of finding something suitable for illustrating a press article. One in particular attracted my attention. It was taken in the New Forest when I was one of the Crown Licensees authorised to shoot there. That was the best part of twenty-five years ago. It shows me and my wife and my spaniel Bruce at the foot of the sandy, heathery track leading steeply up to Sloden Wood from the west. The camera appears to have gone off unexpectedly as we were debating our route.

One or two details catch the eye: the tail of a cock pheasant sticking out of my Payne-Gallwey game bag; the muddied seat of my breeches resulting from an earlier and undignified mishap; and the evidence of the fresh breeze coming from over the Wiltshire Downs, which is blowing the spaniel's windward ear straight out before him. The gun I am carrying is evidently my 27-inch Henry Atkin, which had then only recently displaced my old 30-inch Purdey, for long my favourite Forest gun. The shadows show that it was towards the end of the day. It had been a heavenly one.

What gave so many of those old Forest occasions their wonderful quality? I can only speculate. The bags were very small. On this occasion, there is no evidence that we had bagged more than one pheasant; and it is true that a single cock, well hunted, well shot and well retrieved was held to redeem many such days. But we had also probably hunted and flushed half a dozen hens, which we were not allowed to shoot, and maybe had been outwitted by another cock or two. So, if we sometimes came home with a clean gun, we usually saw enough game to give these expeditions an authentic character.

But it was not only that. In the solitude of the old, self-sown woods and their heather and bracken-covered margins, there was often no evidence of the existence of the modern world we know so well and love so little; and there were times when, under these influences, we seemed to undergo an atavism. It is hardly surprising, for we were doing substantially what our remote, hunting ancestors might have done over the greater part of the history of mankind, and in surroundings that they themselves would have found thoroughly familiar.

There was no part of this age-old Forest ('New' some 900 years ago) that was better calculated to evoke this feeling than the spot where we were standing. Sloden, a wood on a hill, was the site of an Ancient British town, noted for its pottery. It was surrounded by a bank and ditch, and was no doubt once palisaded. Where we stood, many a Bronze Age Briton will have stopped and hailed the gate-keeper. One can picture them: tillers of the soil and herdsmen returning from their labours at the end of the day; hunting parties; scouts; peaceful travellers and traders; and emissaries from neighbouring tribes. And moving off along the track one can imagine a pack-horse

Where we stood, many a Bronze Age Briton will have stopped and hailed the gate-keeper.

train of sturdy Celtic garrons, with their panniers full of the Sloden pottery, carefully packed in bracken, and destined to be bartered for wool, say from the western downlands, or even bronze ingots from Dartmoor.

'*Do their spirits drift on the wind, the ancient ones?*'

I rather think they do: there were times when I felt very close to these old folk – sufficiently often for it to have given the sport I enjoyed in the Forest a rare and indefinable quality. And whenever I had an exceptional day – perhaps four pheasants or the equivalent, including mallard, teal and woodcock – I used to think that shooting could yield no greater delight. For all the opportunities I enjoyed of more sociable and more productive sport, this, I used to say to myself, is the real thing.

SHOOTERS, IN ACTION

'George,' said an eminent trapshooter to a friend who had gone off his form, 'why don't you stop thinking and just shoot.'

8 Workmen and Their Tools

When I was a young chap, already using a 12-bore, a teenage friend of mine, who had done some shooting with a ·22 rifle, both in the field and on the range, aroused my indignation by expressing contempt for the whole art of shooting with a shotgun, which, in his view, was not an art at all. With the large spread of shot issuing from the muzzle, it was obviously too disgustingly easy for words!

A little later, he himself acquired a shotgun, and so far justified his opinion that he shot well on his very first essay. I am not aware, however, that this early promise was sustained, for when we came together in the same party, several years later, his performance, I noticed, was no better than my own.

Over the years, I have come across quite a number of cases of this sort, with which, I daresay, the professional shooting coaches are thoroughly familiar. All that is needed is for the young beginner to have good natural powers of co-ordination, a free and uninhibited action, and – perhaps most important of all – a serene, unpunctured confidence. That is what explained my young friend's success. He was totally convinced that the thing was easy, and so it *was* easy. At least, it was easy until that early confidence of his was undermined. The shock of his first 'off' day may have done it, or a patch of really difficult shooting. I remember perfectly well my own first really bad day, when it seemed that my cartridges must have been loaded with sand. All that happened, I should say, was that I missed a few birds in succession. Confidence slumped, and so I missed a few more. Then I became like the Irish steeplechase jockey at the Grand National – 'Murther! The dhrink's died out of me, and me on the wrong side of Becher's!' For him, we may be sure, the race was over. So it was for me on that black day. Youthful confidence, a buoyant craft in fair weather, can prove a frail one in a rough sea. The thought introduces my theme.

Alongside these cases of early competence are others of the opposite kind. They are those of beginners, particularly young beginners, who write to me despondently about their performance. A letter from one of them – a 15-year-old Dorset lad – lies on my desk. He says that he has been doing 'quite a lot' of pigeon shooting over decoys, but is worried about his 'continual missing'. He uses a French 16-bore, bored half and full choke, in which he fires Grand Prix cartridges loaded with No. 5 or 6 shot.

There is so much that may have gone wrong in cases of this sort that the only thing I can be sure about is that confidence has been reduced to a very low ebb. So my first task is to try to build it up. I tell my young clients what is perfectly true, and what they should never allow themselves to doubt, namely, that provided they are not suffering from any physical disability, and are possessed of normal eyesight and powers of co-ordination, they can be brought to shoot as well as the next man. Sometimes, when performance is extremely bad, I encourage them to take comfort from the fact, because the indication then is that there is something glaringly wrong, which a professional coach could immediately spot and put right. There is indeed a merit in being a sufficiently rotten shot, like an Eminent Military Personage in my youth, who, according to a friend of mine, who saw him shoot on at least one big occasion, missed everything. It is the merit of consistency, which, given a new direction, is potentially capable of turning a conspicuously bad shot into a conspicuously good one.

So, for the rest, I usually try to persuade my young friends who are in trouble to put themselves in the hands of the nearest gunsmith who, if he cannot offer any regular coaching, can usually spot any glaring fault in gun mounting or pointing (including master eye trouble), or any obvious unsuitability in the gun, such as might arise from bad fit or excessive choke. He can also put the beginner in touch with the nearest gun club, where he would be welcome as a prospective member, and would almost certainly find someone only too pleased to offer him some help.

Fallible guns

It is said that a bad workman always blames his tools. Whether he does or not I cannot say, but I have never yet met a good workman who was prepared to tolerate bad ones. The better the workman, the more critical of his tools he is likely to be, and the more efficient the condition they are likely to be in. So with guns; and I have little patience with those cheerful mentors who say, 'Never you mind about your gun, sonny! Your gun's all right – all you have to do is to point it in the right place.' The gun may be far from right, and is easily capable of letting a young shooter down. An example is a Spanish gun which, though nominally bored half and full choke, gave super-choke patterns – 73 and 77 per cent – with both barrels. This nominal boring, be it noted, is the same as that attributed to his French 16-bore by my young Dorset correspondent. I wonder if it, too, gives super-choke patterns? If so, it is not surprising that he is continually missing.

I have on my desk at this moment a letter awaiting reply from a New Zealand correspondent, who quotes the example of a gun capable of explaining the worst shooting on record – even that of my Eminent Military Personage. It was a Winchester M.1200 pump gun – originally, no doubt, an efficient weapon; but it had had a Continental variable choke attachment fitted. These devices, as I have often pointed out, are in themselves likely to make a gun shoot low, both by their depressing the bore axis in relation to the line of sight and by their adding a negative component to the flip of the barrel. But this particular device had been fitted out of true and at a slight downward angle to the bore. The result was that the gun shot *three feet* low at 40 yds! Would it have needed a bad workman to complain of such a tool? I think not.

As I said before, in my youth my friends and I were usually hard up. But good quality English guns were plentiful and cheap – particularly if somewhat out of date, such as hammer guns or non-ejectors. The result was that many if not most of us fitted ourselves out, or were fitted out, with guns that had been properly regulated when they were built. But now things have changed. Guns of the kind described have become scarce and dear, and we have a flood of inexpensive Continental productions – many of them excellent value – to tempt the flush modern youth into the purchase of a new gun. It may be a thoroughly sound one, but it will not have been regulated at the factory, and until it has been, there is always the possibility that the density or quality of the patterns, or the centering of the charge, may be such as to prejudice performance.

Errors and corrections

I know I harp on this point, but it needs harping on. Some fresh aspects now emerge.

The first is that, although it is advantageous in general rough shooting to have a gun that throws its charge well up – say, 6 in. at 40 yds – this may not be true for pigeon decoying, when many shots are taken at birds dropping in. What is ordinarily an inbuilt compensation for the general tendency to shoot under rising birds may then operate as a source of error. My young Dorset correspondent's gun is particularly suspect on this point, because French gunmakers appear to be more anxious than any others to secure a good charge elevation, often building up their standing breeches to an ugly extent for this purpose.

Then, my New Zealand correspondent's experience of the result of a choke attachment with a slight downward cast shows what could be done with one cast upwards. I have, in fact, previously mentioned the possibility of increasing the charge elevation of a gun by giving a slight upward set to the ventilated part of a choke attachment.

Finally, a Dutch correspondent recommends a French book by Dr R. Bommier on 'How to Shoot Well' (*Pour Réussir dans le Tir de Chasse*) in which several means for altering the point of impact of the shot charge are given, including grinding away one side only of the choke. This resembles the off-set recess choke described on page 244. The evidence is that English gunmakers have not previously given enough attention to these tricks.

9 *Taking One Thing with Another*

Taking one thing with another – a game beloved by our politicians in the manipulation of statistics – is of special significance in wing shooting. I say wing shooting because what I want to say will not bear with the same force on shooting clays. The latter sport indeed has now reached such a pitch that the hitting or missing of a single target out of hundreds may decide a championship. To an aspiring temperament, that may represent all the difference between glory and despair – to say nothing of the money that may be involved. Fortunately there is nothing like that in wing shooting!

Still, the game shooter who finds that what he had looked forward to as a special occasion is turning out to be one of his worst off-days knows enough of despair, and of the effort needed to thrust such weakness behind him, and to shoot grimly on in an attempt to get back to his normal form. One of the things of which I remind myself on such occasions is that a day is not a season, and that one's self-esteem as a shooter should be left to rest with what serenity it can on the general level of past performance. Even an entire season may not afford a fair basis for judgment, especially if there has been some new factor at work, such as some physical disturbance or a strange gun. The shooter must take one shot with another, and one day with another, and assess himself and his equipment accordingly. The need and justification for this will pay for a little further examination.

Marvellous killers

The need to look beyond individual shots and individual days arises with special emphasis on the appraisal of a particular gun. There must be many shooters who entertain the highest opinion of their guns as 'marvellous killers', simply because they now and again pull off spectacular long shots. But any complacency based on such performance may be ill-founded. It is, in fact, fairly easy for a gunmaker to turn out such guns, even in the cheaper grades. All that is needed is a heavily choked barrel, capable of throwing patterns of high density and reasonable quality, and a gun that happens to fit its user sufficiently well to enable him to do it justice.

If such a gun is used more or less exclusively for long-range work – say for flighting at a place where wildfowl are well-educated in the need for maintaining height – it may fully justify its owner's esteem. But if it is used for general rough shooting, its occasional long shots will have to be paid for by an undue proportion of misses at the shorter distances. The trouble in such cases is that the shooter is all too inclined to blame himself for these misses and to remain fixed in the delusion that his gun is a marvellous killer.

But here, as elsewhere, the true test is the game tally, taking one day with another; and if the shooter were still inclined to accept responsibility for all shortcomings, the fact would remain that even in the hands of a perfect shot the gun would be unsatisfactory, for it would fill all game taken at close to medium range with sufficient lead to disgust those who had to cook and eat it.

Hard-shooting guns

We get the converse of this situation in the case of those guns which throw open patterns of superior quality, such as many of the old thoroughbreds did —and still do, if they are fed on a suitable diet. When used on game in the range-bracket last considered, they have a pattern density sufficient to ensure clean kills, combined with a spread that accommodates all but the more exaggerated pointing errors.

Provided that such guns are used for the sort of work for which they were chiefly designed, they may fairly enjoy the reputation they often have of being 'hard-shooting' guns. Most game, whether driven, walked-up, shot over dogs or hunted with spaniels, is taken at ranges within, say, 20 to 35 yds, and the same goes for pigeon shot over decoys or coming in to roost, as well as for ground game and 'various'. This is the field, and it is a very big field, in which the open-bored, moderately charged, and therefore light game gun is supreme. Its efficiency, taking one shot with another and one day with another, will fairly reflect the efficiency as a shot of the shooter using it.

But if a gun of this sort is used for long-range shooting at wildfowl, its hard-shooting reputation will immediately start to suffer. Tapping-in at streams and inland, reedy pools, yes; but not for the kind of flighting mentioned a moment ago.

All the foregoing is, of course, elementary shotgun lore, but it still needs repeating, and not always for the youngest and least experienced of shooters. It is the sort of knowledge that men often hold in their heads rather than in their hearts. Old loyalties are not instantly severed by the maturing realisation that they have been misplaced, and there must be many shooters who continue to use guns for classes of work for which they are unsuited long after the fact has been made plain.

Built-in error

But there are less obvious examples of guns that do extraordinarily well at certain kinds of sport, but not at others for which they may mistakenly be regarded as equally suitable. I am thinking of those guns that print their patterns noticeably away from the point of aim. A gun of this sort came temporarily into my possession during the harvest season some years ago. I used it for shooting pigeon over decoys, at which it performed much to my satisfaction. Later, I used the gun for general rough shooting, when it quickly reversed my original impression. It turned out to be a low-shooter, and thus had a built-in correction for my tendency to shoot over pigeon dropping in to decoys. But what was a built-in correction for descending shots became a built-in error for others which, taking one with another, had a marked ascending tendency.

At the moment, I much favour an AYA XXV, which throws its patterns nicely high. There is no doubt that this gun has improved my shooting by compensating for my tendency to miss rising birds under. There is equally no doubt that it has accentuated my tendency to miss certain birds over — for example, the woodcock or pheasant that gets up at my feet and goes off on an ascending course. By the time the bird is fairly shootable, it is still rising in relation to the ground, but it has passed its apex in my field of vision, in which it is declining, so that it needs shooting under. It is a need that I all too often fail to meet. Nevertheless, this high-shooting gun, taking one type of shot with another, is advantageous, since it is undoubtedly putting rather more game in my bag over the season.

Over-and-unders often provide a special case in this connection, for whereas the two barrels of side-by-sides invariably shoot equally for elevation, the top barrel of an O/U is likely to print its pattern anything from slightly to much above that of the other. This indeed is widely regarded as one of the advantages of the O/U for trapshooting.

A special case

But in the general run of game shooting, the open-bored barrel of a double gun is the one that is called on to do by far the most work, and most conspicuously needs whatever degree of charge elevation is found to be most advantageous. In the O/U, as adapted for game shooting, it is the bottom barrel that is usually open-bored and responsive to the first trigger of a two-trigger model. It is therefore this barrel that most needs the right degree of charge elevation. If in fact it has it, and if the top barrel shoots very conspicuously higher, it could, and should, result in an undue proportion of birds being missed over. If, taking one kind of shooting with another, I found anything suspicious about my second barrel performance with an O/U, this is a matter I should look into.

I may say that I have not run into this trouble with my Winchester M.101, which, with the loads I have so far used, appears to print both its patterns to substantially the same elevation.

10 Developing Latent Skill

It is a fascinating thing to visit a factory where some simple, repetitive, manual operation is being carried out by girls. They grab something, maybe off a belt conveyor, their fingers fly around it with incredible speed, and they drop it into a container, the operation duly performed. Often it is performed so quickly that, try as one may, it is impossible to follow the sequence of movements.

And not only has the operation to be carried out, but it often needs to be carried out with accuracy, and the girls who survive on the job will of necessity carry it out to the standard of accuracy required.

Again, some of these jobs require judgment. The girls who pack matches into boxes with such astonishing speed, grab a handful from a readily available supply, stuff it into a box, fit the box into its cover, and repeat the process many hundreds of times a day. On the box it says, 'Approximate contents 50 matches,' but the girls do not count the matches – they simply grab; but they grab with such judgment that they are seldom more than one or two out, according to what I was once told.

And the girls who carry out these jobs with such speed, accuracy and judgment are not super-human; they are not rare beings endowed with more than their fair share of the common faculties. On the contrary, they are run-of-the-mill girls from the local labour market. Some of the intake, undoubtedly, will not be trainable to the necessary standard, but usually it is they, and not the others, who are in a conspicuous minority.

You will see, of course, what I am driving at. The secret of the amazing skill of these girls is simply practice – sheer, unremitting daily practice. Confidence is admittedly another vital ingredient, but their tasks make little demand on confidence, and such as they require will develop with their proficiency. In the upshot, they will relegate these tasks to their subconscious minds, just as we do the common daily processes of dressing and undressing ourselves, and doing up our buttons; and they will often engage in non-stop chat with their neighbours while they are performing them.

And a curious thing about this non-stop chat is that it does not hinder production – not the kind of production I have in mind; it may actually help it. Surely, it might be argued, the girls would do better if they thought about what they were doing. On the contrary – for the best results at this sort of work, conscious thought must not be allowed to turn inwards. If it does, the fingers will falter, and what should be performed in a smooth sequence of movements will have to be done as it was when it was being learned.

William James once said, and I quote from pretty reliable memory: 'It is often said that we should think of what we are doing. The precise contrary is the case. The more of our common daily tasks we can hand over to the effortless custody of automatism, the more our higher faculties are freed for their proper functions.'

So far, I have not mentioned shooting, but you will have realised how my mind has been running on the significance of practice in cultivating the speed, accuracy and judgment with which simple manual operations such as shooting can be performed, and the importance of not interfering with the free exercise of the acquired proficiency by the intrusion of conscious thought. 'George,' said an eminent trapshooter to a rival who had gone off his form, and was trying to work out the reason, 'why don't you stop thinking and *just shoot*.'

The reward of practice

But it is practice I want to concentrate on in this chapter, and not the evils of introspection. We have had plenty of examples of outstanding game shots in this country, but they have been almost entirely private sportsmen, whose achievements have never gone on record. Such men as Hawker, Walsingham and de Grey are exceptions, as having published diaries, or contributed to books, or having attracted the attention of society gossip writers. All we can say of them in the present context is that they were men who shot on the largest scale that their generous opportunities permitted. They were men, in short, who, in all probability, owed as much to practice as they did to innate skill for their outstanding performances.

But if we want to pursue this matter in quantitative terms we had better go to the U.S.A. There, in the latter half of the previous century, were two classes of shooters who to some extent merged into each other, and who, together, demonstrated to what an extraordinary degree skill with the gun could be developed by lifelong and intensive practice. These were the market gunners and the professional crack shots.

For an account of their exploits, we can best go to Bob Hinman's fascinating book, *The Golden Age of Shotgunning*. One of the most attractive figures in it is that of Fred Kimble, originally a market gunner (though in later life he rejected the description) and celebrated as one of the independent inventors of choke boring. He was a man of gentlemanly character and modest disposition, one of whose favourite maxims was that 'the price of good shotgunnery is constant practice.' How well he practised may be seen from a single record. Shooting in the Illinois River valley in 1872, near his home a few miles up-river from Peoria, he shot 1365 duck in the nineteen days between February 27 and March 16, on only two of which he did not go out. This works out at about 80 a day on the average, and all were shot with a single-barrelled muzzle-loader of 9-bore. One morning at Spring Lake he had bagged 122 duck before 9 o'clock.

The exploits of these market gunners gave rise to their being adopted as local 'champions' and thus to rivalry, challenges and competitions, culminating in such figures as that of Adam Bogardus, who, in 1879, addressed himself to the sterile and mindless task of breaking 5000 inanimate targets in 500 minutes, which he duly accomplished with his English double-barrelled gun by W. & C. Scott. The market gunners at least fed the masses, but all Bogardus did latterly was merely to demonstrate that practice makes perfect. It is a principle that has been more usefully, but no less effectively, demonstrated by Fanny Noakes and her sisterhood of the match factories and similar establishments from that day to this.

11   A Bad Foundation

A well-known shooting writer has suggested that the tables of forward allowances published for the benefit of shotgun users should be publicly burnt. My immediate reaction is in favour.

I take it that we are all familiar with the tables in question. Until 1968, there used to be one published in the IMI *Shooter's Year Book*. It purported to show how far one should aim in front of a bird crossing at 40 m.p.h., at various distances, when using standard cartridges loaded with the popular sizes of shot.

But this table, and similar ones published elsewhere, carry the implicit absurdity of requiring the shooter to distinguish between quantities that are indistinguishable at shooting distances—for example, between 96 in. and 97 in. at 40 yds, according to whether he is using No. 6 or No. 7 shot. The complications arising in practice out of variations in the speed of the bird, and whether or not there is a quartering element in its flight, are of necessity ignored. Conscientious beginners, therefore, who try to make literal use of such tables, are likely to find themselves in difficulties. It is a bad way to start.

Tried and proved techniques

So far as tables of forward allowances have any practical use, they necessarily relate to the lead-and-swing technique. In this one swings the gun at a constant distance ahead of the bird, and pulls the trigger without interrupting the swing. If the distance ahead—the lead, that is to say—has been correctly chosen, and if the swing has been faithfully continued until the shot is away, a hit should certainly ensue, provided that the bird is fairly within range.

The method, therefore, is a perfectly sound one. Its great merit is that it is in no way dependent for its success on the shooter's reaction time remaining

constant, or on the constancy of the interval between the pulling of the trigger
and the discharge of the gun. For this reason, it must of necessity have been
the universal technique in the flintlock days, when guns varied materially in
their ignition time from shot to shot, or were at least likely to do so. But
provided the shooter kept his gun pointing at the right distance ahead of the
bird, it obviously did not matter if the gun went off a bit early or a bit late –
there it was, waiting, so to speak, in the correct relation to the target, for the
shot to emerge at its leisure.

The snag about the lead-and-swing method is the absolute necessity it
imposes on the shooter to maintain the correct forward allowance until the
shot has gone. In other words, he must never check his swing. This is fatally
easy to do, and in two distinct ways. The commonest, perhaps, is to keep the
swing going right up to the moment that the brain says 'fire', and then to
relax. But it must always be remembered that, after the brain has given its
command, there is an appreciable interval before the shot leaves the gun.
Even with modern equipment, the interval may be a fifth of a second, during
which a 40 m.p.h. bird would fly over 11 ft. If, therefore, the shooter gives his
mental order to relax at the same time as he gives the command to fire, he
could miss literally by yards.

Lack of concentration

The other way to miss by lead-and-swing is to fail to concentrate absolutely
and all the while on the aiming spot ahead of the bird. The bird itself must
receive only the same sort of marginal attention that a footballer, concentrating on the ball, pays to other players who may be heading to intercept it.
If for one moment the shooter looks at the bird, his gun is practically certain
to follow his glance and if he fires then, a miss is assured.

For all that, I daresay that if a world survey could be undertaken to find
out the truth of the matter, the lead-and -swing technique would prove to be
the one most favoured. Captain Bogardus, the American who claimed to be
the 'Champion Wing Shot of the World', and who came over here to demonstrate the fact to the locals, and came as near as no matter to succeeding, said
that he *always consciously aimed* his gun; and since he could hardly have
meant anything else, I take it that what he aimed at was the right spot ahead
of his birds – in other words, that he practised the lead-and-swing method.

So, notwithstanding the implicit absurdity of the familiar tables of forward
allowances, there is no corresponding absurdity in the associated technique.
It does not require the shooter to measure off specific distances in feet and
inches, as the tables imply, but rather that he should develop an intuitive
capacity to give his birds a certain *basic angular lead* (which varies little for
game birds crossing in full flight in the familiar range bracket) and to modify

this angular lead according to the quartering element and any obviously special features of the case, such as exceptional speed or slowness or distance. As I sit here, typing these notes, I have no recollection whatsoever of what the allowance tables say, but I have a clear mental photograph of the basic angular lead, which I have obviously been carrying in my head for longer than I like to calculate. I would guess it to be about 3 or 4 degrees, though I have never thought of it before in terms of any figures.

The follow-through system

But although I have paid this testimony to the lead-and-swing method, I have no doubt of the superiority of the follow-through system — more especially for driven game, and generally for shooting fast birds at moderate distances. In this, one swings faster than the bird, so as to overtake and pass it along the line of its flight, and gives the mental order to shoot *when the gun is pointing straight at it*. In the fifth of a second, more or less, that elapses between the mental order and the actual discharge, the gun will have raced ahead and established the necessary lead.

There is an inherent compensation in this method for variations in the shooter's reaction time that is not commonly appreciated. Also, the bird seems to act as a pace-setter to the gun, and to prevent any egregious errors in the speed of the swing, which are clearly not admissible.

For these good reasons, follow-through is a style of shooting that is faster, more spontaneous, and decidedly more artistic than the alternative method. I find, however, that it becomes increasingly difficult to apply to the slower and more distant birds. What I say is that I cannot *get going* on them, and I am sure that is a common impression.

In such cases, I tend to fall back on lead-and-swing, though a really skilled exponent of follow-through would probably adapt his technique to the situation. There is, indeed, a special difficulty in dealing successfully with *very* slow birds by lead-and-swing. It arises from the fact that the correct aiming spot becomes so close to the bird that it is extremely hard to prevent the latter from attracting the shooter's concentrated attention. But if it does, the gun will almost inevitably follow, and the lead, so necessary for success, will be lost.

So, although I find myself prepared to help in building the proposed bon-fire, and would even apply the match, I would not condemn the lead-and-swing method along with the absurdities of the tables. It has a long tradition; it has a proper field of application; and what is of even more importance is that some shooters prefer it, and shoot well that way.

12 Problems of Polyguny

An American correspondent, commenting on one of my books, wrote, 'I particularly liked the brief chapter on "one gun", as my failing, since I got a few extra dollars, has been trying to use different guns all the time, and it just doesn't work! I love fine shotguns, and every year or so bought a new one.'

This falls neatly into line with the doctrine I have expressed from time to time – that, for the best results of which a man is capable, the best battery is one gun, or a matched pair. Accurate shooting, I have said, depends on precise muscular response to visual stimuli, and the man who uses only one gun has deep channels of habit engraved in the nervous, mental and muscular machinery involved in the process. Give him a strange gun, and somewhere along the route a departure from the habitual channel of response will need to be established before he can use it proficiently. Admittedly, the new channel can sometimes be established very quickly. An adaptable man, which usually means one who is fairly young, can sometimes mount a strange gun a mere half dozen times to get the feel of it, and then proceed straight away to acquit himself with credit. But the new channel of response does not eliminate the old one, and there must always be a chance that controlling nervous impulses will take the wrong course, and bring about muscular reactions that may not be precisely those most appropriate to the circumstances. In short, he may sometimes miss when he would have hit with a gun that was thoroughly familiar.

But there is more in shooting than attaining the utmost efficiency as a marksman, and although I preach the one-gun doctrine, I do not practise it in total austerity. Like my American correspondent, I love fine guns, and am prepared to indulge my fondness to a strictly limited extent. But however wealthy I might be, I could never let my acquisitive instincts run riot, as in cases I hear about, in which men accumulate fine guns by the rackful for no better purpose, it would seem, than to gloat over them, as any other collecting crank gloats over his treasures. For all that, having acquired a new gun for what seems to me to be a good and sufficient reason, I am reluctant to get rid of its predecessor in my favour, which may have the character of an old friend. On the contrary, I not only want to keep the old friend, but I want to exercise it occasionally.

I would not like this confession to be taken for more than it is worth. I have never allowed these old friends to accumulate, but have sternly disbanded them, so that if I am no monogunist, I have at least avoided the reproach of keeping a seraglio. What few guns I have I like to use; and on that point two problems have arisen.

The first is posed by an acquaintance whom I recommended, two or three years ago, to try a lighter and shorter-barrelled gun than he had previously been used to. He acted on my advice, and duly reported himself as being very pleased with the change. But now he says he had to send his new gun for repair early last season, and to fall back on his old one, which, I take it, he had not used since he acquired its successor. To his surprise, he found himself strongly disconcerted by the weight of the gun that he had used for many years. It seemed completely out of proportion. 'My new gun,' he explained, 'weighs about 6 lb 4 oz, as against 6 lb 12 oz for the old one – a mere 8 oz difference. Yet the old one now seems pounds heavier, and I am unpleasantly conscious of it all day.' He adds, 'What can I do about it? I certainly do not want to regard it as obsolete, and I should hate to get rid of it. Besides, it has already proved itself to be a useful standby.'

I myself have been up against precisely this trouble, for which I have found only two palliatives. I say palliatives because they are not complete cures.

The first is to do regular mounting and swinging practice with a third gun that is appreciably heavier than either of the two it is proposed to use. This presumably builds up a reserve of muscular tolerance, so that both the normal guns will tend to feel somewhat light by comparison. When I was much younger than I am now, I even used a double elephant rifle, weighing over 15 lbs, for this purpose, and my shotguns certainly seemed to weigh very little after a spell with that ponderous but beautifully balanced weapon. Nowadays, I am not quite so energetic!

A variant of this idea is to use the heavier of the two regular guns for practice. This may preserve habituation, but it obviously does nothing to create a reserve. It is indeed an astonishing side-light on the organisation of our muscular systems that they should be so sensitive to such a minor change in a familiar load – one, moreover, so far within their maximum capacity for exertion.

Mr Rimington-Wilson, one of the noted game shots of the Edwardian era, was reputed to preserve his habituation to the weight of his regular guns during the close season, when the shooting muscles tend to get slack, by carrying around with him a walking stick made of iron or loaded with lead, and of the same or greater weight. But I should hesitate to recommend this heroic procedure to my enquirer.

A more practical trick, and the second one I have practised to dodge this problem, is simply to use a particular gun exclusively for a whole season, and, of course, to do with it whatever mounting and swinging practice con-scientiousness and energy may dictate.

Making a match

The second problem I mentioned is related to the foregoing. It was put up to me some time ago by a shooter who had two similar guns by different makers which he had had matched to make a pair. The matching had been done very well so far as the fit of the guns was concerned, but there was still some discrepancy in weight and balance, and I was asked what, if anything, could be done to make them more truly identical, so that they could not be distinguished if handled blindfold.

I believe that I knew the right answer to this problem, but never heard whether a practical gunmaker had been able to fulfil my prescription. It required that the excess weight of the heavier gun should be divided by two, and that metal corresponding to these half-weights should be added to the lighter gun on either side of the point of static balance, and at distances adjusted until the point of balance of both guns coincided, and both felt the same when see-sawed in the hands.

(Technical readers will recognise that this procedure, if found feasible, would give both guns the same 'least transverse moment of inertia,' and would realise this value at the same position; also that these are the prime requirements for equivalent balance. For further details see *Shotguns and Cartridges*, Chapter 17, 'Balance'.)

Unfortunately, the facilities for adding weight to conventional guns, apart from in the butt, are decidedly limited, though I have boundless faith in the ingenuity of the gun trade, and would like to have heard the outcome of this case.

13   Beware the Tables

'Science is measurement' said Lord Kelvin – or if it was not he who said it, it might have been, for that is exactly the sort of thing he is likely to have said. I doubt if an advanced modern physicist would be happy to endorse that famous dictum in its naked simplicity, but when we are dealing with such down-to-earth subjects as ballistics and the performance of sporting guns it seems unchallengeable.

It is indeed in their lack of any measurements of the things they were talking about that so many of the old writers on shooting, even the best of them, seemed to be vague and uncertain, and groping for terms in which to express themselves with clarity and precision. Usually they had to be content with comparatives – this gun or load, for example, shot 'harder' than another, or was 'quicker' or 'slower'; but exactly what harder meant, or by how much one was quicker or slower than another was left undetermined.

Nowadays, we seem to be in a uniformly better position. We have our shot velocities measured by chronograph over various distances; we have the striking velocities and energies of our pellets worked out and tabulated; we have the density and spread of our pattern, corresponding to various borings, all set out in neat array, and much other ballistical information presented with at least an appearance of diamond sharpness.

With all this data, the modern shooter can work out a variety of problems connected with his gun, his cartridges and his loads, and obtain answers which appear to be firm and authoritative. Yet the appearance may be delusory.

It should indeed be always borne in mind that these answers can seldom be regarded as final and absolute, because a considerable proportion of the published information is based on 'nominal' values of this, that or the other, and is only loosely related to actualities. And again, owing to the frequent lack of a full and clear description of exactly what certain figures represent, there may be anomalies as between one source and another, giving rise to erroneous comparisons.

Some good examples of these things are to be found in the field of velocities. What do we mean by the velocity of a charge of shot? Muzzle velocity is easy: it can only mean the speed with which the charge leaves the gun. But the velocity given for some specific distance can be either the 'remaining velocity', i.e. the actual striking velocity at that distance, or it can be the average velocity over that part of the course.

In this country, when we say 'velocity' without qualification in relation to shot charges, we usually mean the 'observed velocity', which is the average velocity over the first 20 yds (e.g. 1050 ft/sec. for a typical game cartridge). But the Americans might say that a similar cartridge had a velocity of 1250 ft/sec., meaning the muzzle velocity. Our Continental neighbours are usually clearer: they use V_0, V_{20}, V_{30}, etc., to represent the muzzle velocity and the actual striking velocity at 20, 30, etc. metres respectively.

Anomalous information

Now for examples. Some months ago, a reader came to me in a state of considerable puzzlement over differences between British and American data on shot velocities as given by authoritative sources. He took several examples of shot of the same size projected at the same, or practically the same, muzzle velocity, and then compared the velocities and energies given for 40 and 60 yds. One example (shown on page 42) will suffice.

These figures have survived my spot-checks, and assuming them to be correct, they reveal the large anomaly that, at 60 yds, the American shot appears to have a 36 per cent higher velocity than the British, and a 77 per cent greater striking energy. So, a shooter, taking it that a mallard needs a pellet energy of not less than 1·5 for a clean kill, and taking his figures from American sources, might consider American No. 6 (British No. 5) adequate at 60 yds; but not so if he used our figures.

Shot	Velocities (f/s)			Energy 60 yds
	Muzzle	40 yds	60 yds	(foot-pounds)
American No. 6	1250	737	617	1·61
British No. 5	1251	646	454	0·91

The probable explanation has already appeared: the American down-range velocities and energy are presumably the average velocity over the stated range and the corresponding energy, whilst the British figures are the striking velocity and the striking energy at that range. As the shot is slowing down, the average figures will of necessity be higher than the terminal one.

Limitations of theory

Published figures of pellet energy, from whatever source they come, are largely in the 'nominal' category. If we know the weight of a pellet and its velocity, we can calculate its energy with great accuracy. But the energy figures published in the tables are calculated from the nominal size of the pellet and from a velocity which, at best, is probably true only for the leading pellets of what may be a string several yards long at full range. And even if the pellets were originally all of exactly the same size, and perfectly round (which they are not), something like half of them, in the absence of a shot protector, are likely to turn up at the target having lost a material part of their substance through abrasion against the barrel wall. For these reasons, some of the pellets may realise little more than half their nominal striking energy. All these considerations emphasise my preference for properly conducted penetration tests as a measure of the effectiveness of a cartridge in the field.

In view of what I have said on numerous previous occasions about the difference frequently observed between the nominal and effective boring of a gun, I need only add that this difference affects, of course, the 'spread' of the pattern, the published tables of which are thus also in the nominal class.

So I come to my familiar conclusion that nothing can take the place of shooting in the appraisal of a gun. I am all for theory, but in matters of this sort it must be firmly wedded to practice, to which it must adapt itself on any issues in dispute.

14 Rough Shooting v. Driving

There was a familiar silly-season topic in the Edwardian sporting press –
'Who are the best twelve shots in England?' The fact that the favoured lists
invariably contained several names from Debrett must often have provoked
suspicion that possession of a title was a prime qualification for inclusion
among the elect dozen. But although the gossip writers in the society papers
were seldom free from the taint of toadyism, there was good reason for seeking the best shots from among the 'nobility, aristocracy and landed gentry' of
the period. It lay simply in the fact that these were the people who got the
most practice.

The point is relevant to another question that was much discussed during
the period referred to – 'Which affords the more difficult shooting: driving
or walking-up?' This was a much more interesting question than the other,
and is one that was recently put to me by a well-known East Anglian sportsman. But since 'walking-up' strictly implies a rather formal kind of shooting, with a line of mixed guns and beaters, and without hunting dogs, my
correspondent phrased his question in more modern terms – 'Does rough
shooting provide more difficult shots than driving?' It is one that is still good
for an argument.

Rough shooting used to mean any kind of shooting on unkeepered ground,
where no game was reared, and so it could have included both driving and
the more formal kind of walking-up. But in the sense intended it must be
taken to mean what the Americans (not to mention the French, Spanish,
Italians, Germans, Russians and others) correctly describe as hunting, in
which a solitary sportsman seeks his game in suitable cover with the aid of a
hunting dog. If we allow the shooter even a single companion the argument
becomes confused by the consideration that sometimes admirable driven
game shooting can be contrived with the help of a single beater.

Reduced to these terms, then, driven game shooting is shooting from a
prepared position at birds coming towards the shooter from a known direction and during a known interval – the period of the drive; whereas the rough
shooter must be prepared to take game flushing in any direction, at any time,
and when he may be ill situated to shoot.

The driven-game shooter has many things in his favour, apart from those
already indicated. He is, or should be, calm, cool and collected. He has a
firm, unobstructed stand, or can usually contrive one while he is waiting. His
eyes can be focused on the part of the sky where the birds are most likely to
appear; and if he misses the first one or two he is likely to have further opportunities for 'getting set'. If birds are plentiful, he may have an opportunity
of picking his shots, as many serious-minded professors, sensitive about their
kills-to-cartridges ratio, undoubtedly do.

43

During the heyday of driving, the difficulties of shooting the driven bird were much exaggerated by distinguished practitioners who equally exaggerated the ease with which game flushed by spaniels could be shot. The truth, of course, is that both kinds of shooting yield easy and difficult birds. An end-of-season cock pheasant, flushed far back from the line, and planing down from high over the tree-tops of a hillside covert on a bright and frosty day, can be as nearly shot-proof as any bird is likely to be. And grouse, belatedly seen, sweeping down the hillside in the rain like feathered meteors, can reduce the unaccustomed shooter to paralytic impotence.

But pheasants like that described are in a minority. My correspondent says, 'Here in Suffolk, which is mostly flat country, with coverts on hills few and far between, high birds are the exception rather than the rule.' One noble landowner, whose hospitality I was once privileged to enjoy, apologized for his birds, which, he said, could seldom be induced to fly properly before Christmas. And it is no secret that the birds from another famous estate are not received with enthusiasm at Leadenhall.

Equally with grouse: those same birds on a hot August day, when relatively immature and already tired from having been previously driven, could fail to undermine the confidence of a tyro.

Footwork

The driven-game advocate might yield the point; but such grouse, he might say, could never be so contemptuously easy as a great pheasant lumbering up out of a root field. It all depends: if at the time of lumbering the shooter's feet are all wrong; and if, in his hurried attempt to get them right he skids off the side of a great mangold with one foot and stumbles over a second one with the other, he could conceivably miss that well-nigh unmissable bird – and with both barrels. It has been known to happen. To quote my correspondent again. 'Several minutes (or more) go by without seeing a bird; then suddenly a pheasant erupts out of a hedge, and one has the chance of a snap shot. Only one shot is possible, and that has to be taken with one's feet firmly anchored in the mud of a ploughed field. Little chance then of following the technique one learnt in a shooting school!'

The value of practice

In my opinion, the question of relative difficulty cannot be answered without reference to the shooter, and to the amount and nature of the practice he has principally enjoyed. True, some shots are intrinsically more difficult than others, and inasmuch as rough shooting affords a greater variety than driving does, it might be argued that it is bound to include more of the difficult kind. But this consideration, I think, has to give way before the great gain in expert facility of which every man is capable if only he has enough practice. The great shots of the past were not so much supermen as men of super-practice. We see the same thing nowadays with the champion clay shooters. Pistol shooters, too: Colonel Charles Askins, a former American pistol champion, once told me, if I remember correctly, that at the height of his career, he was shooting over 30 000 practice rounds a year. The Marquis of Ripon probably fired something approaching that number of cartridges at feathered game.

So, even if rough shooting is more difficult than driven game, which I am inclined to think, because of the small number and unpredictability of the shots it offers, their frequently unexpected appearance, and the adverse circumstances in which they often have to be taken, we need not be surprised if a competent rough shooter makes a sad mess of his first day's driving.

The converse is well illustrated by an incident related to me by an old friend, now departed. It fell to him in his official capacity in India to offer hospitality to a visiting Central European nobleman – a Count, and a member of a family renowned in history. They were also renowned in sporting annals for the vast scale of the shooting carried on on their various estates. The Count, indeed, was reputed to be, not one of the best twelve shots in England, but probably the best shot in Europe, both with gun and rifle.

It so happened that there were exceptional opportunities for quail shooting owing to the late harvesting of crops in an area near Mussorie, and it was arranged that the Count, accompanied by an attendant, and by my friend and a friend of his, should have an early morning walking them up. This they did in line, the beaters trailing a string with feathers attached at intervals to flush the birds, of which there were many.

But the Count could make nothing of them. He shot so badly that finally he said, 'If I miss another, I shall stop shooting.' As he spoke, a couple rose almost at his feet. He missed them with both barrels. True to his word, he flung his gun to the ground for his attendant to gather, and set out to walk the nine miles back to Mussorie.

15   Fast Loading

Nowadays, the average shooter, even if he is chiefly concerned with driven game, seldom needs any greater firepower than that afforded by a single hammerless ejector. Nevertheless, anyone is likely to run up against occasions when he could do with a pair of guns and a loader – at a good pigeon roost, or a coot shoot, for example – and every man should know how to handle his gun so as to make the most of any opportunity of this kind.

On most occasions, right-handed loading from the jacket pocket meets all requirements. Cartridge belts, however, need to be recognised for what they are – slow and reluctant dispensers, and if one is used, it should be shifted around as the cartridges are used up, so that those remaining always lie conveniently to the right hand. If this is neglected, the shooter may be betrayed by sudden need into chasing ridiculously around his own equator in search of ammunition, like the unforgettable recruit in the stage production of *Oh, What a Lovely War!*, who lost his bayonet hopelessly somewhere in his lumbar region.

I have found it advantageous when loading from the pocket to keep it well filled with cartridges from the bag, so as to make it gape conveniently when the flap is tucked in. Further, if the pocket, thus filled, is shaken up from the outside, it will be found that the cartridges tend to settle with their heads uppermost. This will help to speed up reloading; and if both barrels have been fired, more often than not two cartridges can be grabbed together by their heads. Then, if the shooter is well practised in loading two rounds simultaneously, things can be speeded up still more.

It is worth while practising this trick of loading two rounds together. Churchill has described how it should be done by a right-handed loader, and at Holland & Holland's shooting school, Norman Clarke used to demonstrate the method with impressive neatness. He held the two cartridges side by side, with the lower one slightly forward. This he partly inserted in the right barrel without letting go of either. Then, using the right cartridge as a pivot, he twisted his wrist so as to bring the other in line with the left barrel, into which it was then dropped. The right cartridge was, of course, dropped in at the same time. I have what I believe is a better method, which I will come to in a moment.

Continuing with the right-hand method, if we must use a belt, we should use it properly. Whether worn under a jacket or otherwise, the cartridges are most easily drawn from the left front, the belt being shifted around accordingly. Before things start, and during lulls, it pays to ease a few rounds halfway out.

Alternatively, the belt can be used as a magazine from which to replenish a small supply held for immediate use in the pocket. This has the advantage of transferring weight from the shoulder to the hips, where it no longer impedes action; for if the jacket is cut in the prevailing style – loose under the arms – the contents of the pockets have to be lifted bodily every time the gun is raised to shoot. Forty years ago, the Army & Navy's head cutter, Shepherd, convinced me that the ideal shooting jacket was one with minimum shoulder build-up, and as close-fitting under the arms as possible. His shooting jackets were a revelation: when you lifted your arms you lifted nothing else: the freedom was delightful. But you would have to be very strong-minded to get a modern tailor to make you a jacket of this sort.

Coming now to left-hand loading, this tends to look rather less workman-like than loading from the right, but I believe that it can be developed to give the fastest shooting of all, particularly when using a self-opening gun. The basic fact here is that the breech has of necessity to be opened by the right-hand thumb on the lever. If the gun is a self-opener, the left hand can thus be on its way to pick up fresh cartridges before the gun has even started to open; and if special arrangements are made for them to be immediately accessible, so that two (if required) can be grabbed simultaneously, they can be popped into the breech almost as soon as it is ready to receive them.

All that is needed is some way of having the cartridges ready and the right way up. The best I have found is to use a spring clip type of cartridge belt, worn outside the jacket, and with about ten clips on the left-hand side only. These should be eased, if necessary, so that the cartridges are not gripped tightly.

Two cartridges can then be grasped by the heads between the thumb and first finger of the left hand, held straight, and *broken out sideways* from their clips. They are then transferred to the gun, where they are momentarily rested at an angle on the rims of the breech-ends, so as to space them correctly, whereupon they are tilted over into the chambers.

With this system, a self-opener can approach the fire-power of a pair with a loader, but it will very quickly become too hot to hold. Even with an ordinary gun, it is still very fast, and when neatly performed looks impressively competent, *no matter what the standard of the shooting.* Quite a point for the gallery performer!

The reason, incidentally, for having a few clips on the left-hand side only of the belt is that any on the right are inclined to catch the sleeve and scratch the gun. An ordinary leather belt will hardly serve; but the spring-clip type, otherwise an unpleasant article of equipment, is the ideal thing for the job.

There are, as I know, tricks for fast reloading based on holding reserve rounds between the fingers on the left hand; but I have never found any of these a positive gain, but rather a distraction. Nor have I ever succeeded in loading both barrels of an O/U simultaneously.

16 Who Are the Best Shots?

If, at the turn of the century, we had asked ourselves this question, and had been in possession of the relevant facts, we should probably have arrived at much the same answer as the gossip writer of the period; for in this matter his normal preoccupation with titles would have led him towards the big landed proprietors who, in the ordinary course of events, got the most practice. Other things being equal, Lord Tomnoddy, firing 20 000 cartridges a season, was bound to have his natural powers as a marksman honed to a finer edge than that of his poor relation, Johnny Brown, who only fired 200.

But if, nowadays, we ask the same question, without any limitations of time or space, and consider what reasons may lie behind our answers, we are likely to find at least something of interest, and maybe of value.

One thing we must do: we must confine ourselves to shooting with the gun, for if not we shall quickly find ourselves among the legendary performers with the bow, not to mention those incredible Balearic slingers, whom the Romans organised into military formations. They are worth a passing glance – an envious one, maybe – inasmuch as their ammunition was free and practice unlimited.

Coming to the age of firearms, the earliest period relevant to this brief enquiry is that in which the gun had been so far improved as to make personal skill the dominant factor in determining success – that is, the era of the perfected flintlock. Colonel Hawker springs at once to mind as the greatest shot of his own period – some would say, of all time. So far had he mastered the inevitable vagaries of his weapon as to make missing a comparative rarity, even when he was shooting snipe.

But Hawker was a diarist and a writer, and it is well to remember that there must have been many unrecorded men of his period who approached his performance, even if they did not exceed it. Among the 'mute, inglorious Miltons,' we may occasionally catch a glimpse of someone like a certain Mr Jenkins of Petworth, who in 1812 killed twenty brace of partridges with forty shots, and in four days' shooting never missed.

And even if we leave Hawker in undisturbed possession of his reputation in English shooting annals, there remain the French, the Italians and the

Shooting the ZZ targets at the famous Monte Carlo ground overlooking the Ligurian Sea.

other European nationalities, all of whom, we may be sure, have had their legendary figures. And then there are the Americans, who in their own Golden Age of shooting, produced many remarkable shots. Their Hawker was probably Fred Kimble, who shot prodigiously, and to whose modest and gentlemanly character his contemporaries paid tribute. American records also reveal some astonishing performances by their market gunners, some of which are recalled by Bob Hinman's book, *The Golden Age of Shotgunning*.

The common factor that already emerges from all this is the significance of intensive practice. It acquires greater emphasis as we proceed.

Climate and conditions

A thing about which we know very little, but on which I have occasionally speculated, is whether race and climate have any influence in producing the best shots. It is more than possible. We have only to recall the numbing influence of cold weather, and of the way in which it can slow down our reactions when its effects are not neutralised by stimulating exercise, to incline to the suggestion that the warmer countries may tend to produce the finest performers. The records of the old Monte Carlo live pigeon shooting competitions may throw some light on this point. In them, we see an international concourse of the best and most practised shots, shooting under uniform and intensely competitive conditions. According to Greener, the winners of the Grand Prix de Casino for the thirty-nine years from 1872 to 1910 included – fourteen Italians, thirteen Englishmen, four Frenchmen, three Austrians, two Belgians, one Hungarian, one American, one Spaniard.

For what should be obvious reasons, this cannot be accepted as a serious statistical study of the point in question. What may be a more relevant consideration is the comparative reaction times of representatives of the various nations. It is stated that the Oriental peoples are so quick in their reactions as to make them our natural masters in all sports dependent on this factor. The Maharajah Duleep Singh, the one-time proprietor of the celebrated shooting estate at Elveden, in Norfolk, was noted for the extraordinary speed with which he could get his gun off when required. And if we treat as factual the feats recorded by the seventeenth-century Japanese writer, Nagasawa Shagetzuna, such as wing-shooting from the back of a galloping horse *with a matchlock*, we might as well go home, and leave his countrymen in undisputed possession of the field.

Birds and birds

When we are considering outstanding achievements in game shooting, the relative difficulty of the birds is nearly always impossible to assess. The skill of the old partridge shooters, shooting over pointers or setters, is sometimes written down heavily on account of the alleged tameness of these birds when flushed from the long stubbles of the period. It is a factor that could well be exaggerated, for it is easier to miss close birds than those at moderate distances. The point is more relevant in connection with live pigeon trapshooting. Frank Butler, who accompanied the celebrated Annie Oakley on her 1887 visit to this country, was much impressed by the difficulty of shooting our breed of birds. 'As for pigeon shooting,' he wrote, 'I never saw any until I came here. There are no pigeons in America to compare with the English blue rocks.' Is that, I wonder, one of the reasons for there being only one American in my Monte Carlo list? And ought we, for the same reason, to discount the remarkable straight runs of the earlier American trapshooters, such as Fulford and Brewer, when they were shooting on their home ground?

The common factor

The consideration vanishes when we switch to the more or less standardised targets of the modern competitive trap and skeet shooter. Who are the best shots now? – the Americans, the Russians, the Italians? I have never attempted any broad analysis of recent statistics, and would not publish it if I had. The top scores at the various international championships are sufficiently close to deprive the term 'best' of much of its relative significance. They are outstandingly the fruit of unremitting practice.

That, indeed, is the lesson here. Whether we consider game or clay shooting, the best shots and those who have practised most are almost identical. There are undoubtedly individuals so happily constituted – so quick in their reactions, so well co-ordinated, so free and spontaneous in their movements – as to shoot well with a minimum of practice, but they are exceptional. For the rest of us, it is a case of '*None sine pulveris*' – begging pardon for the pun. But it is well to bear in mind that there is no amount of practice – no degree of expertise – that is capable of earning a man the title of a good sportsman. The best sportsmen and the best shots are by no means almost identical.

17   Pregnant Intervals

I am far from being alone in contemplating the lock-time of a gun, as possibly influencing failure or success. The game shooter, using always the same gun, or guns of the same type, is probably outside this consideration; but the skeet or trapshooter, or one who alternates between guns of different types, may be much affected by it.

When we fire a gun at a target, whether it be an animate or an inanimate one, there is a point in time when the brain of the sportsman says, 'Shoot!' Between that instant and the arrival of the shot at the target – or perhaps I should have said at target distance – there is a measurable delay, capable of being divided into several parts.

First, there is the shooter's reaction-time – the time taken for his finger to act on his brain's order. This is variable, even with the same man, according to his state of freshness or fatigue, his emptiness or fullness, and a variety of other factors.

Then there is the lock-time – the factor with which we are now particularly concerned. It is the time that elapses between the pulling of the trigger and the striking of the cap or primer.

A further delay follows while the powder charge is undergoing ignition, and again while the charge of shot is travelling up the barrel.

Finally, there is the time of flight of the shot from the muzzle of the gun to the target. For present purposes, we can lump the ignition-time and the time up the barrel together, and add them to the time of flight, so that we are left with only two factors, the shooter's reaction-time and the lock-time.

The reaction-time, and more particularly its variability, is regarded as a nuisance, but an inevitable nuisance, which has to be provided for and over-come by the shooter's technique, to which I will return in a moment. The lock-time, however, has been generally regarded as an intrusive factor which should be eliminated, as far as possible. On our best modern sidelock guns, with their low-inertia hammers, their compensating swivels, and their power-ful vee springs, it nearly is eliminated, for these locks are very fast indeed.

But this is not the case with the locks usually associated with American-style repeaters. With their coil springs and long, gangling hammers, their slower action is obvious, even to a not-so-sensitive ear, and is readily percep-tible in shooting. A more extreme contrast is provided by the old flintlock guns, for in addition to the relatively slow movement of the high-inertia hammer or cock, with its load of flint, there is the additional time absorbed in throwing back the frizzen and setting fire to the charge, as opposed to detonat-ing a cap.

Matters of technique

How, then, can these variations affect the shooter's performance? To answer this question, it is necessary to consider his particular technique. The classi-cal method imposed as a matter of necessity by the slow and variable ignition of the flintlock, and still, I would guess, professed (though not necessarily practised) by the majority of shooters throughout the world, is the one we know as the lead-and-swing method. In it, the shooter swings his gun ahead of the bird at a constant angle, dependent, within moderate distances, solely on its speed across his line of sight. Contrary to what is sometimes urged in criticism of this method, no calculation, conscious or subsconscious, of yards, feet and inches is involved. If it were, the method would indeed be impracticable. All that is necessary is an intuitive appreciation of the speed of the bird in relation to that of the shot, and a recognition of the need to widen the familiar angle for shots taken at abnormal distances.

In the main alternative, the follow-through method, favoured especially by driven-game shooters, the shooter swings through and beyond his bird, and gives the mental order to fire when his gun is pointing straight at it. In the interval represented by his reaction-time plus the lock-time, the gun has raced ahead of the bird and established the necessary lead before it goes off.

However, it needs recognising that these two methods are capable of being combined, and I believe that they often are combined, especially by clay shooters. Thus, the shooter can come up from behind his bird on an over-taking course, as in follow-through, but not give the mental order to fire until his gun has overtaken the bird by a consciously recognised amount. This is a more deliberate proceeding than pure follow-through, lacking its speed and spontaneity, but perhaps better adapted to the special needs of the trapshooter, who, with his sharply honed reactions, may well be capable of utilising that brief interval when his gun is running ahead of the target to apply some correction in the light of his final observation of the way it is behaving, for example, under the influence of wind.

Cases explained

It is at this precise juncture that lock-time may be significant, by extending or restricting the time interval in which the shooter may make such correc-tions. An eminent British Olympic Trench shooter, Derek Partridge, con-firms the general proposition, and adds that to those who shut one eye, as he does, extending the time may make the difference between having to take a target momentarily obscured and having it in full view. He provides me with valuable supporting evidence, including the opposite case of another eminent O.T. man, one of slower reactions, who benefited greatly from reducing the lock-time of his gun.

When I wrote in the *Shooting Times* of 5 August 1973 about the 'mystery' of the Remington 1100's apparent superiority as a skeet gun, I could find no explanation other than its soft recoil and absence of jump. But it now appears that the slow lock-time, to which I drew attention, and which I found so dis-concerting, may, in practised hands, be one of the secrets of the gun's success.

Then there was the case of the young American who came over here for the grouse shooting, and found that the British cartridges he used were so much slower than his familiar American brand that he had to double his lead on crossing birds! In fact, the British cartridges were almost certainly faster than the others, and the explanation, I strongly suspect, is that over here he was using a conventional English gun, with its fast lock-time; whereas at home he was more accustomed to a repeater of opposite description.

The effect of this could well have been that if he were using the follow-through method, or, more probably, the hybrid version of it which I last explained, the fast-acting English gun would have deprived him of some of the lead he normally got from the over-swing of his repeater. His only remedy for this would have been to increase his lead, just as he would have had to do if his cartridges had been so much slower. One can forgive the delusion, but hardly its ready acceptance as fact.

18   *Missing by Concentration*

Concentration is often referred to as the key to successful shooting. But concentration on what? The bird, presumably. And yet a distinguished American writer on shooting comes to me with a theory that concentration on the bird may be a prolific source of missing. His views command respect, and may repay examination.

'I really learnt to shoot on walked-up quail,' he says, 'which are largely going-away shots. The problem here is to concentrate on one bird only in the swirling, criss-crossing covey as it explodes from the ground; then, when that bird is killed, and only then, to fasten attention on another. I developed such ability to concentrate that on occasions when a bird beyond the one I shot at was also killed, I never realised that it had even been there until the dog brought it to me.

'But,' he adds, 'I used to have great difficulty in hitting crossing birds of any kind, especially when their approach could be studied for some moments. I missed these birds no matter how much I concentrated on leading them. The only ones I could hit seemed to be those which appeared as a complete surprise, and had to be swung on as rapidly as a ruffed grouse in heavy cover, in true "Churchill" fashion. Yet, if I saw a pheasant or duck approaching, and tried to take it with a swing-through as it came into range, I still rarely connected.

'So,' he continues, 'I arrived at the theoretical conclusion that I was missing crossing birds simply by my intense concentration on them. No matter how much I thought I was leading them, my gun was pointing where I was looking – at the bird, and not some little distance ahead of it. I reasoned that, even if I swung well out in front of a crossing target, I was really still looking at it, and therefore, as I pressed the trigger, the gun, without my being aware of it, tended to point where I was looking – directly at the bird.'

My correspondent goes on to explain how he diagnosed his trouble by practising at crossing clays, and then on flighting duck on a shooting preserve. Finally he came to mastering these crossing shots, but only by *not* concentrating directly on the bird.

He goes on to recognise that with what he calls the Churchill swing-through system, the momentum of gun and body carry the gun past the target, and establish the necessary lead in the brief interval of the shooter's reaction time. 'But I am convinced,' he adds, 'that when an experienced shot who uses this method runs into a spot of trouble, it is simply that he is concentrating on his birds with such intensity that he subconsciously tries to point his gun where he is looking; in fact, he tries so hard that his swing is somewhat slowed, and therefore he shoots behind for no apparent reason.

'This natural pointing of the gun towards the exact spot where we are looking,' he concludes, 'is incredibly hard to overcome. Usually, it is why birds are easy to hit, yet it can cause anyone to miss them.'

As a shooter who has, in his time, explored every conceivable cause of missing, but who can shoot fairly well on those occasions when a favourable conjunction of the planets happens to coincide with a euphoric condition in his liver, I feel qualified to comment on my correspondent's observations.

His early trouble when trying to take crossing birds by the lead-and-swing method was, I consider, nothing out of the ordinary. It is usually said that such birds are missed by stopping the swing; but that must not be taken too literally, because the gun is not normally halted – it is merely checked or slowed down, which is quite sufficient. But how the fatal hesitancy arises is not entirely and invariably clear. It can undoubtedly arise through lack of confidence, amounting to psychological or even physical flinching. Nothing, for example, could impede an easy, natural swing more than the certain knowledge that pulling the trigger was going to produce a painful blow in the face. And there can be other and less obvious causes.

But if we all tend to point our guns where we are looking, as we assuredly do, concentration on the bird, instead of on the appropriate point ahead of it, must inevitably give rise to missing, as my correspondent contends. We need to recognise that, although it is possible to *attend* to several things simultaneously, it is only possible to *concentrate* on one. When using the lead-and-swing method, it is essential to concentrate fully and exclusively on the point ahead of the bird at which intuitive judgment says that the gun should be pointed. Of necessity, this involves taking note of where the bird is, in the same way that a player, running to intercept a ball, and concentrating hard on its course and position, pays marginal attention to the position of other players. But in the case we are considering, it is the point ahead that must receive the concentration, and the bird that must have only the marginal attention. If the concentration is, even momentarily, diverted to the bird, the gun is only too likely to be diverted with it, in which event a miss becomes a certainty.

Lesson of the flintlock

There are, I know, critics who scoff at the whole theory of lead-and-swing shooting: who say that it is impossible to measure off imaginary distances in the air, and that when the shooter thinks he is doing this, he is actually doing something else. I do not believe it. Lead-and-swing does not involve measuring imaginary feet and inches at a distance but merely maintaining an angle of lead determined by experience, and there is certainly nothing especially difficult, still less impossible, about that. It must be remembered that in the flintlock days, when ignition times were long *and variable*, the lead-and-swing method was the only feasible one; yet some remarkably fine shooting was done then.

So, on the subject of crossing birds and lead-and-swing, I agree with my correspondent. But I cannot agree with what he says about the danger of undue concentration on the bird when using the 'Churchill' or follow-through method. I believe that in that case total concentration on the bird is the right thing, and that only marginal attention should be devoted to swinging the gun so as to overtake and pass the bird on the same course. Indeed, with a good, free, swinging habit thoroughly established, the gun does not appear to require even marginal attention. All one has to think about is the bird and its course and pulling the trigger, or, rather, mentally giving the order to pull the trigger, when the gun is pointing straight at it. In the fifth of a second, more or less, that then elapses before the gun actually goes off, the lead will have been automatically taken care of.

Swing must be second nature

But a free, uninhibited swing and follow-through is essential for success on this system. Then we have a situation similar to that of the good tennis player, to whom swing and follow-through have become second nature, leaving him free to concentrate on the ball.

I share my correspondent's experience in finding it easiest to practise the follow-through method with fast birds appearing quickly at moderate range. Slow crossers, long seen approaching, are nearly shot-proof to me. I find it hard to deal with them by the follow-through system – I cannot get enough swing going on them; and so I usually find myself trying to take them by lead-and-swing. But then, especially if they are low-flyers as well as slow-flyers, I find that I have to concentrate very strongly on the point ahead, and not on the bird, if I am to be successful, and to beware of letting my attention wander momentarily back to the bird as I pull the trigger.

If I had to do much shooting at slow crossers, I should abandon my seductively light and fast-handling AYA XXV, and go back to my 6¾-lb 30-in. Purdey, which has much more inertia in it. I might even undertake, as an heroic measure, a course of shooting at slow crossing targets with a flint gun! I think it just possible that, in the click–hiss–bang interval, one might have time consciously to resist any lapse of concentration away from the point ahead and towards the bird. Was that, I wonder, the secret of the flint?

19 Spontaneity

I had a letter a little while ago from a correspondent who had worked out mathematically just where to shoot in order to hit flying targets. His letter was backed by sheets of calculations nicely sprinkled with Greek omegas and cosines which, to my initiated eye, at once conveyed the impression that he knew what he was talking about. But if the calculations displayed knowledge, the letter displayed wisdom. It did so by its recognition of the futility of trying to reinforce or replace intuitive processes, as involved in the high-speed co-ordination of hand and eye, by deliberate calculation. I had, in fact, been through all this before. In my younger days I, too, had gone to work with my omegas and cosines, though I am not aware of their having ever put a single bird in my bag. Nor were they ever likely to. The fact is that over the misty ages we have developed in our brains, nerves and muscles a machinery admirably adapted to deal with the problems of time, space and velocity, as presented by a sport such as shooting; and if only we give that machinery a fair chance of working, it will produce the required result. At least, it will do so with the highest degree of certainty of which we are individually capable.

What, then, are the conditions that constitute the fair chance? I should say that there are three: confidence, practice and one other, representing the overall suitability of the gun as the indispensable intermediary between the shooter and his target. Confidence can hardly be overrated, because the lack of it, in extreme cases, can produce something approaching paralysis. So with practice: the gain in speed and accuracy it is capable of bringing about in the performance of repeated actions of the same or similar type is a matter of daily observation. How, then, can we expect to shoot well without it?

But given confidence, practice and a suitable gun, there still seems to be something required to bring the best out of the shooter. It may be only another aspect of confidence, but even so it is worth separate recognition. I would call it spontaneity of style. A year or two ago, I was discussing this with an American shooter at the Monte Carlo Gun Club, when he complained of the difficulty he had in avoiding the deliberate aiming of his gun, which he recognized as being conducive to a slow or poking style. I then roughly performed a little experiment which I have illustrated.

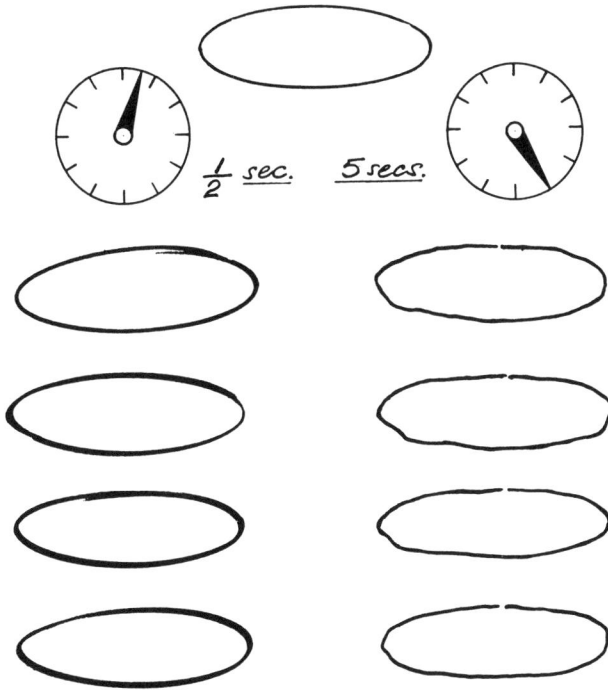

SPONTANEOUS V. DELIBERATE ACTION   The left-hand copies of the figure were each executed in one swift stroke, taking about half a second. The right-hand copies were done deliberately, taking about five seconds.

At the top of my sketch is an ellipse which has been drawn mechanically and which, I say, I am required to copy as accurately as I can free-hand. In the left-hand column are my attempts to do this spontaneously. Each would-be ellipse was made by a smooth, rapid movement which took about half a second to perform. In the right-hand column are my more deliberate efforts to copy the original. Each took just about five seconds — *ten times as long as the others*.

You may well ask, what in the world has this to do with shooting? I would say that it has a great deal to do with shooting, and that it fairly represents the difference between free, uninhibited, spontaneous action and action that is fully conscious and deliberate. The near-perfection of form of some of the left-hand figures is indeed remarkable, and it needs little imagination to equate them with the action of an expert driven-game shooter, taking his birds in first-class style throughout, and killing most of them. By contrast, the right-hand figures reveal the comparative results of a deliberate kind of shot, with a poking style. Whatever may be said for their relative accuracy, it must not be forgotten that they required so much more time than the others – time that would simply not be available if quick shooting were required.

Lessons of the ZZ bird

Shortly after the conversation mentioned, I had an opportunity of trying my hand at the famous Monte Carlo ZZ or robot birds. For the sake of those unfamiliar with these remarkable and fascinating targets, I would say that they comprise a white plastic replica of the ordinary clay target fitted into a thin, red ring of the same material. Projecting from this ring are two wings or propeller blades, about 3 in. long. When the target is struck, it comes out of the ring and falls to the ground.

These targets are spun rapidly by an electric motor, and at the word 'pull' are released with only a moderate forward impulse, whereupon they accelerate in just the same way as a bird accelerates. They leave the ground at an angle from zero to about 30 degrees and in any direction from 45 degrees right to 45 degrees left. Further, the bird appears from any one of five traps; and to complete the picture it should be added that if there is anything of a cross wind, the targets turn off into it, just as a bird would. They behave, in short, like a very strong-flying, walked-up partridge; and M. de Ferdinando, the inventor, told me that he had in fact modelled the characteristics of the target on those of the bird.

I have nothing to say about shooting this target as a formalised sport, ranking with ordinary trapshooting, but it conveys a clear lesson to me in line with my present theme. I myself have had much experience of shooting walked-up partridges and other game, at which I have usually held my own in average company. The same, or something better, could almost certainly be said of most of the shooters at our informal gathering. For all that, the standard of shooting was poor, and decidedly below what it would probably have been if the targets had been live partridges. The reason, then, must be sought in the shooting technique employed. We all took our stand at the 25½ m. mark, shouldered our guns, aimed them just over the middle trap, and called our birds, just as in ordinary trapshooting. By this system, we were more or less committed to an aiming or poking technique, which defeated me completely. Yet, oddly enough, the targets, difficult as they may have been, inspired me with confidence, because of their seeming familiarity. I felt that if I had been free to walk up to the firing point, carrying my familiar light, fast-handling gun (at the ready, but not at the shoulder), and if the bird, or all five of them, could then have been released, I should have been able to give a fair account of myself, according to past experience.

In short, it was a kind of shooting that required speed, freedom and spontaneous action. But it was attempted by methods that imposed conscious deliberation, and in the event proved the limitations of such methods.

20 *Flinching*

A Yorkshire correspondent's simple request for a 'cure for flinching' raises a curious and interesting subject, of wider scope than is commonly realised.

Flinching, according to the dictionary, is a shrinking away from anticipated pain, a wincing, a failure to face a trial or undertaking, and so on. As applied to shooting, it usually implies the existence of some straightforward physical reason for a reluctance on the part of the shooter to discharge his piece. Perhaps it is overcharged, or perhaps it is a bad fit, so that he knows, or has good reason to believe, that when it goes off, it is going to hurt him. By instinct, therefore, he tenses his muscles and screws up his nerves – he may even close his eyes – so as the better to withstand the anticipated blow.

But flinching goes deeper than this. What I have just described may be called physical flinching. It is likely to be fatal to good shooting, especially if the shooter shuts his eyes! But there is also what Barney Hartman, the celebrated Canadian skeet champion, calls psychological flinching. The shooter may have no reason whatever to expect that he is going to be hurt when his gun goes off: indeed, he may know perfectly well that he will not. So, there will be no visible tensing of the muscles, and certainly no shutting of the eyes; yet, somewhere along the chain of nerve and muscle between the shooter's brain and his trigger finger, there will be a hold-up. It may be only a very brief hold-up: the shooter may indeed fire, but he is not likely to do so successfully. Or the hold-up may be total: the bird before him may be eminently shootable, yet the shooter will put up his gun and take it down again without firing, and he may do this repeatedly. It was in these circumstances that the exasperated North Country loader finally blurted out, 'Shoot, man, shoot! – t'crack's worth t'money!'

One basic cause

I was once a witness of a bad incident of this sort. It was at a covert shoot, and for some reason the shooter concerned seemed unable to get his gun off.

Finally, realising how ridiculous this was, he fired. Unfortunately, it was at a low bird, slinking out from the covert edge, and in his desperation he fired down the line. What was worse, he peppered his neighbouring gun. What was worse still, the neighbouring gun was a lady. But, fortunately, there was a doctor in the house – he was, indeed, the gun in question. And when the lady's outraged husband came up and denounced him in thunderous terms, 'You infernal scoundrel! – you've shot my wife!', the poor fellow's flinching was no longer of the psychological order.

I believe that the basic cause of all flinching is *fear*. When it is a case of physical flinching, there is a simple, uncomplicated apprehension of being hurt. Psychological flinching, however, is more subtle and complex: the fear may have several different sources. It may arise from a mere memory, which is possibly subconscious, of being hurt on previous occasions. I have had a horse shy wildly beneath me when he recognised a particular spot as being the one where he received a bad fright months previously.

Again, it may arise from a fear of missing – the fear, that is to say, of being regarded with contempt by other members of the party, or by spectators. This can be a potent source of fear with sensitive individuals. Or the fear of missing may arise from a realisation of the special significance of a particular shot, such as the critical shot of a shoot-off in a clay pigeon contest, or at some unique opportunity in game shooting. I clearly remember missing the first chance I ever had at a blackcock, many years ago. I was shooting well on that occasion; yet the fear that I might miss this wonderful offer induced a fatal hesitation, and provoked an egregious double-barrel miss.

Various fears

I am sure that many rough shooters will share my experience of performing better – perhaps much better – at birds of relatively low esteem than they do at those more highly valued. When there is little game about, and when a single cock pheasant may make the difference between a successful and an unsuccessful foray, I am quite capable of missing the pheasant, and on the same occasion bringing off several brilliant shots at equally difficult, or even far more difficult, pigeon. The fear of missing the pheasant, and the lack of all fear of missing the pigeon, provides an adequate explanation.

In the case of the doctor who shot the lady, the inhibitory fear was, I am sure, simply the fear of missing before what were imagined to be critical spectators. It was what in another context would be described as stage fright. I have known it myself at the opening drive of a shoot where I have been a stranger guest, though I have never been reduced to the point of being unable to bring myself to fire.

But in this discussion I have not yet got down to my Yorkshire correspondent's request for a cure for flinching, though I think I may have exposed some of the causes of the trouble.

If the case is a straightforward one of physical flinching, the remedy should not be far to seek. I should think that some of the worst flinchers are to be found among my young correspondents who so wrongly pin their faith to the heaviest loads they are capable of stuffing into their guns. Further, these same guns will almost certainly include an unduly large proportion that are a bad fit, with stocks too long for young arms ('He'll soon grow into it'). If, in consequence, the butt comes to rest, not in the pit of the shoulder, but on that spot on the upper arm where there is least covering of flesh, where the biceps and deltoid muscles meet, very painful bruising may occur, and a fatal habit of flinching may be established. So it may if some considerate parent or guardian provides a young beginner with a light, well-fitted small-bore, but does nothing to ensure that the load used is light in proportion.

Treatment

The evil consequences of a flinching habit thus formed may long outlast the original cause. Conscious actions are notoriously influenced by subconscious fears, and it may well be that the psychological flinching of an adult is traceable to painful experiences endured in his youth. It is my shying horse over again.

So, the cure for physical flinching is a well-fitted gun, charged in just proportion to its weight, and correctly mounted every time. Note needs to be taken here of the existence of guns – pathological specimens – that give a sensation of recoil out of all proportion to their charge-weight ratio. As I have dealt with this subject fairly fully in *Gough Thomas's Gun Book*, I will not pursue it here, except by saying that the trouble is usually amenable to cure.

Psychological flinching, not traceable to any physical cause, needs psychological treatment. It may be sufficient in some cases merely to recognise the existence of a bad habit, as it is with other bad habits of unrecognisable origin. At other times, the shooter himself can administer the necessary treatment. Fear of missing, as such, is baseless and absurd, and needs recognising in its true light. What the devil! Who cares? The family is not short of food, and the bird will be there for the next day.

As for the fear of incurring the contempt of other members of the party, it is well to bear in mind that most men are far too preoccupied with their own performance to concentrate on that of others. And if anyone does notice that your performance is below par, far from inspiring him with contempt, it is likely to warm his heart towards you, for have you not shown up his own efforts in more favourable contrast?

21   The Blind Spot

Three curious questions of eyesight in relation to shooting have come up together. All give rise to points of interest to enquiring shotgunners.

A correspondent says, 'I am puzzled by what seems to be an unusual defect of vision, which I notice only occasionally, but which could account for some of my off-days when shooting. This is nothing more nor less than my inability to see the very thing I am trying to concentrate on. If, for example, I am looking at a printed page, I see all of it clearly except the very letter I am looking at, which simply disappears.

'I read somewhere that we all have a blind spot in our eyes. Is this it? – and if so, why doesn't everybody have my experience all the time? In my case, I think it tends to be associated with a headache condition.'

If, as I believe, I understand what is happening here, I cannot explain it without firmly separating my correspondent's symptoms from the natural blind spot to which he refers. His symptoms are familiar – I mean, they are familiar to me personally, for I have learned to regard them as a sign of incipient migraine. In my case, the disappearance of the particular letter at which I am looking on a printed page is followed by the growth of the invisible spot into a ragged ring of phosphorescent light, which expands until it finally disappears in the margin of vision. A medical friend of mine, a migraine sufferer in his early days, confirms this as a correct description of familiar symptoms. I should not regard the particular phase described by my correspondent as a good augury for shooting – it is as well to see what one is shooting at – but in my experience it is only a transient one, lasting ten minutes at the most, and could not by itself account for an off-day.

Two spots

The blind spot is a different matter altogether – it is a normal thing that exists of necessity in every eye. I have never previously considered the possibility of its having any significance in relation to shooting, but a simple experiment, which I will describe in a moment, suggests that it is by no means inconceivable.

There are, in fact, two spots of special interest on the retina of the eye – the yellow spot or fovea, and the blind spot or papilla. The yellow spot is a little depression which marks the place where vision is most acute. It is the spot on which, by instinctive movement of the eye muscles, we always try to locate the image of the object in our field of view on which our attention is concentrated. This, it would appear, is the spot that temporarily goes on strike in the circumstances first described – how and why I have no clue.

The blind spot is simply the spot on the retina where the optic nerve comes in from the back. Here, the essential means by which light waves are converted into nerve impulses are missing, being displaced by the incoming bundle of nerve fibres. In a one-eyed man, *or one who closes one eye, as in the act of aiming*, the blind spot, if I may use an Irishism, is always visible; but, curiously enough, provided that one has got the thing to which one is paying attention nicely located on the fovea, the existence of the blind spot completely escapes notice.

How a bird can disappear in the shooter's blind spot.

Still, it is easy to pin it down, and by a familiar experiment. In the diagram above, close the left eye and gaze fixedly at the cross. Then move the page slowly to and fro, when it will be found that at a distance of about a foot the bird totally disappears. Astonishing, but true! When both eyes are open the experiment fails, because whatever falls on the blind spot of one eye will not do so on that of the other. The game or skeet shooter who shuts his left eye and practises the lead-and-swing technique, may well speculate furiously on whether this experiment is capable of explaining any of his misses. The point is worth examining.

The visual angle between the fovea and the blind spot would appear to be about 12 degrees; and it would be necessary to lead a crossing bird by this amount only if it were travelling at over 150 m.p.h. at 20 yds distance, or nearly 130 m.p.h. at 40 yds. Then, and only then, would the bird disappear from the shooter's sight when he was correctly concentrating on the appropriate point ahead. I have known grouse, partridges and teal in particular that *appeared* to be flying at 100 m.p.h. when they had the wind in their tails, but even that was probably no more than 60 or 70; so I think we can rule out any possibility of the blind spot being of practical significance in shooting.

The transparent gun

My second questioner makes a good point. 'You wrote somewhere,' he says, 'that one of the great advantages of shooting with both eyes open is that an oncoming bird, which would be blotted out by the gun if one were shooting with a non-aiming eye shut, remains visible if both eyes are open, *and in the correct relation to the gun barrels, which then appear to be transparent.* But surely that must be wrong. If the bird is blotted out to what was the original aiming eye, and the other eye takes charge, surely one will get an entirely different view. Either the gun will appear to be pointing in the wrong place or, if it is re-aligned, one will miss for certain, owing to cross vision.' To make things clear, my questioner adds a convincing-looking sketch to the foot of his letter which I now reproduce.

A familiar demonstration which does not apply.

But although, as I say, this is a good point, the conclusion is false. The appeal is to practical experiment, which is best conducted sitting at a table before a window commanding an open view. Take a gun, and resting the elbows comfortably on the table, sight it at some clearly defined object out-side, both eyes being open. Now raise the muzzle slightly so as to blot out the object, as one would with an approaching overhead bird. If, keeping every-thing steady, visual impressions are then analysed, they will be found to comprise three things – the left-eye view of the object; the right-eye view of the gun; and the combined view, in which the object appears below the muzzle of what then looks like a transparent gun, and in the right relation to the line of sight, just as I originally said. I must leave it to my questioner to work out where he went wrong. It should not be too difficult.

Keeping things in focus

The third question was put up by a young friend. 'How long does it take to focus the eyes,' he asks, 'and how far could a bird fly in that time?' Rough experiment suggests that it takes me personally about two-fifths of a second to change my focus from a near to a distant object. In that time, a 40 m.p.h. bird would fly over 20 ft.

The point here is that, when waiting to take a shot, one should focus one's eyes on the place where the bird is expected, and not on the gun, or the foresight, or one's finger-nails.

22 *Shooting Habits*

Among the many advantages of being young there is one that is less well recognised, and far less publicised, than it was at times when people were more prone to moralising than we are at present. I am thinking of the ease with which we can fall into good and useful habits if only we give ourselves, or are given by someone else, a push in the right direction before we become set in our ways. Whether we regard shooting as a game of skill, as in clay pigeon shooting, or as an outlet for the hunting instinct, or as a social amusement, it offers more scope for good and bad habits than anything else of its kind that I can think of.

William James, having explained habit in terms of reflex channels formed in our nervous system, says, 'The great thing, then, in all education, is to make our nervous system our ally instead of our enemy. It is to fund and capitalise our acquisitions, and live at ease on the interest of the fund. For this, we must make automatic and habitual, as early as possible, as many useful actions as we can, and guard against growing into ways that are likely to be disadvantageous to us, as we would guard against the plague. The more details of our daily life we can hand over to the effortless custody of automatism, the more our higher powers of mind will be set free for their own proper work.'

I must apologize to my younger readers if this sounds anything like what, at school, we used to call a pi-jaw; but I am not writing about morals, but about shooting, and the ways in which we can make habit work for us in improving our standard – and standing – as sportsmen.

The most obvious scope for good habit formation in this context, then, is in the act of shooting. Many of us who are now getting long in the tooth must wish, as I do, that we had been better trained and better disciplined at an earlier age in those habits which constitute a first-class technique. If we had been, we might be better and more consistent shots than we are. It is no doubt a fine thing to be given a gun or a horse at an early age, together with the freedom to use it without adult interference; but it is equally a fine way to acquire an extensive collection of bad habits in shooting or equitation that may prove difficult, or even impossible, to eradicate later. A bold and enterprising youngster will thus show his mettle better by seeking out some sound instruction than by going his own way. If there is no one in the family circle competent and willing to afford such instruction, the local gunsmith is almost certain to be able to help. He may himself undertake coaching at his own ground; and if not, he will be able to put the young sportsman in touch with the local gun club, where there is usually a senior member only too pleased to help beginners. There, the essentials of mounting, pointing and swing may be learned, and the foundation of good marksmanship properly laid.

65

If good habits account for a large part of good shooting, as they certainly do, they are of even greater significance for good sportsmanship. For this, the first requirement is undoubtedly a deeply-rooted set of gun-safety habits. There is no standard of marksmanship that will atone for any shortcomings in this department – indeed, the man who has taken the time and trouble to acquire a first-class shooting technique, but who is indifferent to the safety code, bears the mark of a bounder in any company. The young shooter, however well grounded he may believe himself to be, should unfailingly get a copy of the *Gun Code* from his local gunsmith, and exercise the simple precautions advised in that short and simple booklet until they become engrained habits. It is not clever or smart to cut corners, and he should not be influenced by the examples he will see of his elders doing things that he has learned are wrong.

There is more in this than the avoidance of the horrible possibility of being responsible for a serious gun accident, at an impressionable age, and of having to carry the memory of it for ever after. There is worldly advantage, too, because a youngster who sets an example in this matter will be noticed and remembered, and will attract invitations and encouragement that may lead in advantageous directions, far beyond shooting.

Moving upwards, we come to another set of good habits that the young shooter should cultivate. They relate to more general behaviour in the shooting field – to good shooting manners, in short, which, like all other good manners (as distinguished from mere etiquette), are based on consideration for others. 'Do unto others . . .' is really the all-comprehensive guide here. Do you like to have another gun shoot at a bird that you feel is fairly yours? Do you like to have to listen to another gun while he explains just how he came to miss this bird and that? Would you like it as a keeper, a beater, a flanker or a picker-up, if a gun ignored an obvious opportunity of expressing his recognition of your part in a successful day? Would you like it, as a farmer who had offered a stranger a day's pigeon shooting, if he departed without a thank-you, and without picking up his litter or stooking-up once again the sheaves he took to make his hide? And, finally, if you were a dog who had spent himself in his master's service throughout a long day, would you like it if you were left wet, cold and hungry, for a minute longer than necessary, while your master fortified himself? The moral in each case is as obvious as the answer.

Section 3

GUNS

'The gun ... for all its loud voice and domineering manner, is a highly impressible thing, and, like some people with similar attributes, can be cruelly deflated in unfamiliar surroundings.'

23 Value for Money

I have had to submit (not for the first time) to a blunt confrontation on gun prices. Everybody knows, I am told, that a cheap gun will shoot just as well as an expensive one, and that you can get a good cheap boxlock for about £100. If you want a sidelock with every refinement, you can have it for £500 – or you could when this was written (1976). For something around the latter price, in fact, you could get a gun which, without your reading glasses, was indistinguishable from a best English gun costing ten times as much, and for which you would have to wait years for delivery. What possible justification can there be, then, for buying one of these fantastically-priced weapons? Who buys them, apart from Arab sheikhs, Texas oil barons and non-shooting hedgers against inflation? Surely no simple sportsman, however wealthy, who merely needs a good gun for shooting which will in no way discredit him, and which he is prepared to subject to the inescapable hazards of the field.

As I am in no way connected with the gun trade, I cannot answer these questions concerning buyers, but I can say something about the differences between the very best kind of guns, such as those which are still being turned out by our top-flight English gunmakers, and those imported ones which are designed to imitate them closely, but which cost maybe only a tenth of the price. And I can also say something relevant about that old axiom that a cheap gun will shoot just as well as a good one – as good an example as one could wish to find of a half-truth.

The imported gun

Can the imported gun shoot as well? I will deal with this point first, and chiefly with reference to the sort of guns already indicated, because these are the ones which my questioners had in mind. I have no doubt that it is the essential differences between them that most keenly exercise the curiosity of a large class of British shooters nowadays, for it is obvious that of all the men who would cheerfully have laid out £100 or so on a best English gun before the war, only a small fraction would be prepared to pay the £5000 or more that must now be contemplated as the settling price, after a long wait, for the same class of weapon.

On this point, then, the truth is that the superior foreign gun *may* shoot as well as the other, though whether it actually does so, and is capable of doing so over an extended period, is another matter. The foreign gun, indeed, offers little assurance of satisfactory performance as compared with a good bespoke weapon. The latter is usually bored to the buyer's specification, having regard to the class of sport for which it is chiefly intended, and he is free to witness its final trial at the gunmaker's plate, and to satisfy himself that it duly fulfils his requirements as to the density, quality and consistency of the patterns.

This procedure, and the opportunity it affords of checking the fit of the gun, is of inestimable value in giving the shooter confidence in his weapon. He knows *how* it shoots and *where* it shoots, and when he has an off-day, his gun at least is above suspicion.

By contrast, the shooting of the imported gun, with a cartridge arbitrarily chosen, is conjectural. It is practically certain that it will never have been shot by the makers, except for proof, and the boring assigned to it affords no firm assurance of the kind of patterns it throws. But it must nevertheless be admitted, and it should be emphasised, that its performance can readily be checked after purchase, and that it can be regulated here – probably to the same standard as the other, and without undue expense.

Critics of the kind of imported guns I am writing about sometimes say (and they used to say it with libellous embroiderment) that they were no good, or even dangerous, because they were made of rubbishy material. I have never believed it. I have no intention of mentioning any particular make of gun, so I will only say that I have investigated at source the material used for what probably remains the most popular of all the imported guns in the price class under consideration. What I found is likely to be true of comparable grades of other makes.

The barrels are made of a 3 per cent nickel steel, slightly stronger but slightly less ductile than the similar steel favoured by our best gunmakers. (Approximate British equivalent: B.S. En 23). The actions are made of a tough, malleable, low-carbon manganese steel of eminently suitable characteristics. (Approximate British equivalent: B.S. En 2).

The lockwork is made of a high-grade chrome-vanadium steel, of an ideal specification for the purpose. (Approximate British equivalent: B.S. En 47).

These are all electric alloy steels, made of a superior imported ore. But the suitability of these steels depends, in the final issue, on correct heat treatment. In the particular guns I have in mind, the hardness of the lock parts is continuously checked by a direct reading Rockwell machine, and I have not succeeded in faulting any of the many parts I have tested. The action bodies, however, are casehardened by the cyanide process, which is inferior to the prolonged baking in bone-dust still favoured for the best guns here, but not always efficiently carried out by some makers.

The representative guns of the particular make and grade I now have in my mind are well made in their essentials. The barrels are straight and well struck up, so that they are free from the bumps and hollows seen in the lower-grade sort. They are admirably jointed into the action – a point which scores heavily with me, and a guarantee that they will not come off the face after short service. The filing of the (unseen) lock parts is, of course, not up to the highest English standard, but is thoroughly adequate. The stocks, though not exotic, are quite satisfactory, as are the stocking and chequering. I have had several of these guns through my hands, and have used one of them continuously and with every satisfaction for about eight years. All of them have attracted my criticisms, but never ones of any gravity, and I cannot recite examples without appearing captious. Moreover, such minor defects of manufacture, adjustment or function as I have found have almost invariably been easily remediable. Finally, I have had many reports of these guns having given satisfactory service to others over several years, and the accounts I have had from gunsmiths who have sold them are uniformly favourable.

For all these reasons I consider them thoroughly acceptable in their intended market and good value for money, and I usually recommend them. But I always say, buy the best you can afford.

24   The Gun Comes Last

An article I wrote on guns for light loads brought an appreciative letter from an American soldier stationed over here. He is a devotee of the 28-bore, and has a magnum over-and-under of that gauge, with which I picture him wandering forlornly about the country, unable to find anyone to share his enthusiasm, unable to find suitable ammunition for it, and even having to endure the scepticism of a gun shop proprietor as to the very existence nowadays of such a thing as a 28-bore gun. That must have hurt!

But since I wrote impartially about it, and freely acknowledged the possibility that it might represent the best opportunity in certain circumstances of matching man, gun and sport, my correspondent recognised me as a potential sympathiser, and has left me in no doubt that he regards the 28 as the supreme all-round game gun.

Not that he agrees with everything I said. Chiefly, he disagrees with my statement that the 28-bore fires only about half the charge of the 12; whereas, as he points out, the $2\frac{3}{4}$-in. American 28-gauge cartridge carries as much as 1 oz of shot, a 'potent load', with which he scornfully compares the Eley 28-gauge load of $\frac{9}{16}$ oz.

But my comparison stands. What I said was that whether we consider the Eley range or the American magnum range, the 28-bore fires only about half the charge of a 12. Thus the Eley range of standard cartridges runs from $1\frac{1}{8}$ oz for the 12 to $\frac{9}{16}$ oz for the 28, whilst the American magnum range runs from $1\frac{7}{8}$ oz for the 12 to 1 oz for the 28 – which is indeed about half for the latter gauge in each case.

Logical choice

But in maintaining this point, I am in danger of starting the sort of discussion that I always seek to avoid – I mean, the discussion of the relative merits of guns *in vacuo*, independently of the two other factors I have already mentioned: the man and the sport concerned. Every gun and every load suits *somebody* best for *some* particular purpose, and before we can decide whether one gun is better than another, we must define the purpose, and check our decision against the shooter. To proceed in this way, we must first consider the kind of game chiefly in view and the range bracket within which most of our chances are likely to fall. This tells us, not what kind of gun we need, but the kind of shot charge, and the minimum pattern for reasonably consistent performance. It also tells us the weight of the gun for comfortable recoil; and if we can appraise the shooter's skill, it further gives us a guide to the best boring.

Only at this stage do we have to consider what gun to choose to shoot the charge we have decided on. The gun, indeed, comes last. In this country, we seem to have followed this line intuitively, and to have assigned to each shot charge the bore or gauge in which experience has shown it to go best. If, for example, for some light task, we need only $\frac{1}{2}$ oz or so of shot, we assign that to the 28-bore, which accounts for the existence of the Eley cartridge that aroused my correspondent's contempt; but if we want 1 oz, or $1\frac{1}{16}$ oz, or $1\frac{1}{8}$ oz, we take to a 12. We do not, in the absence of some special need or justification, consider what is the smallest gauge capable of handling the charge in question on the magnum principle.

Advantages

It is, nevertheless, a principle that has a legitimate field of application. As I said in *Shotguns and Cartridges*, the more walking and less shooting a man does in the course of a day's sport, the more he will be willing to buy lightness at the expense of recoil; and under these conditions a small-bore magnum may be well justified. Again, in the hands of a one-gun man, it can provide the flexibility of the old muzzle-loader – a light charge for dogging or walking-up birds shootable at easy range, and a heavy charge for an occasional go at wildfowl.

But my correspondent does not mention lightness, recoil or flexibility. He appears to belong to the school that claims equality of performance for the small-bore as compared with the gun of larger gauge, when firing the charges normally associated with the latter. Individual guns may, admittedly, give extraordinary results, but I can find no evidence to support the general proposition. It has not been for lack of trying: some years ago, I cast my net

very wide in an attempt to gather any such evidence, but none came my way
that would stand up to critical examination.

Handicaps

The familiar argument against the small-bore magnum is that the long shot
column unavoidably incurs more pellet-damage in the gun, so that, even if the
charge leaves the muzzle with equal velocity, it will not be so effective as that
from a normal gun. The pellets will not have the same average ranging power;
there will be more erratic 'fliers'; the shot string will be longer in flight, and
the total striking energy will be less.

But there are two sources of pellet-damage – abrasion against the barrel
wall and compressive deformation; and the former, which is the more
serious, can be prevented by the use of the modern plastic wad with protective shot-cup. Compressive deformation, however, is proportional to the
maximum pressure, to its duration, and to the number of layers of shot in the
cartridge, and in this respect the small-bore magnum is bound to be at a
disadvantage. For the charge to attain the same velocity, the maximum
pressure must either be higher or longer sustained; and even with modern
progressive powders, it is likely to be both.

The following average results from tested loads listed in the Lyman handbook are probably typical.

	Max. Pressure	Muzzle Velocity
12-ga. 2¾-in. 1 oz loads (quick-burning powders)	8270 p.s.i.	1265 f.s.
28-ga. 2¾-in. 1 oz loads (progressive powders)	10 080 p.s.i.	1170 f.s.

So, with a 22 per cent higher maximum pressure acting for a longer time on
the base of a shot column one-third greater in length, there is no possibility
of the small-bore charge surviving in such good shape as that from the normal gun; and if this increasingly damaged charge is launched with a 7½ per
cent lower muzzle velocity, it could only compete in the field with the other
if it were thrown to make a pattern of superior regularity. But I do not believe
that there is a barrel regulator in existence who could undertake, as a regular
thing, to get better results from inferior pellets, other things being equal.

So, I come back to where I started. I freely acknowledge that in certain
circumstances the small-bore magnum may be a better choice than a normal
gun, but I am sure that the policy we have hitherto followed in this country
of allotting the charges appropriate to various classes of sport to the calibres
that have been proved by experience to suit them best is conducive to the best

results. The prime object in sporting gunnery is the delivery of the most effective charge of which other factors admit. The gun, as such, comes last.

The hidden factor

Here, as elsewhere, a factor emerges that is capable of redressing any marginal disadvantage of one gun as compared with another, but that does not admit of quantitative evaluation. I am referring, of course, to confidence.

It needs to be recognised that in much or most of our field shooting, our normal guns and loads have a liberal reserve of power. The ordinary 12-bore, for example, loaded with $1\frac{1}{16}$th oz of shot, is traditionally recognised as having an effective range of 40 yds if bored improved cylinder and 50 yds if full choke. But most of the average man's shots with such a gun will be taken in the 20-30 yds range bracket, within which marginal differences in ballistics are not practically discernible.

But more or less of confidence can make a world of difference to performance, so that, *for him*, my correspondent's 28-bore may truly be the best game gun in the world.

25 Gun for Wildfowling

By the time the leaves begin to turn, another wildfowling season will have opened, and a new entry of wildfowlers will have taken the field. Some of them will have come along with the guns and other equipment that they have previously used for rough shooting or pigeon decoying, or even for trap or skeet; but others, and particularly the younger beginners, will have armed themselves anew for the game, or will be prepared to do so by the time the season gets fully into swing. Some points for their consideration may thus not come amiss.

The only young shooter in this category who has come under my immediate notice may be fairly typical. The first thing he *ought* to have done was to join WAGBI – not only to add his weight to the furtherance and protection of the sport which, like all other field sports, is open to constant attack, but also to get the benefits of membership, which are substantial, more especially as affecting access to Crown foreshore and third-party insurance. But I suspect that my young man has not yet joined, though I hope he may be induced to do so before he is much older.

But what he has done, I notice, is to buy himself a new gun. It is a well-known make of American repeater. It is a 3-in. 12-bore, weighing, at a guess, $7\frac{1}{2}$ or 8 lbs, and probably carries a full choke. This gun, I have no doubt, is proved to at least 3½ tons, and would therefore officially rank as being safe and suitable for shooting the Eley 2¾-in. 1½ oz magnum cartridge, but not the 3-in. 1⅝ oz load unless it were specially 'magnum proved'.

Unnecessary handicap

But 1½ oz of duck or goose shot makes a fine, powerful load for a shoulder gun, and according to what often passes for sound wildfowling tradition, the young shooter has fitted himself out in a proper manner. He may indeed have done so if, in due course, he finds himself using the gun chiefly for long-range flighting at dusk and dawn. But from what I know of him and his background the only wildfowl shooting he is likely to do is tapping-in to inland streams and pools – what the Americans descriptively call 'jump-shooting' – combined, perhaps, with some flight-pond work. In the intervals, he will most probably use the gun for shooting pigeon, either as they come in to roost or over decoys. So, it comes to this: that for every kind of sport I can see before him, this young shooter, for all the popular weapon-lore of wildfowling, is likely to find himself handicapped by his gun.

I have done a lot of 'jump-shooting' in my time, and provided that the water level has not been so high as to give fowl a view over the approaches, I have seldom had any difficulty in getting within easy game shooting range of them. Indeed, far from needing a heavy load in a fully choked gun for this kind of work, I would often have been best equipped with a light game load in a true cylinder. And as for the gun, a normal 12-bore game gun, or, better still, a fast-handling short-barrelled one, would have been far better for getting quickly on to birds jumping from the water than would any forward-heavy repeater. This applies particularly to teal. As for the other kinds of shooting that I can see ahead of my young sportsman, an ordinary game gun, with an improved cylinder right barrel and a moderate load, would, without the slightest doubt, fill his bag better than would the gun he has bought.

Another opinion

It may be thought that I am making too much of an individual case, and that even the shooter in question may, if not now, at least in future, extend his wildfowling into other spheres in which his gun could prove to be the right choice. As to that, of course, I cannot say, but it would be poor tactics to take to an unsuitable weapon for no better reason than that, at some future date, and in circumstances that cannot be foreseen, it *might* prove to be suitable.

On this point about other uses and other circumstances, another defect in his present weapon clearly emerges, namely, its lack of flexibility. An ordinary double gun, with an open-bored right and a choke-bored left can cope properly with both near and distant shots, as offered, which no heavily choked repeater can do. Because of the tight patterns it throws at close range, near birds are likely to be missed. If not, they will be filled disgustingly with lead; and no system of choke tubes or variable choke can provide that instant choice of close or open pattern offered by the double-triggered double gun.

Many will recognise these as familiar arguments of mine, but they are shared by other writers more worthy of attention. Max Baker, for example, equally distinguished as a writer and practical wildfowler, and the inventor of the famous pigeon decoys that bear his name, had this to say in the chapter on wildfowl shooting in *British Sporting Birds*; 'As to the guns needed for wild-fowling, fancy, especially on the part of the novice, usually dictates something of the blunderbuss order, as unhandy in weight as in dimensions. To the study of this question . . . I have naturally devoted a considerable amount of time, and at the finish remain faithful to the ordinary style of game gun having the right barrel true cylinder, and the left perhaps full choke. This view was early formed by meeting a wildfowler of supreme understanding, now, alas, dead, who used only the simple type of gun, actually without choke in either barrel. This he used for all his work, and he was out most days, the punt gun being his next larger weapon. His view was that if you are properly hidden the birds are as likely to be too near as just out of range, and therefore, that the gun is best which handles easily and delivers its charge with maximum spread.'

Yet he added – 'That many wildfowlers do favour powerful guns is a fact to which all due respect must be paid. In all probability the choice is dictated by conditions where, over and over again, long shots or none at all are imposed . . . The harder hitting gun then comes into its own.' True, *but not until then*. Success in wildfowling, as in so many other things, lies in being best equipped to cope with the normal situation, not with the rare contingency.

Gains and losses

There is more in this matter than choosing between one kind of gun and another. It lies in recognising to what extent they differ in their performance. This is where even experienced shooters go astray. A man may have been schooled by experience to recognise, say, 40 yds as his maximum effective range with an ordinary gun. But give him a heavy fully choked magnum, loaded with a magnum cartridge, and he will be only too likely to blaze away at fowl 60 or 70 yds away. Yet it is a fact that every eighth of an ounce of shot adds only two or three yards to effective range, so that the difference between the $1\frac{1}{8}$ oz that might be fired from the choke barrel of an ordinary $6\frac{1}{2}$ lb game gun, and the $1\frac{1}{2}$ oz that my young shooter is likely to fire from his $7\frac{1}{2}$ lb magnum is not 20 or 30 yds, but something less than 10.

Unlike Max Baker, I arrived at my views on the uncritical adoption of magnum guns for all wildfowling, not by contemplating the example of others, but by sheer practical experience. I can assure the reader that I did not lightly abandon my made-to-order, fully choked, long-case gun. But I did abandon it, and shot more fowl in consequence.

For my last point, I must trot out another of my hobby horses, but one requiring regular exercise. I am referring to *where* the magnum gun shoots.

Heavily choked guns, more than any others, need accurate marksmanship. But the best of marksmanship is no good unless the gun shoots where it is believed to shoot, and any gun firing a heavier load than that for which it was designed, or for which its weight renders it suitable, is almost certain to shoot low, so that the dense part of its pattern may pass clean below the point of aim. This is a point particularly needing attention from those shooters with modern $2\frac{3}{4}$-in. 12-bores, weighing $6\frac{1}{2}$ to $6\frac{3}{4}$ lbs, and designed for game loads, but used on occasions with the $1\frac{1}{4}$ oz Alphamax cartridge. Such guns, so loaded, are quite likely to shoot a foot or more low at extended range, whereby all the advantages of the heavy charge may be lost, and birds may be missed or only pricked that should have been brought to bag.

26   *Where Does It Shoot?*

Shooting literature teems with arguments, discussions, theories and experimental evidence concerned with *how* shotguns shoot — that is to say, with the quantitative and qualitative aspects of their patterns and their ballistical properties. By comparison extremely little has been written about *where* they shoot. Yet this aspect is as important as the other, for the finest patterns ever made obviously put no game in the bag unless they are placed on the target. This is a matter which, as I have said, has been much neglected in the past by both gunmakers and shooters alike.

There are good reasons for this. The spread of the pellets of an ordinary gun is sufficient to mask very considerable discrepancies between the point of aim and the centre of the charge, to such an extent that the owner of an in-accurate shooting weapon can use it for years without realising how much his performance is suffering on that account. The maker of cheap guns can thus neglect all proper measures to ensure accurate shooting and still get away with it. I say he can; and it is probably not unfair to say that he nearly always does. In consequence, his customers, even if they are accurate shots, will often be taking their game with the less efficient, off-centre parts of their patterns, and doing slovenly work when they ought to be killing outright.

For these reasons, I have written much about the things that affect the relation between the point of aim and the charge centre; and, looking back, it would seem opportune to clear up some points I have not previously elaborated, and to mention some new ones.

Elevation

In an article I wrote in 1967, I suggested that there was one kind of inaccuracy – a somewhat high-shooting tendency – that could be counted as merit in a gun, both for game and clay target shooting. It seems that I could have been more positive in what I said, for a friend having read my article, telephoned to ask me, in what I took to be a tone of mild reproach, whether, when writing, I had remembered what Hawker had to say on the subject. I had to confess that I had not. But I have since looked him up, and our great English master-gunner is certainly positive enough. Referring to the argument, current in his day, to the effect that short-barrelled guns shot better than those with barrels of 34-in. or so, as then favoured, he says: 'But still the short guns have often *shown off best* in the field. Why is it? Because the gunmakers regulate their guns to shoot well *to* the bull's eye; whereas they ought to shoot *above* the bull's eye; *and the longer the gun, the higher must be the elevation!*' Hawker's explanation contains no reference to the smaller negative flip of the shorter barrels, and their inherent tendency to shoot higher, about which he probably knew nothing, but he is in no doubt about the practical effect. Referring to long shots, he says that 'if the gun is not kept well up, the shot will fall from its own gravity; that a long snap-shot is always at a *rising*, and not a straightforward-going bird; and that if a good shot misses through being nervous, it is always *because his left hand drops as he flinches*.' He adds, 'We should rarely err by somewhat over-elevating our guns.' So there we are, with all the emphasis of Hawker's italics.

I subsequently had an opportunity of discussing this matter in Birmingham with one of our finest English gunmakers. He appeared to agree with what I have said on the subject of elevation, and added that he normally regulates his game guns to shoot about 3 in. high at 40 yds. In my article quoted, I suggested about 6 in, which I feel inclined to let stand. The difference is unlikely to be significant.

Cast and spring

In another article, I explained how cast-off, as normally applied to right-handed English guns, tended to produce a lateral error in the left barrels only of side-by-side guns, and in both barrels of an over-and-under. Only two cases have come to my notice of this error being sufficient to be detected in the field by the shooter of a side-by-side gun, and then only with heavy charges, but it seems to be conspicuous in some over-and-unders carrying considerable choke. Indeed, the celebrated Joe Wheater has been quoted to me as insisting that O/U trap guns, for this reason, should on no account be cast-off.

A criticism of my reasoning has, however, arisen out of consideration of the special case of guns with cross-eyed stocks, as adapted to shooting left-eyed from the right shoulder or *vice versa*. It has been suggested that if a normal cast-off, not exceeding, say, half an inch, can produce a measurable lateral error in the left barrel, the relatively enormous cast of a cross-eyed gun should produce an intolerable error. So it might seem; but in this case a compensation occurs due to the springing of the stock in the hand portion. Sketch (a) shows what happens better than any verbal description. I have never tested a cross-eyed gun for lateral error, but I should be prepared to find nothing serious, for the reason now given.

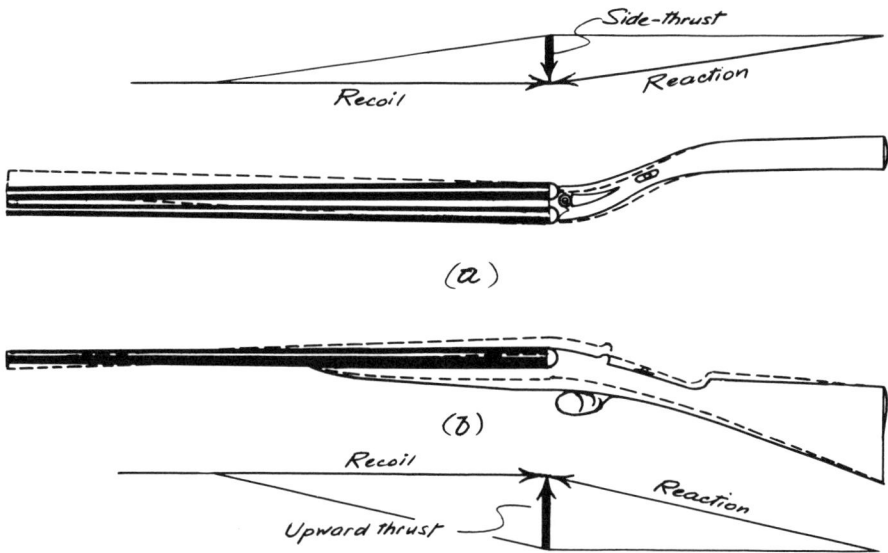

HOW STOCK-FLEXURE AFFECTS THE SHOOTING OF A GUN   In a gun with a cross-eyed stock (*a*) the side thrust developed on recoil would by itself cause the gun to shoot strongly to the left; but flexure, shown dotted, introduces a compensating tendency to shoot to the right, as indicated. In an ordinary gun (*b*) the upward thrust developed on recoil causes vertical flexure, as shown, which increases the tendency of the gun to shoot low.

In the case of a normal gun, with or without cast, it was apparent to me that this springing of the stock in the hand could contribute seriously to a low-shooting tendency, as indicated in sketch (b). I was accordingly much interested the other day to come across an account, published in *The Field* of 30 July 1892, of a light game gun which was proved to shoot low for this reason.

The gun in question was a 30-in. 12-bore, weighing only 6 lbs. With the relatively heavy charge, for a gun of this weight, of 3 drams of powder and 1⅛ oz of shot, the gun placed its charge centre 12 in. low — sufficient to prejudice performance quite seriously, particularly that of the choke barrel. The cause having been correctly diagnosed, the hand of the stock was reinforced experimentally by glueing splints of wood to it, whereupon the gun shot true to the point of aim.

This source of error could obviously be a serious matter in the case of guns made exceptionally small in the hand, such as a pair by Stephen Grant I once owned. The writer of the account, who appears to have been a gunmaker, made the proper point that the springing of stocks in the hand could be reduced by hollowing and lightening the butt portion, and transferring the weight saved to the action and the breech ends of the barrels.

Regulating the shooting

I have referred elsewhere to the better-known ways of regulating the shooting of guns for elevation, including the adjustment of the elevation of the rib in the course of manufacture, and the bending of the barrels, as practised by the Americans in the course of fitting choke attachments to single-barrelled guns. I have also pointed out the significance of the weight-stiffness ratio of barrels, and the way in which the vibrational whip, or 'flip', can be influenced by the distribution of weight fore and aft. In barrels of given overall weight and of the same length, I should expect those with the more forward distribution of weight always to shoot lower than those of opposite case. This, I suspect, is much neglected as a manufacturing control.

Unfortunately, none of these considerations is of much help to those correspondents who come to me, having found by practical test that their double-barrelled guns shoot unduly low; for although the bending of the barrels of such guns is feasible, it is not a technique that is practised in this country. Neither is eccentric choking or recess-choking, though I fail to see why some enterprising maker or repairer should not develop the technique and offer to re-regulate low-shooting guns accordingly. Journée quotes a St Etienne barrel-maker, M. Breuil, as practising eccentric or oblique choking, and he himself experimented with two guns so choked. In this way, he obtained a correction of about 9 in. at 40 yds. I myself have a gun with an eccentric recess choke – confined, that is, to the lower part of the bore near the muzzle. This gun throws its charge well high, though I have no means of checking how it shot originally. Still, as an elevation-correcting device, this has highly attractive possibilities, which our more enterprising repairers could easily and profitably explore. In many cases it would be more acceptable than the familiar expedient of straightening the stock.

27   Is the 30-inch Barrel Dead?

A member of the gun trade recently commented adversely to me on the value of a certain high-quality English game gun for the reason that it had 30-inch barrels. I had every reason to respect his opinion on guns in general, and the occasion made me ask myself, just what is the present status of the 30-inch barrelled gun?

For trap guns, this, of course, is a favoured length, but not for game guns. For these, it became established as the best length for a 12-bore at the end of the black powder era; but by the time smokeless powder had ousted the older kind, 28 inches had come to be recognised as the longest barrel strictly necessary for the efficient combustion of the charge. From this limited viewpoint, therefore, the 30-inch barrel had become obsolete; and since shooters everywhere were only too ready to shed a few ounces from the weight of their guns, provided that they could be assured of sustained performance, 28 inches became the fashionable length.

But even from the restricted viewpoint of the combustion of the charge, there is nothing critical about 30 inches or 28, and for a proper appraisal of barrel length, there are several other factors to be taken into account. The first, perhaps, is the one I touched on last – that of fashion. It would be easy, but misleading, to underrate it.

The influence of fashion

We tend to think of fashion as being the preoccupation of the light-minded, but we all come under its influence, and it is significant here as affecting, perhaps very considerably, the re-sale value of a gun.

But there is another aspect of fashion where guns are concerned, and the knowledge or belief or suggestion that the gun we are using is out of date could materially affect our confidence in it – worse, if we had already dubbed it in our thoughts as being 'obsolete'. For best results, we undoubtedly need complete confidence in our weapons, and any niggling distrust, whatever the cause, and however unfounded, will take its toll of performance. We see the converse of this in the improved standard of shooting we often enjoy when we take to a new gun – a gun, that is to say, which has never had an opportunity of letting us down, or of being associated with any off-days or hoodoos.

So if we are inclined to look askance at our gun, or at any gun, for no better reason than that its barrels are of an unfashionable length, I suggest that we should suspend judgment until we have considered some of the other, and more weighty, factors concerned.

Performance

This brings us to the performance of 30-inch barrels against those of any shorter length, and by that I mean, in the first instance, the performance independently of the shooter. Here we are on firm ground, because all the factors concerned can be measured, and have in fact been measured so often in the past as to leave little room for doubt or uncertainty.

Thus, 30-inch barrels have a slightly higher velocity than those of 28 inches. or less; the terminal pressure is lower, giving less muzzle blast and some prospect of a marginal superiority in the patterns; and other things being equal, they weigh more and recoil less, and in movement have a greater inertia. For what it may be worth in terms of pointability, they provide a longer sight-base.

But when we bring the shooter into the discussion, and consider the performance of man and gun on a joint basis, as we always should do in these cases, the only really significant factors we are left with are weight, recoil and inertia; and the point I want to bring out is that with some individuals they may operate more or less strongly in favour of the longer-barrelled weapon.

Take weight: there is no doubt that after handling a $6\frac{3}{4}$ lb gun, one of $6\frac{1}{2}$ lb or less is disproportionately pleasant to use. And I say disproportionately because, to a healthy man, a mere few ounces of weight cannot be as significant as it appears at first. It is really chiefly a matter of habituation, and so long as a man does not expose himself to the seduction of a lighter gun, he is likely to remain happy with his old 30-inch barrelled favourite until old age demands some relief.

Until then, he remains in enjoyment of its lesser recoil, which may be important if he does much shooting, and its greater inertia, which may impose a beneficial deliberation.

Blessing or bane?

One of the main advantages claimed, and justly claimed, for shorter barrels, and especially the spell-binding 'XXVs', is their faster handling, arising from their reduced forward inertia. But the other side of this medal is that the reduced inertia exposes the shooter to checking his swing, and it is for this reason that some men simply cannot get on with them. A deliberate, unhurried style is generally recognised as being advantageous, and such a style is encouraged by the greater inertia of the longer barrels. The point here is, when and to what extent is faster handling advantageous? It depends on the kind of shooting, as well as on the man; and I recently had a relevant lesson on this point.

I had been missing my crossing shots, and was having some practice clays under the good guidance of Ken Chard of Exeter. He was sending me fast birds from the trap, invisible to me, on a high bank, and my situation exactly resembled that of a flank gun at a partridge drive. Now this is a kind of sport for which a fast-handling, short-barrelled gun would normally be considered ideal. Yet, though I was using my 28-inch Lang, I was reacting too quickly, as Chard succeeded in convincing me. Indeed, I found that on the birds' first appearance, I had plenty of time to say, 'God save our gracious Queen' before I moved a muscle to start mounting and tracking them. Then I started hitting them in good style. What is more, sometimes they vanished completely in a hazy sun, yet the inertia of my gun carried it forward at the right pace to score a hit. I am sure that I would have done better, not worse, with my old 30-inch Purdey, which had restored my lost timing on several occasions.

This and much related experience, both direct and vicarious, has convinced me that, far from being dead, 30-inch barrels, whether fashionable or no, are the right thing for many men on many occasions. To say this is not to retract a word I have written about short barrels in the past; it only puts the case for critical and independent judgment in the light of all circumstances.

28 The Well-Integrated Gun

In a letter I once received, a correspondent, describing the result of an ingenious conversion job, said that, after all, it was not 'a well-integrated gun, if you know what I mean.' I certainly knew what he meant, and have used the phrase myself, without perhaps being clear as to its precise significance. Yet there is a very real something here. It is a something that represents a large part of the difference between a thoroughbred gun and a mechanical shot projector; and it represents nearly the whole of the difference between a gun of high-class origins and workmanship, but which lacks a certain *je ne sais quoi*, and one that does not.

What I am concerned with here is no idle fancy, but a stage in the attainment of ultimate efficiency. As such, it is worth attempting to analyse.

Some years ago, I met a yeoman farmer at a shoot who had a gun with an unusual feature that caught my eye. When we stopped for lunch I asked him to let me have a look at it. It was indeed a beautiful gun so far as workmanship went, and it bore the name of a celebrated maker north of the border — a maker, I hasten to say, who is no longer with us. Noting my admiration, the farmer said that the gun was one of a pair, which he never used as such; and that if I was interested, he would consider an offer for the other one. So I arranged to have it on trial; but it needed very little trial to convince me that the gun was not for me: it was beautifully made, but it lacked balance and handling quality, as well as that something else which I am trying to define. It is a help to be able to say that it is nothing to do with the performance of a gun, but is a quality, or combination of qualities, that can be appraised without shooting.

Apart from shooting, then, how do we size up a gun? In the present sense, we can only appraise it by its appearance, and by the muscular and tactile sensations arising from carrying, handling and manipulating it. Three of our senses are thus involved.

Appearance is important; and in saying that I am not concerned with such superficialities as engraving or the figure of the stock. I am not even concerned with the external evidence of workmanship, but rather with what conformation implies in a gun, as in a horse. Sporting guns are what I have described as intimately manual implements, and centuries of development have given the best kinds a certain line and certain proportions which provide the connoisseur with immediate indications of the suitability of the gun for its purpose. The shape and size of the stock, and of the grip, and their relationship to the main masses of the gun, tell an immediate story to an experienced judge — so do the form and position of the trigger, the lever, and even the safety catch. Triggers can be well- or ill-shaped, and close up to the action or otherwise. The lever can go very wrong. One that is too short, that has too large an opening angle, and that combines these defects with an inadequate thumb-piece, can be a constant irritant in active shooting. There is a just rightness here that not all our best gunmakers have always attained.

So with the safety catch. As something requiring frequent manipulation, it, too, can go wrong — and not only in its positioning, as in the decorative but unhandy Greener side-safety, but in its size, shape and roughening. I recall two safety catches so smooth and unobtrusive that I sometimes thought I had pushed them off when in fact I had not; and I recall plenty that were offensively otherwise. Every one of these defects can be spotted by eye.

There was a music hall song years ago which asserted that all girls are alike in the dark — a proposition I would be prepared to dispute. Whether or not, these other objects of men's affections — guns, I mean — have qualities that need no daylight for their appraisal, not even when weights are the same — for that matter, not even when balance is the same. Two remaining senses arrive at their judgments without calling on visual evidence; the muscular sense and the tactile sense. The former assesses the energy called for in the active handling of the gun, and the proportionate contributions required from the two hands, whilst the latter assesses the shape and surface condition of the parts handled, as affecting the sense of touch.

To satisfy the muscular sense it is necessary that the gun should be light, and that its inertia or stored energy when swung from one position to another should be low. (For every man, there will be an optimum in these matters, depending partly on his physical reactions and partly on the kind of use he requires of the gun.) It is also necessary that the point of static balance should fall nicely between the hands; for this is the point about which the gun tends to turn in all turning movements, and if it occupies a materially different position the gun will give the impression of trying to resist its user, and going its own way. I have explained this matter more fully in *Shotguns and Cartridges*. It involves consideration of a measurable quantity known to engineers as the 'least moment of inertia'; and I can only say now that this is a prime factor in determining the handling quality of a gun, and that no gun is well integrated if it fails to realise this quantity at the right place along its length.

The tactile quality of a gun is seldom or never mentioned, as such. Yet a wise old gunmaker, when examining a gun, will often be seen to feel it carefully all over. Clearly, there is a matter of some importance here, for a gun so rough as to be distracting, or so smooth and slippery as to elude a firm grip, would be at once rejected. The chequering, of course, should be just right, but there is more involved than that; the well-integrated gun must have fluent lines and surfaces, and the right surface quality to be acceptable and pleasant to the hands. If everything is realised to perfection in this department, there will be a positive pleasure in handling the gun. A woman friend, writing about her John Dickson 20-bore, once said to me, 'It *feels* so lovely – like an old violin.' That puts the matter very nicely.

But if the gun trade does not usually refer to well-integrated guns, or to moments of inertia, or to tactile aesthesia, our best gunmakers have a keen, intuitive appreciation of these things, and have taken them as some of their guiding lights in evolving the finest kinds of traditional guns. They are, as I said, no idle fancy, for inasmuch as they largely determine the pleasure and economy of effort with which a gun can be used, and the extent to which it enables the shooter to forget it, and to concentrate on his shooting, they make a real contribution to efficiency. Happily, a well-integrated gun does not have to be costly, but a costly one should certainly be well integrated.

29   *The Impressible Gun*

The modern science of ecology, which treats of the mutual relations between living things and their environment, could fairly be extended to cover some of the things that these organisms produce – outstandingly those of that restless two-legged creature who above all others makes the angels weep. Whatever he has brought out over the years can only be fully understood and appraised in relation to the environment in which it was evolved, it being understood that by environment we mean all the physical, economic and historical influences to which it was subjected in the process. This is true of a host of things: domestic utensils, agricultural implements, means of transport, clothes, furniture, tools and weapons – all reveal its influence, and often its nature. A Chinese junk, a Dutch galiot and an Italian felucca express more than the differences between Eastern, Western and Mediterranean idiom in ship design, and if interchanged would no doubt reveal marked incompatibilities with their environment and a lower standard of efficiency than the native product.

So with guns. Few things have done more than these tubes stuffed with lead and 'villainous saltpetre' to change human environment and to bring it under control, and few things have in turn been more amenable to its influence. The pioneering man, utterly dependent on his gun, as he so often was, for food and defence, will have been made sharply aware of its deficiencies and limitations, and constantly spurred to remedy or remove them. Under settled conditions, with the gun reduced to the status of an implement of sport, the needs of sportsmen, the spirit of emulation between them, and commercial competition between gunmakers will have replaced necessity in stimulating improvement. The gun, in short, for all its loud voice and domineering manner, is a highly impressible thing and, like some people with similar attributes, can be cruelly deflated in unfamiliar surroundings.

Rifle of Empire

Outstanding examples of mutual reactions between gun and environment, in the physical sense, readily occur. The opening up of the old British dependencies in Africa, like the establishment of the British Raj in India, brought many explorers, traders, ivory hunters and sport-loving Army officers into contact with the dangerous big game of those regions. The development of that unique British speciality, the large-calibre, double express rifle, with its terrific stopping power and its almost perfect reliability for a quick second shot, followed as it were automatically. In its heyday, its impact on big game, both in the literal and figurative sense, was unmistakable. In 1907, Carl Larsen, a Danish hunter in Portuguese South-West Africa, shot seven lions in thick bush in two minutes with a Jeffery ·600 double express. I once possessed one of these fine rifles, and for all its 15 lbs, so beautifully was it balanced and so fast-handling that one could almost have used it for shooting rabbits in covert. But sad to say, as we abdicated from our Imperial role, our production of these magnificent weapons declined in proportion, and the highly specialized skill needed to make and regulate them must now be nearly lost.

Rifle of Independence

An even better example of firearm ecology is provided by the American so-called Kentucky rifle. The original German settlers in Pennsylvania brought with them the typical German Jäger rifle of the period – a weapon developed for forest shooting in Northern Europe. This was a heavy short-barrelled rifle of large bore. It was effective against anything from deer to European brown bear, and in particular was capable of stopping the charge of that notoriously touchy, aggressive and dangerous beast, the wild boar. But the weapon was unsuited to the conditions of eastern North America, where there was no dangerous game, and where its weight and that of its ammunition was excessive for frontiersmen whose rifles seldom left their hands. Besides, its appetite for powder and lead must have been disadvantageous at a time when these commodities were likely to be scarce and dear.

Accordingly, the rifle underwent a forced evolution, and eventually became what was essentially an accurate deer rifle, and one that was incidentally effective against hostile Indians. The calibre was reduced from, say, ·700 to around ·450; and since the powder charge was proportionately much increased to bring about a corresponding increase in velocity, the barrel was greatly lengthened to enable the charge to be burnt efficiently.

Thus adapted to its changed environment the rifle in turn reacted on that environment sufficiently to have become a significant factor in American history. It is even credited in folk-lore with having been the decisive weapon of the War of Independence; and if that is not historically true – if the decisive weapon was really the Committee of Safety musket, or the Charleville musket, or simply British ineptitude – the Kentucky rifle at least dominated the early phases of the campaign. Nobody seems to know, incidentally, how this rifle of Pennsylvanian origin came by its familiar name.

The influence of history

'History is bunk,' said the first Henry Ford in one of his less inspired moments. Yet guns, no less than other things, are deep-dyed by history. Pistols, and more particularly revolvers, which in Europe are largely regarded with distaste because of their criminal associations, appear to have a fascination for the average American citizen which can only be explained on historical grounds – their association with a phase of American history which, though tinged by much that was lurid and brutal, may yet be seen as one of the great folk-migrations of all time.

By contrast, our English double-barrelled gun, according to my interpretation, reflects a phase of our sporting and agricultural history when the partridge flourished everywhere on arable land, and was shot over pointers and setters. Then, the appropriate weapon was obviously one that could take a brace out of a covey. Similarly, the height of perfection later attained by these double guns – their lightness and elegance, their speed of handling and their superb balance – reflects the heyday of driven game shooting, and the tastes and demands of the wealthy and critical sportsmen who did so much to stimulate their production.

Equally redolent of history are the American repeaters. If there had never been an American Civil War, the repeating rifle might never have been developed when and where it was, and American arms manufacturers would have lacked the inducement they later felt to produce a repeating shotgun. Similarly, but for the historical fact that, after the country had settled down, there was still a vast quantity of wild game outside the settled areas, and a large tribe of market-gunners busily exploiting it, there would have been little demand for such a shotgun, if produced. Also a matter of history is the impact of the repeater on American game and wildfowl; whilst the reaction to that impact may be seen in the conservation laws and the plugged magazines of these guns, and their tendency to evolve from five-shot into three-shot and two-shot types, such as the short-recoil Browning and the new Armalite.

The gun for the job

These thoughts bring me round to a point to which I often return, by one way or another, in the course of my writings. The best kind of gun, and the best load – even the best size of shot – for a given kind of sport in a given country are almost certain to be those evolved on the spot and generally favoured by the more experienced resident practitioners. Anything exotic imported by a stranger will be likely to put him at a disadvantage in one or more respects, which, if they do not reveal themselves immediately, may yet do so over the long term. Even an overall ballistical advantage could be disadvantageous if it gave a man what might appear to be an unfair or greedy start on his companions: he might suffer not only an inevitable loss of popularity, but a future loss of shooting invitations.

But if few men are likely to fall into this particular trap, many, I am sure, fall into that represented by trying to use, for general mixed shooting in this country, a heavy and heavily choked, 2¾-in. chambered gun, with load to match, instead of the lighter, more open-bored, indigenous weapon.

30   Eumatic Principles

The *Penguin Dictionary*, the B.B.C. were at pains to assure us, contains, in addition to other things, certain obscenities hitherto ignored by respectable lexicographers. If they could find room for such superfluities, I wish I had suggested that they include the word 'eumatic', which will not be found in any existing dictionary. It is a pity, because it is a word well adapted to denote principles of much importance to all manually operated implements, such as guns, and ones that should pervade the minds of all concerned with their design. It is ironical comment on an age that invented the word 'functionalism' that many such designers have either never become acquainted with the principles concerned, or, if they have, that they should so often forget them.

Broadly speaking, 'eumatic' may be taken to mean 'convenient', but, in coining the word, I have much more in mind than can be fobbed off in that way. The manufacturer of a mechanical appliance may say in his instructions, 'The so-and-so can be *conveniently* operated by a knob close to the operator's right hand.' The knob may be close to the operator's right hand, sure enough, but to operate it he first has to turn his wrist over in order to hook his forefinger around it. He then finds that the direction of motion is such that he can only exert a fraction of the strength normally available in his arm and hand. Worse is to follow: the wretched thing springs surprises on him. A strong initial resistance suddenly collapses, so that the motion continues headlong, until brought up with a jerk; or, alternatively, it starts easily, and then develops a sudden increased reluctance to proceed, so that the operator has to signal for reserves of muscular power to overcome it. And, anyhow, it should not have been a knob; it should have been something much better shaped to accommodate a hooked finger.

'Eu' and 'non-eu'

By this simple example of a thoroughly non-eumatic contrivance, I have almost escaped the necessity for a definition. But not quite. So I will define my verbal bantling by saying that it expresses that quality in a manually operated device whereby it is *totally* correlated to the human being who has to use it. This means that parts requiring to be handled shall be fully conformable to the hands or fingers, as the case may be, and shall be placed so that they are accessible, and can be worked without assuming any forced or unnatural postures. Further, that the direction and range of motion, and the resistance to be overcome, shall be such as to employ to best advantage those muscles which the operating posture brings most naturally into readiness and play. Lastly, that the quality of the motion shall be in conformity with the operator's expectations, free from all harshness and from any sudden changes in resistance or direction.

As a fairly obvious rider to all this, it may be added that full observance of eumatic principles is most important when extensive movements and considerable exertion are involved at frequent intervals, and least so when things are otherwise. Nobody minds very much if his cigarette lighter is non-eu, provided it lights.

But, generally speaking, there is no doubt of the pleasure to be derived from using some mechanical implement or device that has been designed on the best eumatic principles. There is an aesthetic quality in smooth, sweet action, responsive to easy control, that recalls a bridle-wise horse with easy paces, as opposed to a hard-mouthed brute that seems always to be travelling down-hill.

Our guns, regarded in the light of eumatic principles, are a mixed lot, and reveal some unexpected weaknesses. They would reveal more, were it not for our wonderful adaptability, whereby a truly non-eumatic feature in design can sometimes be overcome by a simple knack. For example, although I am a staunch believer in the superior overall merits of the conventional side-by-side gun, I must confess that the motion of opening it by turning over the left wrist is strictly non-eu. That explains the curious difficulty in opening and closing the gun frequently observed when someone tries to do it for the first time, or when a new gun is somewhat stiff. The essential unnaturalness of the movement is most noticeable with the exaggerated opening-arc of most over-and-unders, when it is emphasised by the undue size of the lever (that is to say, the barrels and fore-end) that has to be handled. The self-opener avoids the charge of contravening eumatic principles during the opening phase, but may run into it on closing, if there is any undue resistance. The earlier Purdeys were open to criticism on this account, and also because of an element of unexpectedness in the opening action. When the gun had not been fired, there was a momentary hesitation when the lever was pressed over, followed by an unduly precipitate opening. These criticisms have long since been overcome by subtle improvements in design.

Another highly non-eu feature of the conventional drop-down gun arises from badly designed or regulated Southgate ejectors. I once had a gun, bearing a famous name, that was conspicuously defective in this way. After both barrels had been fired, the reclosing of the gun met with strong resistance during the recompression of the ejector springs, which ran up to a sharp peak and then suddenly collapsed with a disconcerting clack, as if something had broken. This is merely an exaggerated instance of what is normal with this kind of ejector.

But perhaps the worst offender on the present calendar is the hammer gun – at least, when the hammers are cocked in the way usually recommended, with the barrels pointing to the ground. Fortunately, however, the gun can recover its lost eu-rating by being pointed to the sky while cocking and uncocking.

Truly eumatic

Under the present terms of reference, some curiously high performances are put up by the repeaters. Indeed, I hope it may count in my favour as an unbiased observer if I say that the standard American pump-gun is probably the weapon with the highest eumatic rating of all. It was surely a stroke of genius to make the business of cartridge ejection, recocking and reloading ensue, more or less automatically, from the convulsive reaction to recoil and the instinctive recovery from it. Who the earliest inventor of the principle was, I do not know – it may have been Alexander Bain, whose British pump-gun patent was dated 1854, but in the American Spencer shotgun of 1885 it appears in modern form. All credit to John Moses Browning for his perspicacity in adopting it for his 1888 and 1890 patents, subsequently exploited with such success by Winchester.

The undoubted merit of this basic feature of the pump-gun is what chiefly gives me the respect for these weapons to which I have previously confessed here, and, although I got into trouble the last time I made the impious suggestion, I still think it is a pity that some mechanical genius has not taken this honoured relic of the Victoria era in hand and designed a truly modern version, free from the crudities in respect of balance and other imperfections of those now made.

But to return to my muttons, lever-actions and bolt-actions are both without serious criticism from the eumatic viewpoint. True, the bolt-action involves interrupted movement, but this seems to be pre-eminently a case where an easily acquired knack fully overcomes a theoretical disadvantage. Witness, if required, is the little favour commanded by the straight-pull principle.

The pursuit of perfection

I am sure there will be some readers of these notes to whom my observations will appear, if not meaningless, at least not significant. But, in fact, they express something vital to the progress of mechanical design in its present context. In these days, when the rising generation of shooters usually have to put up with guns inferior to those their fathers possessed, they provide a basis both for criticism and appreciation which, if abandoned, can only result in a further decline in the standards of gunmaking. The gun trade, like any other, could quickly get tired of taking pains over products which their customers lacked the knowledge or critical faculty to appreciate.

31   The Anatomy of Elegance

The idea of elegance is inseparable in my mind from fine sporting guns. It is, indeed, the first attribute that impresses me when I look at a favourable specimen, and the first thing I miss when it is not present. Snobbery would suggest that it is a quality largely monopolised by high-class (and more than correspondingly high-priced) English guns; but that is not true, because elegance is largely a matter of external form, and to that extent is realisable in a relatively inexpensive gun, provided that the maker has the taste and discernment to recognise its constituents. Conversely, not every expensive gun is elegant, even though it may be above reproach on the quality of its material and workmanship.

If that is so, it might be argued, then elegance is obviously a matter of no importance. I would not agree; I consider that it is a matter of notable importance, and that every sportsman who seeks the utmost enjoyment from the possession and use of a gun should learn to recognise it and value it, and understand its significance. So, I will try to define this elusive element, and to show why it is important to all but hardened Philistines. If, to you, a gun is no more than a mechanical shot projector, turn the page: but if you are conscious of its being more than that, please bear with me while I try to explain.

What it means

Among the many shades of meaning associated with 'elegant' in my dictionary, the most appropriate here are, 'marked by finish and simplicity; neat and apt'. And again, 'marked by careful and tasteful selection or execution; characterised by grace, propriety and refinement'.

With the help of these definitions, I think I can say what I mean by an elegant gun. It is one of graceful and simple outline, neatly and tastefully finished, of which all the external features have been carefully designed and executed. Above all, it is one which is *refined* in the best sense of the word, as being of a shape that has been fined-down over the years to the irreducible simplicity consonant with its function; purged of all excrescences, and totally adapted to the human being who has to use it. In short, it is a gun that has the highest degree of functional beauty; and therein lies the key to the value of elegance, for a manual implement or weapon that has functional beauty will always be more pleasant, satisfactory and efficient in use than one that lacks it. Thus, the elegant gun will not only please the eye, but also the hand, irrespective of whether it is merely being carried or actively used. The grip

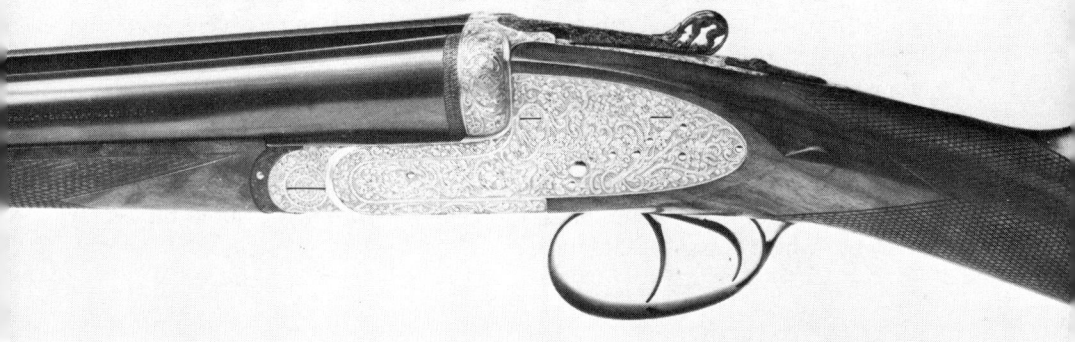

An outstandingly elegant 12-bore made by Luigi Franchi and presented by the President of the Italian Republic to Prince Philip in 1965.

will be of the right shape, correctly disposed in relation to the triggers, and the lever and safety catch will be just where the thumb most readily seeks them, and of a shape and surface quality best adapted to respond to its pressure. In the course of its evolution, the elegant gun will have been blind and deaf to the exigencies of mass-production by machinery.

Stocks and decoration

The true, austere doctrine of elegance eschews all mere decoration, as its high priest, Beau Brummel, did when he designed our masculine evening dress, in which most men still look their best. One of the most elegant guns I ever saw was a flintlock made for the Duke of York by one of the Manton brothers. The metal work was finished a plain black, and bore no trace of engraving – not even border engraving. The name 'Manton' was inlaid in gold – that is all.

Still, the decoration of sporting arms is a matter of ancient tradition, and I would not deny my elegant gun some engraving. I recognise two sorts: craftsman's engraving and artist's engraving, between which there is no clear, distinguishing line. Curiously, one of the best-known engraving styles — the so-called Purdey engraving — is pure craftsman's engraving and makes no pretence at all to artistic merit. It conforms to no overall design, but has the advantage of being inconspicuous. Engraving which is conspicuous must, if elegance is not to suffer, be designed as a whole and possess genuine artistic quality. Schiller's maxim, 'The artist is known by what he omits', is very true here.

But even the most artistic and finely executed engraving, including chiselling and gold inlay, can never by itself endow a gun with elegance, and a gorgeously decorated repeater reminds me of a woman who tries to make up for a lack of natural dignity and distinction by an ostentatious display of jewellery.

Exotic stocks also confer no elegance, though they may add distinction to an otherwise elegant gun. But insofar as they may, by obvious weakness, be less efficient than plainer ones, they detract from that assured fitness for purpose which is part of elegance.

A thing of beauty

When, in the course of one of my solitary forays, I come to one of those little secret places on the fringe of the woods, and call in my dog as I sink into an armchair of dried bracken to eat my midday bite, and the sun comes out, I prop up my gun where I can see it to advantage. Then its panther-like elegance, combining repose and menace, its beauty of line and feature, give as much pleasure to my eye as the food does to my palate. It is a pleasure that never palls.

32   Who Made It?

Nothing that I have written over the past years has served to stem the flow of correspondents' enquiries about their guns — their history, their age, their grade, what they cost when new, and what they are worth now. Very often, my replies seem to me to have a rubber-stamp quality, as indeed have the enquiries themselves, and I have to remind myself that what is to me a stereotyped set of questions is nothing of the sort to the correspondent concerned. So I dutifully search for the required information through my scattered records of the gun trade, which, with the recent acquisition of a copy of

AN OLD-FASHIONED GUNSMITH The late R. Blanton, of Ringwood, Hants, not only served as a small market town gunsmith, but also worked for the London trade, making among other things sidelocks for best guns.

Merwyn Carey's book, *English, Irish and Scottish Firearms Makers*, now include some 4000 names of gunmakers or ostensible gunmakers. Many of these are, of course, duplicated, but even allowing for all redundancies, there remains a formidable list.

What is so striking in the circumstances is the fact that, in about a third of all the cases, I can find no trace of the name engraved on the gun. My consequent admission of failure must, I am sure, often disappoint my enquirer, and seriously undermine any reputation I may have acquired (though I have abjured it on every convenient occasion) as a know-all in these matters.

But there would be less disappointment over these negative enquiries if it were not for the widespread misconception among shooters as to how the traditional gun trade works. Many men take it for granted that the name on the gun is that of the maker, and the air of obscurity that frequently surrounds it does nothing to put them off. There it is, boldly engraved on the rib, 'J. Smith, Little Muckington, Loamshire', and J. Smith is duly envisaged as having a gun factory, large or small – or, say, small – in which rough forgings and timber blanks go in at one end, and finished guns come out of the other.

When I fail to find any trace of J. Smith among my identifiable 4000, the probability is established that he is (a) a small market town gunsmith, and that the guns bearing his name are made for him in their entirety by one of the firms working anonymously for the trade; or (b) that he is not even a gunsmith, but perhaps only an ironmonger, who finds that he can sell one or two guns in the course of a season, and who procures them from trade sources.

Only a little while ago, I had just completed one of my familiar researches, when I said to my waiting secretary, 'No – nothing doing'. 'Are you sure?' she said. 'The name seems very familiar'. 'Not to me,' I replied, whereupon, after a moment's cogitation, she got up and came back with a receipt file, through which she quickly thumbed. 'There you are,' she said triumphantly, pointing to one of the receipts. It was from a firm who had recently supplied a loft-ladder. They were the alleged gunmakers in question, but their bill-head described them as 'Builders' Merchants and Ironmongers.'

A popular misconception

Enquiries of this sort assume something of a pathetic character when they relate to an old gun, perhaps seventy or eighty years old, for which the en-quirer needs a minor repair, which he says he would like carried out by the 'original maker'; for J. Smith never repaired a gun in his life, and anyhow, he died from overdoing his personal celebration of Queen Victoria's Diamond Jubilee.

But even when we cut out all the builders' merchants and ironmongers, and all the little market-town gunsmiths who do nothing more than minor repairs, and get down to the manufacturing gun trade, properly so-called, there is still a great – indeed, an astonishing – paucity of information about past members, even though they may have been distinguished in their day. Merwyn Carey's book reveals this at every turn, despite the thirty-three years of 'careful and diligent research' that, it is claimed, went into it. This is at least partly due to the author's typically American preoccupation with pistols and pistol makers, and to the extent to which gunmaking has always been a combined operation, involving the efforts of several separate trades, all employed and co-ordinated by a gunmaker who may himself make very little, or even nothing. This way of working does not highlight individuals; but the number of firms who have assembled all these trades under one roof, and who can claim to produce guns from rough forgings and timber blanks has always been extremely small. Greener did it in his day, and so do Webley & Scott, save for the new Webley-Beretta over-and-under. Purdey and Holland & Holland go as far in this direction as any of the crack London makers have ever gone; but the rest – the great mass of London and Birming-ham makers – have always made full and proper use of outworkers.

An admirable illustration of the discrete nature of the gun trade is pro-vided by one of my sources of information. This is a Birmingham Trade Directory of about 1850. In it, the various component trades are listed separately, and include the following –

97 Gun and Pistol Manufacturers
38 Gun Barrel Makers
 2 Gun Barrel Riflers
 6 Gun Barrel Browners
32 Gun Furniture Makers
74 Gun Finishers
87 Engravers
25 Gun Lock Makers
 4 Gun Nipple Manufacturers
41 Gun Stockers
 6 Gun Stock Dealers
 3 Gun Stock Polishers and Varnishers
40 Gun Implement Makers
 4 Gun and Pistol Bag Makers

It must be remembered that this was in the muzzle-loading days, when guns were simpler. Later, there would have been the machinists, actioners, single-trigger and ejector specialists and so on. Many a small gunmaker of well-deserved repute would thus have very few of the craftsmen he employed under his own roof. The rest would call for their jobs, take them away, and do them in their own workshops. One of the commonest sights in the old Steelhouse Lane gunmaking district of Birmingham, now swept away, was that of boys and men running about with gun barrels and other components in their progress from one specialist to another.

A sad lacuna

In a trade so loosely organised, and so individualistic in character, it is perhaps not surprising that there should be no regular archives, and that the names of even distinguished members of the past should have no durable memorial apart from their identifiable work.

I came up against a striking example the other day. In reply to a correspondent, I had to confess that I could find no information about a William Baker, whose name appeared on his gun. There have been Bakers a-plenty in the gun trade, but nowhere in my records could I find any trace of a William Baker.

Subsequently one of the leading figures in the Birmingham gun trade, no less than Mr G. E. Lewis, the Chairman of the Proof House Guardians, was able to enlighten me.

It appeared that he himself had been apprenticed to William Baker, whom he described as 'one of the cleverest of Birmingham gunsmiths, originator of the single-trigger, the Baker ejector (a coil-spring powered rod ejector which, unlike the ubiquitous Southgate, will operate even when broken) and the single-barrelled, top-lever, semi-hammerless ejector gun, now made by Webley & Scott, but which he originally made for Vickers.

'He also made an excellent self-opener and, in later years, invented box-lock and sidelock under-and-over actions. He also made a hammerless lock which, in an ingenious manner, used the one coil spring both as mainspring and sear spring. He died in 1934, aged 75. His workshop was in Snow Hill, next to the Metropole Theatre. He then moved to Bath Street, where his premises had the doubtful distinction of being the first to suffer from German bombs.'

The Baker ejector and the Baker single trigger are classics. Strange that their inventor should not be conspicuously on record.

33   Nostalgia in Firearms

Pedants and purists will insist that 'nostalgia' means nothing more or less than home-sickness; but in modern parlance it has come to connote any looking back with yearning, and in that sense I use it here.

Nostalgia in relation to firearms, then, is only one of those many manifestations of a longing for things of the past — one of the more human and venial weaknesses of our common nature, deriving largely from the belief, not uniformly supported by a study of social history, that life long ago was generally more truly satisfying and enjoyable than it is today. So far as it is based on a desire to recapture the beauty, elegance and taste of our more civilised periods, nostalgia is on firmer ground.

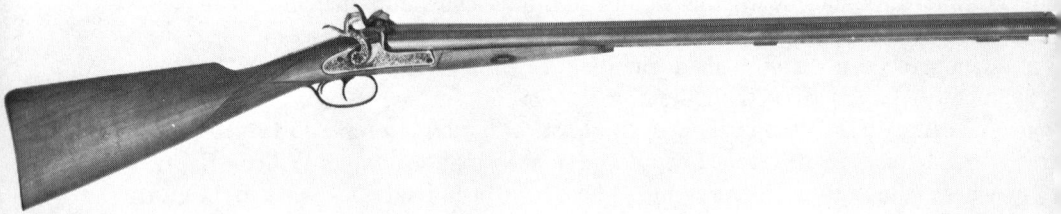

A modern Italian double 12-bore replica percussion muzzle-loader by Pedersoli. This is a 6 lb. gun intended for active shooting. (Courtesy of the importers, Parker-Hale Ltd.)

But this particular manifestation is something more than a wave of sentiment — it has become the basis of a new and substantial industry. Not so many years ago, shooters satisfied their nostalgia for antique or outmoded guns by acquiring and using surviving specimens of the kind in which they were particularly interested. They still do, of course; but unless they are collectors to whom 'genuineness' is all-important, they can satisfy their longing to follow the ancient ways by means of one of the faithful modern reproductions now on the market. They cover an impressive range. The Americans, with their longing for 'history', not to mention their numbers, obviously afford the best market for reproduction firearms, and shooters there have for some time been offered well got-up versions of the long, Pennsylvania (miscalled Kentucky) rifles, both in flint and percussion, and, outstandingly, Colt revolvers in what appear to me – a non-collector – to be their many tedious variations. But in recent years the range has extended to cover an astonishing variety of guns, rifles and pistols, both flint and percussion, including such unlikely things as stubby Derringer pistols, mail coach blunderbusses and large-bore elephant guns. And these are not merely wall ornaments: they are all shooting guns, though what kind of sport some of them would be suited for is hard to say. But three particular weapons, whose appeal is largely nostalgic, impress me now.

Three personal choices

The first is British, unlike the majority, which are probably Italian. It is the Enfield Model 1861 percussion carbine, manufactured by Parker-Hale. The production of this celebrated Service weapon was conceived and carried out with a thoroughness which I greatly admire. In effect, Parker-Hale picked up the production just where it had originally stopped, using the original sealed model as the pattern, and even the original gauges. As a master stroke, they issued it with the original instruction manual, reproduced in facsimile. Deservedly, demand out-stripped capacity.

The second is indeed Italian, and is a weapon of entirely different character from the preceding. It is the Armi Famars 'Castore' self-cocking hammer ejector, exhibited at the Game Fair. This is a very costly and beautiful weapon, and, inasmuch as it functions like a hammerless ejector, the reversion to external hammers must rank as a nostalgic element.

The third is as different again. It is the Ruger single-action revolver, introduced in 1953. From the early 1900s to the outbreak of the Second World War, production of the functionally obsolete single-action weapon had declined to practically nothing, and it says much for Wm. B. Ruger's percipience that he recognised the existence of a large latent demand for the old kind of revolver on nostalgic grounds. But even he must have been surprised by the enthusiasm with which the Ruger Single-Six was received – it quickly became, and is stated to remain, by far and away the most popular revolver on the U.S. market. What is its secret? Chiefly, it would seem, that it recaptures in form and function a type of weapon closely identified with a phase of American history—the settlement of the West—which, for all the false glamour through which it is now seen, remains one of the epic movements of the English-speaking people.

A projected success

I have mentioned these three very different weapons because together they indicate the breadth of the nostalgic appeal of firearms, and support the suggestion that there may be other winning ideas waiting to be exploited. It will be noted that the present state of the English gun trade imposed no obvious impediment to Parker-Hale's brilliantly successful exploitation of the Enfield carbine idea, and it is pleasant to contemplate another English success-story of a similar sort. For obvious reasons, it would have to have an export setting.

The weapon I would cast for the leading rôle in this success-story would be a shotgun—a self-opening or easy-opening, double-barrelled, side-by-side shotgun, with hammers, but self-cocking and with automatic selective ejectors. With an eye on American predilections, it could advantageously take the external form of a classic and identifiable model, such as one of the Marquis of Ripon's favourite Purdeys, and would be marked and marketed as such.

It will be objected that the sort of gun I have contemplated might meet its potential market on nostalgia, but it would certainly miss it on price. I wonder? Back-action hammer guns are immensely strong, and the action bodies would appear to be ideally suited to production by the investment casting process, thereby eliminating nearly all machining. So with hammers, lock-plates, etc.: but there would obviously need to be a well-judged adjustment of grade and price to the potential market.

An eminent American writer on the shotgun, Roger Barlow, invests my daydream with an air of reality. 'Hunting,' he says, 'is a sport rooted in tradition. We enjoy it most . . . when we are conscious of a link with the past —hunting where our father or grandfather hunted, perhaps above all with guns themselves having roots in the past. This is why the modern hammer gun . . . has so much to offer the perceptive shooting man.' Barlow was writing about the Armi Famars 'Castore' gun in the *Gun Digest*, but his nostalgia could obviously have been satisfied on much easier terms.

34 *Meeting Modern Hazards*

Some years ago, a famous American gun manufacturer showed me a 12-bore game gun of his make. Among other things he enlarged on its strength, in evidence of which he mentioned its proved ability to fire without damage a succession of proof loads – I forget how many, but it may well have been two hundred.

The gun was a weapon of superior grade, but, judged by English standards, it was unduly heavy. Commenting on this fact, I said that an English maker, faced with a gun of such weight, would consider it to possess unnecessary reserves of strength on which it would be both justifiable and desirable to encroach in the interests of lightness and balance. My American friend agreed, but then he pointed out that gunmakers in his country of necessity took a different view. Our English makers, he said, designed their guns for a definite maximum load, and were justified in so doing by the implicit co-operation of our ammunition manufacturers, proof authorities and shooters; whereas in America, guns had to be made strong enough and heavy enough to withstand whatever loads could be crammed into them.

American influence

When I was in Birmingham recently, I examined two guns which had burst mysteriously in the chamber, and heard accounts of several others. Coming on top of the case I reported in the *Shooting Times* of 26 May 1973, in which a careful home-loader was producing 5-ton loads and the indications that many others may be doing the same, these bursts made me realise that, since the last war, we have moved significantly over to the American position. Thus, before the war, a regular 12-bore game gun invariably had $2\frac{1}{2}$-in. chambers, and was marked '$1\frac{1}{8}$ oz.' A so-called pigeon gun had $2\frac{3}{4}$-in. chambers, and was marked '$1\frac{1}{4}$ oz.' And a wildfowling gun had 3-in. chambers, and was marked '$1\frac{1}{2}$ oz.' *All* these guns were suitable for firing *any British* cartridge of the appropriate gauge and chamber length. All cartridges were loaded into cases of the same length as that of the chambers for which they were designed; and, in addition, there was very little home-loading. My impression is that what there was, was done overwhelmingly with black powder.

All these things have gone by the board. Regular 12-bore game guns now frequently have $2\frac{3}{4}$-in. chambers, but not all British cartridges so marked are safe to use in them. The same goes for 3-in. chambered wildfowling guns. Further, home-loading has greatly increased, and smokeless powder has taken the place of the old, tolerant black variety. Accordingly among the cartridges nowadays loaded with insufficient knowledge or care, there must be many more than ever previously giving excessive pressures. Again, the prevalent use of $2\frac{3}{4}$-in. cases, suitably loaded, for guns with $2\frac{1}{2}$-in. chambers may be perfectly satisfactory if the guns have normal cones, but not if the cones are exceptionally abrupt, as some are, when the use of the longer case may give rise to objectionable, or at least enhanced, pressures.

For example, a Haywards Heath correspondent has acquired one of the famous French 'Robust' guns – a 12-bore with 65 mm. ($2\frac{1}{2}$-in.) chambers. This gun shoots the Impax cartridge, with its $2\frac{1}{2}$-in. case, very satisfactorily. But with cartridges with $2\frac{3}{4}$-in. cases, though designed for $2\frac{1}{2}$-in. chambers, it recoils unduly and makes his right arm numb. Three out of four crimps were shot right off; the fourth was bottle-nosed, and I have no doubt that pressures were well above their proper level. The gun was found to have abrupt chamber cones, and it is fortunate that it is of exceptionally strong construction.

A weak spot

With all these considerations in mind, I consider the time has arrived when we ought to be taking a critical look at the reserves of strength available in our guns.

The weakest part of a gun barrel, in relation to the stresses it is called upon to bear in regular service, is just where the chamber ends. This part has to withstand the maximum pressure set up by the cartridge; and if it is strong

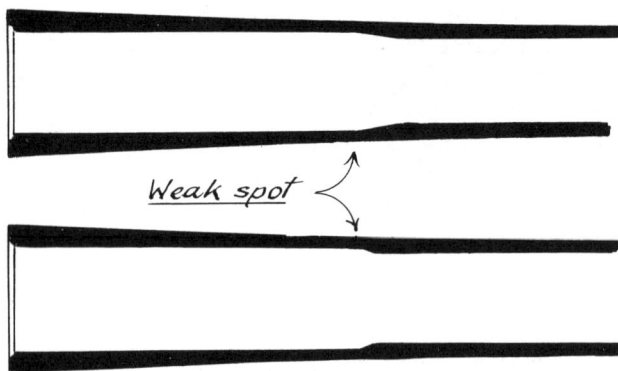

The weakest part of a gun barrel, in relation to the stresses it is called on to bear in regular service, is just where the chamber ends. Above is shown, truly to scale, a 12-bore breech-end (top) with a normal cone, and (bottom) with a sharp cone.

enough, and the barrel is of normal form, it will be of adequate strength anywhere else along its length.

The prime criterion of strength in a normal gun barrel is accordingly the wall-thickness at the end of the chamber in relation to the maximum working pressure and the strength of the material. For present purposes, the strength of the material is taken as its elastic strength, which is the maximum tensile stress from which the material makes a complete elastic recovery when the stress is removed; and it is considered good gunmaking practice to work to half this elastic limit, or, in other words, to a factor of safety of 2.

On this basis, I have worked out what should be the minimum wall thickness of a 12-bore barrel with $2\frac{1}{2}$-in. chambers and designed for a maximum service pressure of 3 tons per square inch.

As for the strength of the steel, I have deliberately taken a superior grade of Spanish chrome-nickel steel – the Bellota Urko 1, such as is used by leading Spanish gunmakers. From personal investigation I believe this to be a high-class product. The published specification gives an elastic limit of 32–41 tons per square inch; and taking the lower limit, and applying our factor of safety of 2, we get 16 tons as the maximum permissible stress under the working pressure of 3 tons.

With this information, and according to my calculation, the minimum wall thickness should be ·084 in. or 84 thousandths of an inch.

A practical check

Now for a check on actual guns – the only ones I could immediately lay my hands on. Their wall thicknesses were as follows:

Gun	Period	Wall-thickness (in.)	
1 English	Post-war	0·115	
2 English	Pre-war	0·122	All these barrels had been reblued at
3 English	Pre-war	0·106	least once. In addition, No. 3 had been
4 English	Pre-war	0·113	freshly struck up.
5 English	Pre-war	0·115	

Average 0·114

6 Italian	Post-war	0·085	
7 Spanish	Post-war	0·084	
8 Japanese	Post-war	0·090	All these barrels were in their original
9 Spanish	Post-war	0·086	state.
10 Spanish	Post-war	0·076	

Average 0·084
Diff. 0·030

The first thing that stands out from these figures is that the makers of the foreign guns (except the maverick No. 10) appear to have built them closely in accordance with my interpretation of the minimum requirements of good gunmaking practice, so that they should be perfectly safe to use with their proper cartridges. For all that, the English guns, assuming equally good material, have a substantially greater reserve of strength.

If, therefore, my sample is representative of the mass, which its consistency suggests; and if, for the reason I have given, there is a case for increasing the strength of our traditional double guns, it is on the foreign ones that the onus chiefly falls. I see no good reason why British importers should not ask them to discharge it. One eminent Spanish maker tells me that he has already done so.

Section 4

SPECIAL GUNS

'The prime object in sporting gunnery is the delivery of the most effective charge of which other factors admit. The gun, as such, comes last.'

35 New Light on the Pump Gun

A curious and interesting point arises on the manipulation of the pump or slide-action gun, which, though never seen at regular English shoots, is still fairly to be regarded as the national shotgun of America.

The point arises from the scepticism – not to say the incredulity – of an English shooter regarding an observation attributed to an American writer on the subject of these guns. The writer in question is stated to have said that if you are conscious of working the slide of a pump gun, you obviously don't know how to use it. My enquirer admits that he has never regularly shot with pump guns, but he insists that he is quite familiar with them. You pull the trigger to get off your first shot; and then, to get off your second, you yank the fore-end back some $3\frac{1}{2}$ inches, against a resistance that is by no means inconsiderable, in order to unlock the breech, eject the fired case and recock the mechanism. Then you have to execute the movement in reverse before you can fire again; and my doubting Thomas regards the possibility of performing this double action subconsciously as being too remote to be worth consideration. Is it? Let us see.

Facts and beliefs

Although I have an unswerving belief in the superior merits of the conventional double-barrelled gun for field shooting in this country – a belief based on a detailed appraisal of its qualities, and not on any ideological concept – I nevertheless have a respect for the pump gun, both for its long record of reliable service and for the special reasons set out on p. 91 of this book. As I said there, it was surely a stroke of genius to make the business of cartridge ejection, recocking and reloading ensue, more or less automatically, from the convulsive reaction to recoil and the instinctive recovery from it. The significant thing about that here and now is the phrase 'more or less automatically'.

I have never made the point before, but I wonder if the man who first invented the pump gun, probably the Englishman, Alexander Bain, in 1854, realised how near he was to inventing an automatic, or, more strictly, a self-loader? The ordinary pump gun has, in fact, an innate tendency to work automatically. This arises from the fact that when the gun recoils, the fore-end and associated parts are compelled to recoil with it. But when the gun is brought to rest by the resistance of the shooter's shoulder, these same parts are free to continue their rearward course, and if only they had enough inertia, they would do so and would eject the spent case and recock the gun. What is more, if there were a light return spring, the fore-end would then return of

Demonstrating the inherent tendency of the pump gun to act as a self-loader.

its own accord to its original position, feeding a fresh cartridge into the chamber in the process, whereupon the gun would be ready to fire again. (This, incidentally, is how the new Benelli repeater works. The recoil of the entire gun kicks an internal inertia weight and sends it flying back against the action of a light return spring to perform all the functions just described.)

But how much weight would it be necessary to add to the fore-end of a pump gun to make it work as a self-loader? My immediate answer to the doubt that has been raised is that the hand and forearm of the shooter, added to the weight of the fore-end, and reinforced by anticipatory pressure, are, in my opinion, quite capable of achieving the first part of the double-movement without conscious effort; and that the second part can equally unconsciously be achieved by the instinctive recovery from the recoil.

So, I do not think that there is anything remote about the prospect of working a pump gun subconsciously. I do not know if my enquirer has ever seen the Winchester film, *Showman Shooter*, depicting the late H. Parsons in action. Parsons would throw as many as seven clay targets into the air and break the lot with a pump gun, which I have been specifically assured by Winchester was a normal gun, worked normally. And then we have the case of our own Percy Stanbury with five dead pigeons in the air simultaneously in the Teign Valley. He, too, was using a pump gun; and I cannot believe that these accomplished shooters were devoting conscious effort to the mechanical operation of their guns.

A significant experiment

To get an idea of the extent to which the pump gun acts automatically, I have made a significant experiment. Taking the deadweight value of the shooter's hand and forearm as being only 1 lb, I added this weight to the fore-end of a Model 37 Ithaca 12-bore gun by clamping a piece of sheet lead around it. Also, I smoked the slide and fitted a pointer bearing on it to record the movement under recoil.

I had admittedly hoped that, even with this modest added weight, the gun, when fired with the fore-end unsupported, would have ejected the spent case automatically. But the recoil from a 2½-in. Grand Prix (1⅛ oz) was insufficient to bring this about. Nevertheless, it showed that, under the test conditions, some 35–40 per cent of the inward movement of the slide took place without outside aid. More would have taken place with the gun's normal American load of 1¼ oz, and still more with a more generous, and probably more realistic, deadweight than the pound I allowed. Circumstances prevented my extending the experiment, but it was sufficient to reinforce my conviction that the pump gun can indeed be worked subconsciously, a fact of which I have since had undeniable personal testimony.

36 Improving the Boxlock

The other day I was handling a top-quality boxlock gun. It bore every indication of having been made to the best standards of the London gun trade, and apart from the difference in mechanical design, was in no visible respect inferior to sidelock guns fetching the highest prices. There is, of course, no reason why a best gun should not be made on the boxlock system, and the specialized weapons of certain firms, such as Westley Richards and W. W. Greener, usually have been. But since the ordinary Anson & Deeley boxlock is a simpler weapon than the sidelock, and lends itself to more economical manufacture, it is usually regarded as the honest hunter, and the sidelock as the thoroughbred.

It is for this reason, I suppose, that the designers of boxlocks have almost invariably taken the sidelock as the *beau idéal* of an elegant sporting gun, and have modelled the boxlock on it as closely as possible. Thus, the high-quality boxlock to which I first referred had an action body with perfectly flat sides, such as a sidelock would have, more or less as a matter of necessity. It also had panels and points at the head of the stock in imitation of a feature imposed on the stock of a sidelock gun by the need for neatly accommodating the rearward portion of the lock-plate.

There was a mental inertia in all this, reminiscent of the designers of the

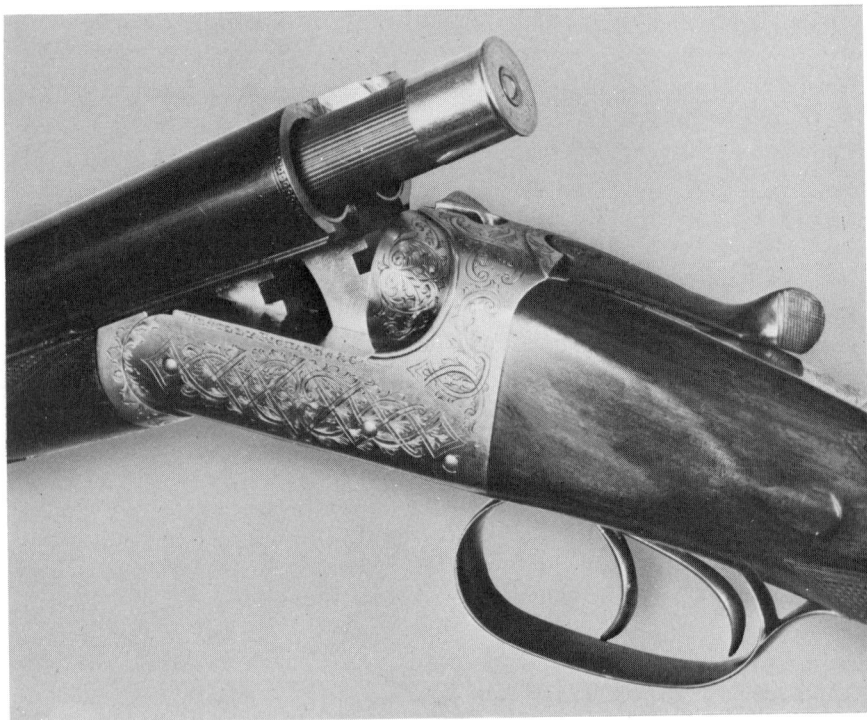

INCONGRUITY OF DESIGN   Stock with panel-and-point unhappily associated with
a round-bodied action.

early railway coaches. The stage coach having been so long established as the
normal form of vehicle for public passenger transport, the railway coach
almost inevitably became three or four stage coaches stuck end to end. Even
the external form of the panels and the mode of painting long followed the
stage coach pattern. And the boxlock gun that was so unimaginatively
modelled on the form of the sidelock revealed essentially the same approach.

But what was overlooked in all this was that the boxlock action not only
opened up new aesthetic possibilities, but offered a prospect of mechanical
advantage in their exploitation. In the event, both beauty and utility were
sacrificed to purposeless imitation; but if only we forget the sidelock and start
designing a boxlock with a fresh mind, with a view to realising all its poten-
tialities, we undoubtedly arrive at something different from the admittedly
fine gun that started me on this subject. It would be a more elegant and
streamlined gun; it would be stronger; and it would be less susceptible to
superficial damage.

A practical suggestion

To begin at the beginning, we have to consider that familiar feature of box-lock actions, the top extension. Every one of these contrivances, from the most efficient to those that have no merit beyond eye-appeal, embodies a defective principle. If correctly designed and accurately fitted so as to hold the standing breech firmly up to the barrels, the top extension of necessity prevents any flexing of the action bar; and since the action bar cannot develop any resistance without flexure, it follows that a perfectly fitted top extension would take the full force of the impact delivered to the standing breech on firing. If it has the capacity to resist an indefinite succession of such impacts, well and good: the action bar is thereby permanently relieved of any onerous duty.

But what ordinarily happens is that the top extension is not fitted sufficiently accurately to perform in this manner. It usually has enough working clearance to allow the standing breech to come back by the minute amount needed to develop the bending strength of the bar. Or if, when new, it has no such clearance, it quickly develops one, and thus becomes functionally

AN AYA BOXLOCK   The gun could be stronger as well as more elegant with a rounded action like that in the previous illustration.

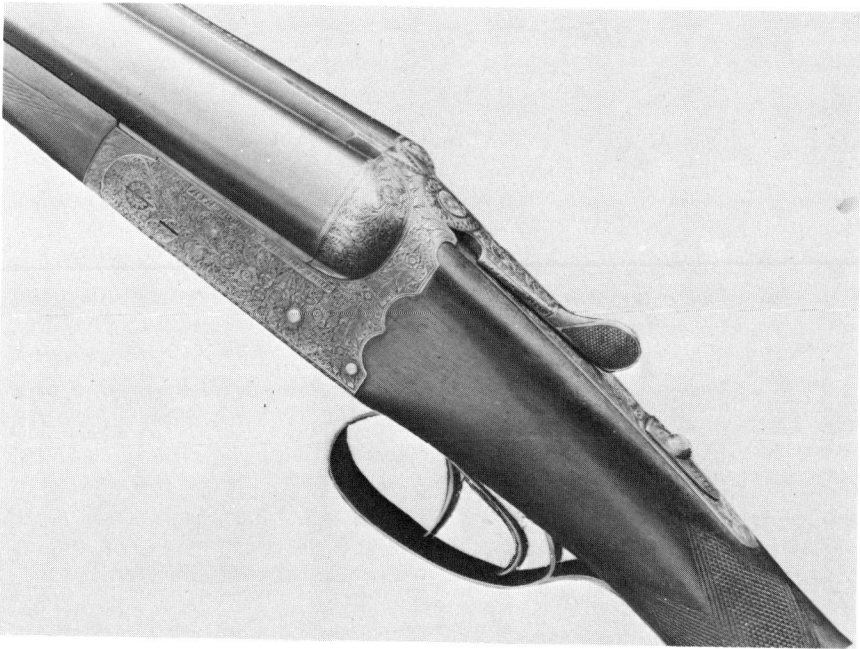

degraded from a first-line rôle to a supporting one. I have proved this experimentally by applying a brittle seal between the barrels and standing breech of a cross-bolted gun. Although this was a strong gun – a Greener 'Empire' – with a well-made cross-bolt, and in tight and sound condition, the seal broke on firing a normal load, thus demonstrating the movement of the breech and the flexure of the bar.

Since all top extensions have a nuisance value, both as an impediment to quick loading and when cleaning a gun, far more boxlocks are nowadays made without any form of top extension, so that they rely for their strength and safety on the bar of the action. It thus becomes a matter of prime concern to the gunmaker to see that the bar is fully strong enough, especially at the most highly stressed section, which is at the foot of the standing breech.

My main suggestion, therefore, is merely that the makers of boxlock guns should follow some distinguished examples in abandoning all deference to the sidelock form, and should strengthen their actions by widening them at the top and rounding them off to minimum normal width at the bottom; also, that they should forswear all panels and points on these guns, and open their eyes to the striking simplicity and elegance thereby attainable. The model for external form here is the Dickson 'Round Action' gun. For sheer thorough-bred lines and perfected functional form, this gun yields nothing – nothing whatsoever – to the finest sidelock ever built.

Elusive elegance

Yet there is one further point. The traditional sporting gun having evolved over centuries, it has come to acquire somewhat of an organic character, as exemplified by the almost total absence of any visible straight lines. This being so, I find something discordant in the hard, straight line at the back-end of the action body of the typical boxlock gun. This is the only imperfection that might be charged against the Dickson. In my view, this straight line should be modified or broken, as by the scroll back-ends that Westley Richards used to adopt for their best pre-war guns. They also used to round off their action bodies on the lines suggested here, with an overall effect that was highly pleasing.

Their inexpensive 'Heronshaw' model, shown in the photograph on page 110, shows this rounded action to perfection; but it also reveals a lamentable gaffe: the action having achieved this admirable rotundity, the stock breaks out into a horrible, mutilated panel-and-point.

My favourite AYA XXV, shown in the photograph on page 111, also just misses the boat. The clean, rounded surface of the stock, instead of running right through to the fore-end, is broken by the slab-sided bar. It is like a beautiful woman with a flat on her leg. If only the bar had been rounded like the 'Heronshaw', the gun would look shallower and more elegant, and, the bar being wider at the top, the gun would be stronger. It is time that all boxlocks were given this new look.

37 The 2-inch 12-bore

A pre-war partridge-driving day in Wiltshire comes back to my mind. The stranger guest in our small party was, it duly emerged, a lawyer, and a specialist in forensic medicine, so I forgave him the tendency he displayed at lunchtime to press questions on common conversational topics somewhat as if he were extracting evidence from a reluctant witness. One must not grumble at dyers if their hands are stained.

But he was a good and experienced shot, and highly knowledgeable on shooting matters; and so, having parried some of his questions, I turned the tables on him by asking him why he shot with a 2-in. 12-bore. Surely, I suggested, the limitations imposed by its light, $\frac{7}{8}$ oz load, and the difficulty in obtaining ammunition, were too high a price to pay for any advantages it possessed.

This modest challenge touched off a dissertation on the merits of the most neglected of all the 12-bores that was sufficiently eloquent to have swayed a hostile jury. Indeed, I believe that one of my most cherished and hard-ridden hobby horses – I mean, the one concerned with the need for matching man, gun, and sport – was sired at that instant.

My lawyer made a good case. His shooting was mostly driving in which partridges predominated. He had no need for a long-range weapon, since the range-bracket within which optimum efficiency was needed for maximum success was perhaps between 20 and 30 yds. Further, his kind of shooting called for the active manipulation of his gun; and since he had reached an age when a man realises that his physical energy is not a bottomless well, he found much virtue in a gun weighing considerably less than 6 lbs. Lastly, he insisted that it threw patterns of marked superiority, so that he felt at no disadvantage whatsoever on the score of the lightness of the charge. What his personal share of the bag was on that day, I do not know, but I shrewdly suspect that he killed more than his quota.

Since that occasion, the subject of the 2-in. 12-bore lay largely dormant in my mind. It was sharply revived by a letter from a veteran English sportsman and by another, of identical purport, from an Irishman who described what happened when he borrowed one of these guns from his son, for pigeon shooting. This was a Jeffery, with 26-in. barrels, bored half and full choke and weighing only $5\frac{1}{4}$ lbs.

The stock was $\frac{5}{8}$-in. shorter than that of his regular gun, but that may have been advantageous in the circumstances, for my correspondent says, 'It was a vile afternoon, with heavy wet snow falling so that I had to wear a heavy sweater and heavy mackintosh – quite the wrong clothes for good shooting.

'The pigeon,' he says, 'were coming over a high beech wood from an estate half a mile away, where half a dozen guns were busy. The birds flew straight in across open ground. In about an hour's flighting I shot properly every pigeon that came over me, shooting much above my usual form, and finished up in the dark by dropping a lone bird which came flying low and straight for me. It was dropped dead fifteen yards out in front.

'What impressed me was the ease of handling, and the speed and killing power of this little weapon. I feel that it is well ahead of any 2½-in. 20-bore in killing power and speed of handling.'

Pros and cons

One swallow, of course, does not make a summer, nor do single episodes of this description establish any general superiority on the part of the type of gun employed. Yet, in this case and in the others, one can see indications of a general pattern that may be worth examining.

Notable is the fact that my Irish correspondent is also a veteran sportsman, so that the lightness of the gun will have made it especially suitable in his hands for active shooting. A younger and more vigorous man might have done just as well with a markedly heavier gun; but then many of us who shoot are on the wrong side of the grand climacteric, and would have benefited equally from the reduction of weight. So for all shooters to whom weight is significant, the lightness of the 2-in. gun counts as a general merit.

But other guns weighing no more can be had to shoot a ⅞ oz load, and the real point of interest here is whether the 2-in. 12-bore can be expected to outshoot any such rivals. It could certainly do so if, boring for boring and pellet-count for pellet-count, it threw better distributed patterns – patterns, that is to say, with a more uniform spread over the circle, and with fewer vacant patches. If, in addition, it delivered its pellets with a somewhat higher velocity, or in a shorter string, indicative of a higher average pellet energy, its superiority might well be apparent, even on early acquaintance, as in the case of my Irishman.

The conditions for attaining this superior effectiveness from a given charge are well known. They are that, for a given muzzle velocity, the pellets should leave the gun, so far as possible, in their original condition – that is to say, they should have suffered the least possible damage from compressive deformation or from abrasion against the barrel wall. Also, the length of the shot column within the gun should be sufficient to bring the charge as a whole most favourably under the influence of the choke.

A compromise has to be sought here. A bore that is unduly small for the charge means a long shot column. A long shot column needs a higher and/or more sustained pressure to achieve a given muzzle velocity. Pressures that are higher and/or more sustained mean more compressive deformation of the pellets, and are also bad for pattern. Again, a long shot column exposes a larger proportion of the pellets to abrasion.

On the other hand, whilst a bore that is unduly large for the charge avoids all these disabilities, the pattern quality may suffer from loss of that degree of pellet control which even the slightest degree of choke, if skilfully introduced, is capable of affording.

Some conclusions

But, on balance, the small bore is at a strong *prima facie* disadvantage, and, to bring its performance up to an acceptable level, pressure has to be reduced and something of velocity sacrificed. This point is well brought out in the American *Lyman Shotshell Handbook* which publishes a wide range of tested loads together with their appropriate pressures and velocities.

It will be appreciated that I have contrasted the performance of over-small and over-large bores, firing the same charge, in order to bring out the relevant principles. They apply equally to the comparison between large and small charges in a bore of given size.

What is admittedly the elusive factor in this case is the precise point at which the length-diameter relationship of the loaded shot column attains its greatest potential for good results. It is probably something that varies to some extent with every gun, or at least, with every degree of choke. But all indications, both theoretical and practical, encourage the expectation of superior performance from the 2-in. 12-bore; and it is significant that the light 2½-in. gun of that gauge, firing the 1-oz Impax cartridge, which represents the same school of gunning philosophy, is probably nowadays the combination most favoured by the most experienced game shooters in this country.

38   The Handicapped ·410

I have been asked to give an appreciation of the ·410. Regrettably, it is a task I do not feel fully competent to undertake, for I am conscious of being better equipped with prejudice than I am with experience respecting these little weapons. I know, of course, that they are very popular; that they can be usefully employed in certain limited spheres; and that they are widely regarded as being ideal for starting a boy in shooting. What is more, I believe there exists a select company of enthusiasts who can give chapter and verse for their successful employment even against geese. So, having confessed my prejudice, it may not be a useless exercise to see what justification I can find for it.

Apart from imported brands, there are three Eley cartridges of this gauge, the Fourten, the Fourlong and the Extra Long, of which particulars are set out in the table below.

Cartridge	Length	Charge	Shot sizes available	No. of pellets (nominal)	Max. service pressure (tons)
Fourten	2-in.	$\frac{5}{16}$ oz	4 5 6	50 69 84	$3\frac{1}{4}$
Fourlong	$2\frac{1}{2}$-in.	$\frac{7}{16}$ oz.	BB 3 4 5 6 7	30 61 74 96 118 149	$3\frac{1}{4}$
Extra Long	3-in.	$\frac{5}{8}$ oz*	4 5 6	100 138 169	5

* Also available with $\frac{11}{16}$ oz in imported brands

Geese or a goose?

I have made the point with sufficient emphasis elsewhere that birds are not killed by guns – they are killed by charges of shot, and one that is struck by four or five pellets of adequate penetrative power cannot derive any consolation from the fact that they may have been fired from a mere ·410, nor can it plead exemption from its fate on that account. On these grounds, I am quite ready to hear authentic accounts of individual geese being killed well and truly by the Eley Fourlong cartridge loaded with its $\frac{7}{16}$ oz of BB, and, what is more, at full range. But what I am not prepared to hear is that they can be *consistently* killed at that range. It is one thing to pull off an occasional fluke by hitting a goose with a single pellet of large shot in what may *happen* to be a vital spot, and quite another to rely on hitting it with sufficient pellets to ensure that, even after allowing for the inevitable variation in the number of strikes from round to round, the bird will receive enough to make reasonably certain of killing it. With the 30 pellets of BB, or the 61 of No. 3 in the Fourlong cartridge, there is no chance of making a killing pattern for use against geese at other than very short range.

But I recognise that most supporters of the ·410 would not attempt to make out a case for the use of this gauge against geese, and might well press their case on the 149 pellets of No. 7 in the same cartridge, or the 169 of No. 6 in the Extra Long, when used against small to medium game.

Here, of course, we are getting much nearer to practicality. A fully choked ·410 may be capable of giving 60 per cent patterns at 40 yds, though that, I believe, is being generous. But let it stand. It represents half-choke performance, and may give, according to the book, an 83 per cent pattern at 30 yds. That would mean about 124 pellets of No. 7 or 140 of No. 6 in a 30-in. circle from the charges mentioned; and if they were patterns of good quality, comprising a normal proportion of full-energy pellets, they would give good results at that moderate range.

But the trouble with the ·410 is that everything is against its satisfying these conditions. Good quality, killing patterns can only be made with pellets that arrive in good shape. Those which are badly abraded by friction against the barrel wall, or deformed by high initial pressure in the gun are not fully effective. For a charge of given weight, the number of pellets exposed to abrasion is 34 per cent more in a ·410 than it is in even the little 28-bore; and since compressive deformation, other things being equal, is proportional to the number of layers of pellets in the charge, which in turn is inversely proportional to the square of the bore diameter, it follows that the ·410 charge would have almost exactly twice as many layers. Worse is to follow: other things are not equal, for to accelerate the ·410 charge to an acceptable minimum muzzle velocity would require a pressure twice as high for a given grade of powder, or, for its avoidance, a powder of advanced progressive character. The practical shortcomings of this expedient are sufficiently well indicated by the fact that, whereas the 28-bore is proved for a service or working pressure of 3 tons, the 3-in. ·410 is proved for 5 tons, which is the highest of all the regular pressures for which English guns are proved, and a bad omen for performance.

For what I regard as these good reasons, I would back a 28-bore with its $\frac{9}{16}$ oz load against any ·410 with its $\frac{5}{8}$ oz for effective performance in the field.

Starting a boy

Despite these prospective disadvantages of the ·410, there must be many people who would continue to regard it as the ideal thing with which to train a boy in the safe handling of a gun. Here we are up against matters of opinion, on which I should be anxious to avoid appearing dogmatic. My own view is that the sooner a boy can be entrusted with an adult style of gun the better.

This, I recognise, is a matter that must be regulated largely by his physical development, but the transition from a toy-like ·410 to a 12-bore is bound to be uncomfortable, as well as disturbing from the viewpoint of performance, if it is unduly deferred. When I see a strongly built boy, well on in his teens, with a ·410, I always think what a horrid, heavy, clumsy thing a 12-bore will seem to him when he belatedly takes to one.

An incidental point

It is a well-known fact that ·410 paper cartridges are much more prone to splitting than are the larger gauges, but the reason is not always appreciated. It is because, for a given clearance between the outside diameter of the cartridge and the inside diameter of the chamber, the paper of the small gauge has to undergo a greater proportionate degree of stretching to take up the clearance when the cartridge is fired. In fact, the clearance is somewhat less, but not sufficiently so to equalise the risk of splitting.

Did I say that I was prejudiced against the ·410? No doubt I am, but it is not altogether a blind, unreasoning prejudice.

39   Case Salvage Made Easy

A Lincolnshire correspondent writes, 'Having taken up reloading, I am anxious to save my empty cases; but my gun is an ejector, and I cannot get out of the habit of opening it in the ordinary way, so that I have to search for the cases in the undergrowth, or pick them up out of the mud. As I do not really need an ejector for my sort of shooting, I should like to convert my gun to a non-ejector, and I have heard that you have a trick for doing this by means of a simple screw. This sounds like something that I could do myself. Would you please elaborate.'

There is so much misconception behind this letter that I certainly think I ought to elaborate, more especially since there must be many reloaders in the same position.

What needs to be understood is that if a gun is fitted with the ordinary Southgate or two-piece ejector, it does not need my correspondent's 'simple screw' or any other mechanical device to convert it into a non-ejector, nor does it need any kind of surgery. All that is necessary is to remove the ejector springs, whereupon the gun will operate as a non-ejector. This is so simple a job that anyone with a minimum of mechanical *nous* can do it for himself. All one has to do is to remove the woodwork from the fore-end, replace the latter on the gun, and cramp one of the springs, so that it is incapable of opening.

Then pull the corresponding trigger and open the gun. The ejector spring, being prevented by the cramp from operating the kicker, will then be loose, and can be lifted out of its place in the fore-end iron. The operation should be repeated for the other spring. If at any time it is required to reconvert the gun into an ejector, all that has to be done is to restore the springs. Incidentally, they should be carefully marked so that they can be put back in their original places, because if they are crossed over, the timing of the ejectors is likely to be affected.

Despite the simplicity of this procedure, there are one or two points that need attention. To remove the woodwork of the fore-end, first undo the little set-screw that locks the push-rod in the slide. Then unscrew the push-rod, and remove it together with its spring. This will expose another little screw, which is then visible through what is often mistaken for an oil-hole at the top of the push-rod tube. Remove this screw, which fastens the tube to the fore-end tip. Then remove the big screw or screws passing through or into the woodwork, when the latter should come away. The thing that may be overlooked by anyone not familiar with these details of gun construction is the small hidden screw at the top of the push-rod tube, and I have known men miss it when trying to gain access to their ejectors, and to wonder why the fore-end iron will not come away. I daresay that many guns have suffered some damage from this oversight.

The other point concerns the cramping of the ejector springs prior to their removal. Few shooters keep any kind of spring cramp, but one of the best for this purpose can be made by filing a rectangular slot in the side of a stout piece of mild steel strip, and near to one end, the width of the slot being adjusted so that it fits fairly tightly over the legs of the spring in its compressed state. When the spring is released from all other restraint, it remains securely in its cramp.

The optional ejector

But so far I have only dealt with the routine operation of converting an ejector semi-permanently into a non-ejector; whereas my correspondent's reference to a 'simple screw' evidently arose from some proposals I made a few years ago for an 'optional ejector' – a different thing altogether. This was an added facility which I suggested should be incorporated in all good ejector guns, and which would enable them to be switched from ejectors to non-ejectors at will. My idea was that with the salvage value acquired by empty cases, now that reloading has become so popular, and with the litter problem posed by the scattering of plastic cases across the countryside, we were no longer justified in using ejectors except when required by the nature of the sport in hand. This idea seemed to appeal to my correspondents, including, not surprisingly, some Americans; but, so far as I know, the only English gunmaker to take it up was the ever-enterprising firm of Westley Richards, who unfortunately found it rather expensive to adapt to the ordinary Southgate ejector.

What, then, about my original correspondent's 'simple screw'? This was undoubtedly a reference to suggestions I made for converting the special form of Southgate ejector incorporated in the AYA guns – not into a non-ejector, but to give it the optional facility.

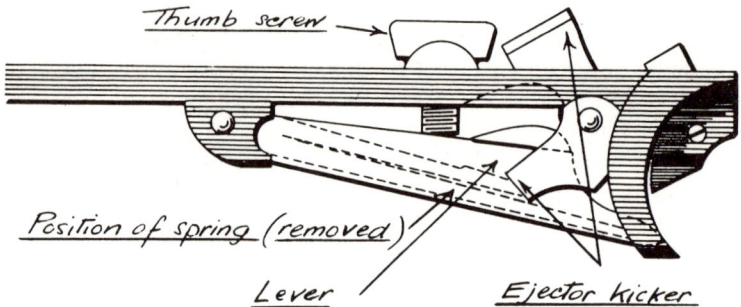

Converting an AYA gun to optional ejection.

The AYA guns are fitted with powerful ejectors, and to enable the springs to be recocked smoothly after ejection, they have an additional part. This is a lever, as shown in my sketch, which lies between the ejector springs and has two transverse projections bearing on the lower part of the ejector kickers. The rearward end of this lever is held down by a small fixed projection from the knuckle of the action, which can be described as the ejector cocking dog. The opening of the gun after firing frees the lever from the restraint of the cocking dog, and when the ejector kickers have been pushed around sufficiently to pass their dead centre, the springs are free to flick them forward, raising the lever to its uppermost position in the process.

All that is necessary, then, to convert this system to optional ejection is to fit a thumb-screw, as shown. The downward projection of this screw must be carefully adjusted so that when it is screwed right home it makes contact with the upper edge of the lever just as the ejector kickers reach their dead centre position *and not before*. The springs will then be unable to flick them forward because they will be restrained by the transverse projections on the lever, which, in turn, will be restrained from any further upward movement by the screw.

Fore-end of gun showing completed conversion.

To go back to automatic ejection, the screw is turned back until its point is flush with the underside of the fore-end iron, whereupon the ejectors are free to work in the ordinary way.

This is obviously a job well within the capacity of any amateur mechanic possessing drills and taps. I have converted two AYA XXV's in this manner, and find the added facility a boon. In my case, I used $\frac{3}{16}$-in. Whitworth screws, which require to be turned back five half-turns for the restoration of full ejection. There is no need for any locking arrangements, as the barrels prevent any undue movement of the thumb-screw when the fore-end is in place.

Since writing the foregoing, I have heard that at least two foreign firms have adopted optional ejectors. The first is the Spanish concern, Armas Ego of Eibar, and the second is the well-known Japanese firm of Miroku, whose O/U model, as imported into the U.S.A. by Charles Daly, now incorporates a neat version of this device.

40   The Famous Purdey Action

Of all the innumerable hammerless gun actions brought out during the latter part of the last century, two, in their different ways, stood out above the rest, and have most triumphantly survived. They are the Anson and Deeley action, representing ultimate simplicity, and the Purdey action, representing ingenuity and functional refinement.

Every sportsman with the slightest pretensions to a knowledge of guns understands the Anson and Deeley action, as used in nearly all English and foreign boxlocks, and it is not my purpose to make any further reference to it. But not every sportsman understands the Purdey action. Indeed, so little is it understood that I have never yet come across an explanation of its method of working that is correct and free from mechanical fallacies. Even our leading authorities, such as Greener and Burrard, have betrayed a failure to understand it, and a more recent book has appeared which perpetuates their errors. This is Richard Akehurst's otherwise admirable volume, *Game Guns and Rifles*. So, with the Purdey action now nearing its centenary (it was patented by the inventor, F. Beesley, in 1880), and still going as strong as ever, I think it is high time that someone did it justice, which I will try to do, if only for the record.

The single-spring action

The Purdey action is a self-opening, rebounding action. When the trigger is pulled, the internal hammer or tumbler falls and hits a spring-loaded striker, which, in turn, hits the cap and fires the cartridge. The hammer, and with it the striker, then instantly rebounds a fraction of an inch, so that the latter clears the cap indentation and leaves the gun perfectly free to open. When the top lever is pressed over, the gun opens of itself, independently of the weight of the barrels, and in so doing recocks the hammer. On reclosing the gun, the mainspring is compressed. All this is achieved by a single vee spring.

Greener says that 'the principle employed is a spring having two arms, one of which is stronger than the other, the stronger cocking the lock and the weaker firing it.' Burrard says that 'the principle of the cocking system lies in the fact that the two arms of the mainspring are of appreciably different strengths. The upper arm is the more powerful and is used to produce the rebound action . . . and also to cock the tumbler when the gun is open. The lower and less powerful arm is used for rotating the tumbler in the firing of the gun'.

These explanations do the ingenious inventor less than justice by representing his mainspring as being, in effect, two different leaf springs, brought into action at different times and for different purposes. They also carry the mechanically monstrous implication that the two limbs of a vee spring, freely pivoted at its head, are capable of exerting different pressures at their extremities, provided that one limb is made stiffer than the other. I call this a monstrous implication because, if it were true, it would be possible to make a powerful perpetual motion machine by pegging such a spring to the centre of a turntable, with its limbs compressed between two pins fixed at equal distances from the centre. The unbalanced force (if it existed) would then spin the turntable strongly forever!

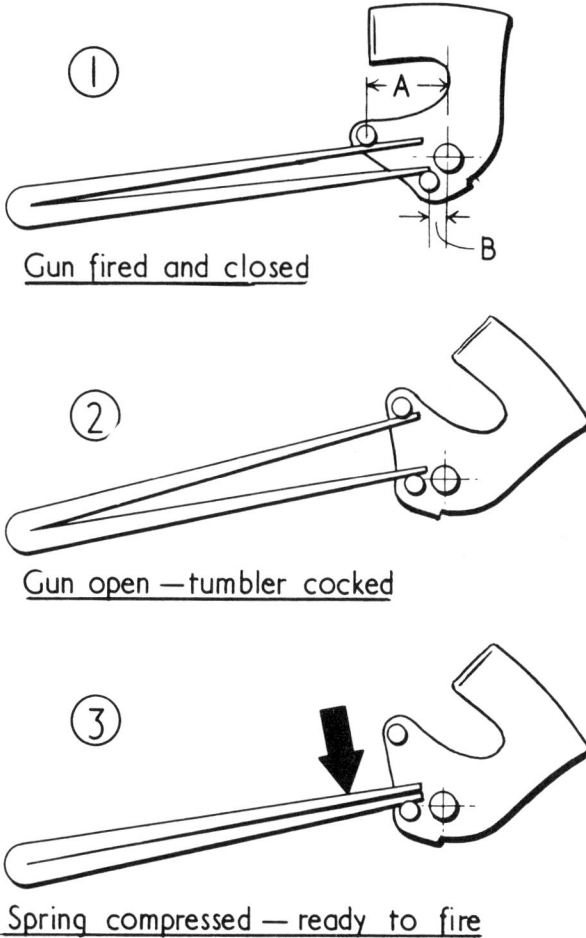

Working principle of Purdey action.

The truth is that the Purdey action does not depend on its mainspring having arms of different strength. It can be shown to work perfectly well with a mainspring made out of a uniform strip of metal of obviously equal strength throughout. Also, it does not depend, as Richard Akehurst says, on 'alternate

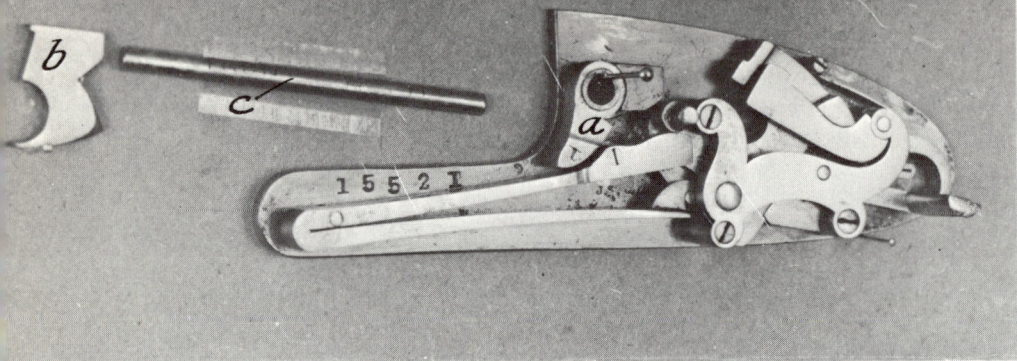

A PURDEY SIDELOCK Showing (*a*) cam which compresses mainspring; (*b*) cam which rotates with barrels; and (*c*) push-rod which communicates motion from (*a*) to (*b*).

use' being made of the two arms of the spring. *Both arms are, in fact, equally involved in all the operations of the gun — opening, closing, firing, and rebounding — and give out, or take in, equal amounts of energy at each stage.*

Having got that out of my system, where it has been festering ever since I first read Burrard's book in 1931, I would like to run over the whole of the working cycle of the action by reference to principles, and without confusing mechanical detail.

In most guns, such as the Anson and Deeley, only one limb of the mainspring bears on the tumbler, tending all the time to cause it to fall and fire the gun. In the Purdey action, however, both limbs of the mainspring bear on the tumbler whenever they are free to do so (see (1) p. 123), the lower one tending permanently to run it left-handed or anti-clockwise, and thus to fire the gun, and the upper one tending to turn it in the opposite direction, and into the fully cocked position. And since the upper limb works on the long arm *A* of the tumbler, whereas the lower limb works only on the short arm *B*, the upper limb, if free to do so, will always overcome the lower one, and force the tumbler into the fully cocked position (2). This is the position of the lock when the gun is open after firing.

When the gun is closed by the shooter, a cam, operated by a push-rod connected to the barrels, presses the upper limb of the mainspring down clear of the tumbler (3), on which only the lower limb then bears. When the trigger is pulled, and the sear thus freed from the bent, the spring behaves like any other, and flicks the tumbler around to the left and fires the gun.

The reaction of the spring to the pressure exerted on it by the push-rod and cam tends *at all times* to throw the gun open, and actually does whenever the locking bolt is withdrawn; so, in the transition from 1 to 2, the mainspring not only cocks the tumbler, but also opens the gun, irrespective of whether or not it has been fired.

I said 'at all times'; but this is not strictly true, because at the instant of firing, the long arm of the tumbler makes contact with the upper limb of the mainspring and momentarily depresses it very slightly by virtue of its inertia. It then rebounds to the first position.

It is doubtful if this splendid action has ever been beaten. The disadvantage commonly attributed to it—that it makes the gun hard to close—disappears with very little use, and the acquisition of a certain knack. An advantage seldom recognised is that, by keeping the rear hook or bite right up to its locking bolt, it stops the gun from shaking loose as soon as it otherwise would do, and is eminently adapted for long and hard service.

41   Barrel Shortening

Who really invented the modern 25-in. barrelled gun? A correspondent raises the question on what he considers the undue share of credit I have given to the late Robert Churchill for this development. The point is of wider interest than the question implies.

But on the narrow issue of priority of invention, Churchill certainly has no claim to have 'invented' short barrels of a particular length, any more than James Watt can be held to have invented the steam engine, or George Stephenson the locomotive. The steam engine was a large, self-acting machine in commercial use and production long before Watt was born; whilst the locomotive made, patented and demonstrated by the wayward Cornish genius, Trevithick, anticipated Stephenson's 'Rocket' by a good quarter-century. Similarly, short gun barrels saw the light long before Churchill did, and had their advocates—both sportsmen and gunmakers—little inferior to him in enthusiasm and conviction.

But we all tend to pin a name on every innovation, even if it is not always quite the right one, and Churchill must be allowed to bear his tab as the inventor of the modern, short-barrelled sporting gun. And rightly so, for he not only recognised, perhaps more fully than any of his gunmaking contemporaries, the good case that could be made out for barrels shorter than the prevalent 30- or 28-in., he redesigned his guns around the 25-in. barrel, and redisposed to the best advantage the weight saved from the muzzle. That, at least, was his contention, for I recall that he always insisted that his guns were 'no mere hacksaw job', as were those, he implied, of some of his imitators.

The Churchill rib

Churchill must also be credited with the introduction of the distinctive high, narrow and tapered rib that bears his name. In this matter, I believe that he made a virtue, and a true merit, of necessity. I suspect that he was at first embarrassed by the unduly high shooting of his short barrels, and that he was constrained to adopt a high foresight to counteract it. The idea of connecting this high foresight to the breech by means of what we now know as a Churchill rib may well have come a beat of time later; and later still, a full recognition of its advantages as an aid to pointability. Here, as elsewhere, the processes of invention may have been intuitive rather than rational: many a first-class idea has arrived by passenger train, leaving its logical exposition to follow by slow freight.

Apart from these mechanical matters, Churchill established, or caused to be established, the truth about the ballistics of the 25-in. barrelled gun. It was easy to say, as his detractors did, that his gun did not shoot so hard as one with barrels of a more conventional length, but when, under his provocation, the matter was subjected to a rigorous course of experiments, it was found that the inferiority was of no practical significance. The average loss of striking energy at game shooting distances, was, in fact, less than might be found in individual cartridges from the same batch, when fired from a conventional gun. This, as Churchill did not fail to point out, was likely to be compensated, and more than compensated, by the faster handling quality of the short-barrelled gun, whereby the shooter could get on to his bird a trifle quicker.

A new orthodoxy

But although, from a broad viewpoint, there was little originality and no true invention in his 'XXV' gun, Churchill was undoubtedly the father of the modern short-barrelled arm, and the founder of the new orthodoxy it came to represent. For years, he fought its battles and gave its detractors blow for blow. He was indeed a bonny fighter, and in the end had the bonny fighter's reward of seeing most of his opponents lowering their swords to him. I count myself among his converts, but not as a doctrinaire convert, for I am sure that the XXV is not everybody's gun. But for many a shooter like myself, who, I repeat, is on the wrong side of the grand climacteric, and whose reactions are not so fast as once they were, it is an undeniable boon, and a means whereby performance can be noticeably improved.

To return, then, to my correspondent's original question, who did invent the short-barrelled gun? The answer, I am sure, is nobody. Nobody invented it; but it is possible to discern a true inventor whose invention marked a turning point in this particular aspect of shotgun development. I refer to Henry Nock, an eighteenth-century gunmaker, whose 'Patent Breeching', brought out about 1787, was destined to chop more inches off the barrels of sporting guns than any invention of any gunmaker had done before, or has done since.

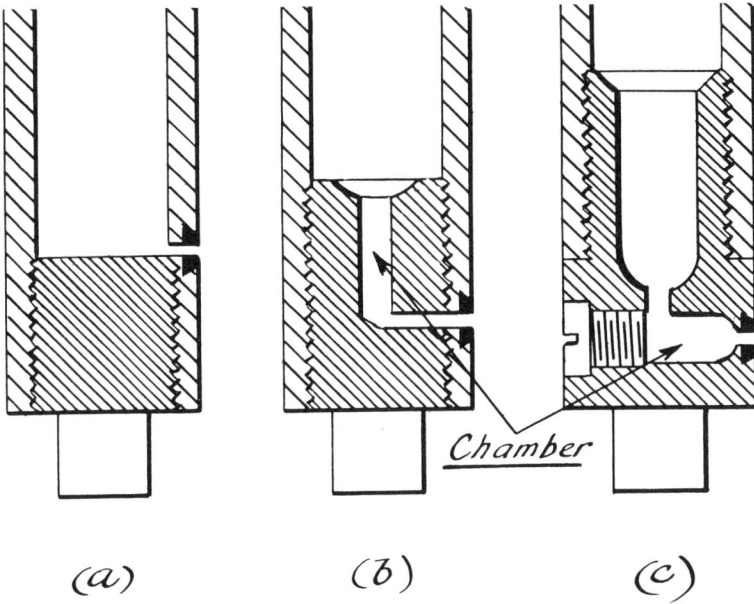

Evolution of the flintlock breech plug.

Early firearms, because of the inferior quality of the powder and the slow means of ignition available, had, of necessity, to have long barrels – otherwise there would have been incomplete combustion of the charge and inadequate ballistics. So, the shotgun of Queen Anne's day had barrels of anything up to about 46 in. in length. Ignition was, of course, by flint, and the breeching was a plain screwed plug as shown in my sketch (a) above. The flash from the pan thus ignited the charge at one point only.

Two great innovators

An improvement on this arrangement was the chamber plug (b). In this, ignition was transferred to the base of the chamber shown, with the effect that the powder in this chamber, on burning, shot the main charge through with flame, and thus ignited it more thoroughly and more quickly. Unfortunately, however, the full merit of this arrangement was not realised because of the delay involved in the passing of the flash along the much extended touch-hole.

The grand merit of Henry Nock's breech (c) was that it made the best of both worlds. In it, the chamber was turned sideways, thus cutting out the long communication between the flash pan and the base of the charge, whilst retaining the full advantage of chamber plugs of the earlier kind.

The effect of Henry Nock's invention on the performance of the shotgun was revolutionary. It improved the efficiency of combustion of the charge to such an extent that it became feasible to reduce barrel length by a foot or more. At the same time, the reduction in weight made double guns a thoroughly acceptable proposition, and gave wing-shooting a great fillip, not only by the improved speed of handling of the shorter gun, but by its improved performance. At the same time the old, full-length Queen Anne stock disappeared, and guns became conveniently demountable, so that they could be stowed and carried about in cases such as we know today. In short, the Henry Nock breech was the culminating improvement of the flint system, besides which all subsequent inventions, up to the arrival of the percussion system, were comparatively unimportant.

So, I always like to think of Henry Nock and Robert Churchill as standing at the beginning and the end respectively of a single process—that of delivering the sporting gun from the burden of all barrel length and weight not required for ballistics or for the convenient handling and pointing of the weapon. If there is a laurel wreath awaiting a head in this matter, I suggest that it should be divided in two, and shared by the two celebrated gunmakers named.

42   *Hammer Gun Revival*

I have been trying to make up my mind recently as to whether we are witnessing a genuine revival of the hammer gun. The qualifying condition for such a revival would be an upsurge of desire on the part of many shooters to possess and use guns of this kind. It would not be enough for them to be driven to use them by the shortage or high cost of hammerless weapons, both new and second-hand, as I suspect that many are. For all that, ever since the 1880s, during which the various hammerless actions were brought to perfection, the hammer gun has retained a body of faithful adherents. At first, it was a large body, headed by many eminent and distinguished sportsmen, and made up, as to the mass, chiefly by men of mature age who had used hammer guns all their lives, and wished for nothing better. It included some fierce partisans of the hammer principle, who could not see merit through the fog of prejudice; and others who were genuinely apprehensive of what they considered to be the danger inherent in guns, the state of which – whether cocked or uncocked – could not be instantly seen. Others again took great exception to hammerless guns on the score of their appearance, their oft-quoted objection being that they looked 'like a dog without ears'.

Declining fortunes

But as the merit of the hammerless principle became unmistakably established; as the dangers attributed to it were seen to have been delusory; and as time thinned the ranks of the old hammer gunners, partisan and non-partisan alike, their guns themselves descended in the social scale. Many were handed over to keepers; others were part-exchanged for hammerless guns, and were in due course bought by shooters not so long in the purse as their original owners. In time, as their market value declined, they fell increasingly into the hands of shooters of the kind who abused and neglected them – unworthy

The Lefaucheux pinfire, the earliest form of breech-loading hammer-gun, was viewed with grave suspicion at its first appearance in this country, as this Leech cartoon of about 1855 clearly indicates. The original caption read: 'Don't think much o' him – he's gone and bruck his gun the werry fust shot.'

THE IRONMONGER DIARY.

Wonderful Value in Guns.

New Prices.

New Patterns.

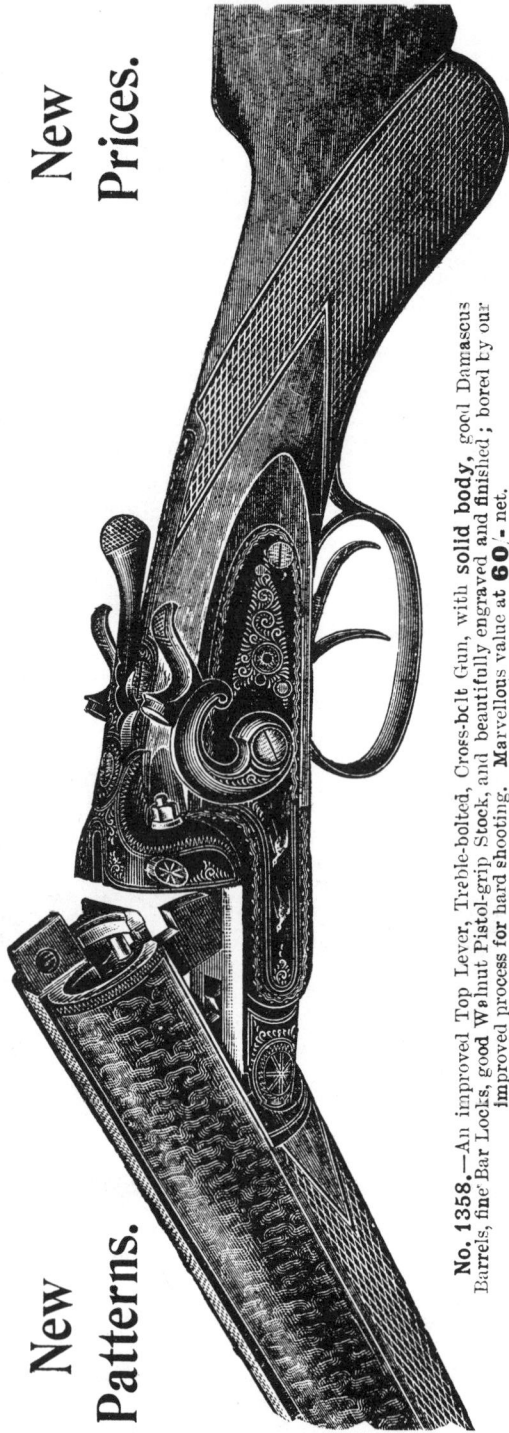

No. 1358.—An improved Top Lever, Treble-bolted, Cross-bolt Gun, with **solid body**, good Damascus Barrels, fine Bar Locks, good Walnut Pistol-grip Stock, and beautifully engraved and finished ; bored by our improved process for hard shooting. Marvellous value at **60/-** net.

For every kind of GUN, RIFLE, and REVOLVER of the Highest Quality at the Lowest Possible Price, write to—

MIDLAND GUN COMPANY, Bath Street, BIRMINGHAM.

A nostalgic advertisement from a trade journal of 1900. At this period best quality London hammer guns fetched 50–60 guineas.

custodians of what were often fine old thoroughbreds. So they were to be found, scattered across the countryside and in longshore villages, with barrels grossly pitted and maybe perforated, stocks broken and whipped with copper wire, locks dangerously rusted up – but still, more often than not, bravely digesting modern smokeless ammunition.

But while this process of degradation was going on, hammer guns continued to be made, though increasingly in the lower grades. There was good reason for this. No longer were those of higher quality so much in demand, for discriminating shooters who could afford the hammerless variety were taking to them as a matter of course. At the same time, the simplicity and natural strength of the hammer gun made it the obvious choice for makers catering for the cut-price market. The competition in guns of this kind must indeed have been intense. Before the First World War, English (or what purported to be English) hammer guns could be had for as little as 60s. My illustration, culled from a trade paper of 1900, shows the kind of thing. And Belgian guns of a similar kind were still being offered at this price as recently as the mid-1920s. It was notable, however, that at least one respectable Birmingham maker who listed them, was anxious to make it clear that they were sold without any kind of guarantee whatsoever.

A changing status

At that period, the status of the hammer gun was fairly clear. For firing ordinary game charges it was simply an obsolete type. Those that were still being made were chiefly made for cheapness. Gunmakers who were prepared to prostitute their craft produced them as a matter of course. Good and high-class specimens made in better days had mostly come down in the world – often, as I said, very badly. But a few survived in the hands of careful users – men who valued them, perhaps, not so much because they were hammer guns, but because they were old and well-tried favourites. A still smaller number, retired from active service while still in good condition – 'widow's guns', maybe – were all set to last into our own times, when they occasionally come to light.

But something like half a century has passed by since the time of which I am speaking, and since then the status of the hammer gun seems to have undergone a perceptible change. No longer is it simply an obsolete type: it has acquired something of the status, not perhaps of an antique, but of a veteran motor car. And if a particular gun was originally a fine specimen, and has survived in first-class order – moreover, if it has been nitro-proved – it has now become an article of value. I suspect that there is now a considerable body of shooters who use hammer guns, either regularly or occasionally, for reasons similar to those that inspire others to use muzzle-loaders. No doubt there is a nostalgic element here—part of the impulse that most of us feel at times to turn away from the harsh realities of our own era, and towards the days when we feel (perhaps quite mistakenly) that life was simpler, better, easier and more truly enjoyable.

But there will be other and more concrete motives. These old guns, in their higher manifestations, are really beautiful, and afford conscious aesthetic pleasure. Then again, the demands they make on the shooter for their manipulation, far from being an unrelieved drawback, can be a source of pleasure to the enthusiast. Many a keen motorist prefers a manual to an automatic gearbox for precisely the same reason.

But on the question of nitro-proving these guns, I should warn owners of fine specimens that, to some keen collectors, nitro-proof may actually reduce their value.

A TRANSITIONAL HAMMER GUN   A striking example of the persistence of the hammer tradition. The gun, by Thomas Turner, is virtually a hammerless boxlock in which the hammers have been transferred to the outside of the action.

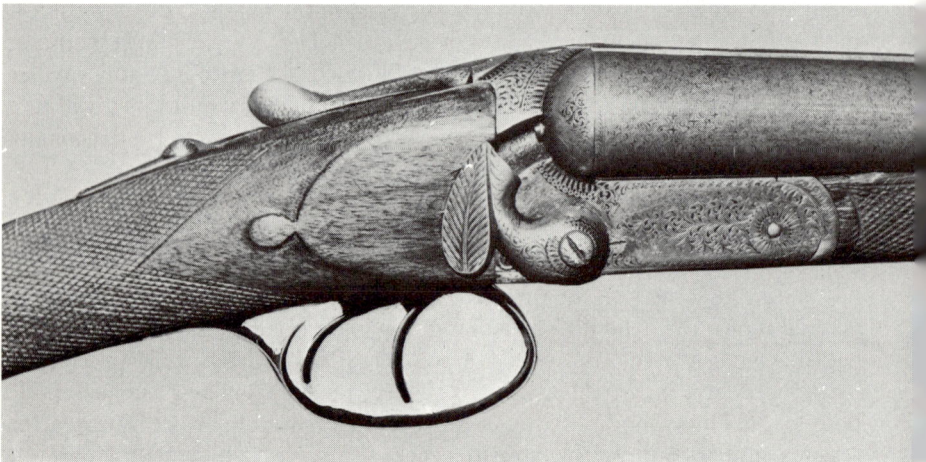

Section 5

PATTERNS

'Birds are not killed by bangs ... good patterns are indispensable for the best results, more especially for the longer reach.'

43 *Pattern Quality Tells*

I have many times stressed the importance of good quality in shotgun patterns, for it is a fact that, within wide limits, uniformity of distribution is more significant than mere pellet count in determining the success and consistency of a shooter's performance. It has often been assumed that if a bird presents an area of, say, one fiftieth of the area of the pattern circle in which it happens to be caught, it will receive one fiftieth of the total pellets. Nothing of the sort! – it may receive that number on average; but birds are not killed by averages, only by actual hits, and the essential point is that, with good quality patterns, the actual number of hits from round to round will tend to keep more closely to the average than they will if pattern quality is below par. In the latter case, the number of birds slipping through the pattern untouched, or receiving a superfluity of pellets, may greatly exceed the corresponding number when the patterns are really superior.

This is all very well as general doctrine, but I recognise that it needs backing with figures. Several years ago, I made an interesting experiment, which is described on pages 160–164 of *Gough Thomas's Gun Book*. What I did was to take an actual good pattern, and to apply to it, by a suitable random process, a transparent cut-out representing the vulnerable area of a mallard. I repeated this 100 times, each time counting the number of pellets covered by the cut-out. The average number of hits was six, but the individual numbers varied from one to twelve, and in only 72 per cent of the cases did the target receive the four or more pellets considered necessary to bring the bird to bag. Subsequent and independent evidence strongly supports the validity of these conclusions.

But the pattern chosen was, as I said, a good one, and so I decided to repeat the experiment with two patterns of similar pellet count, and the same overall spread, one of good quality and one of poor. The good pattern I selected was the actual one shown on the left (page 136). It contains 163 pellets, and rates as being of 'excellent' quality by the Oberfell and Thompson method described in the above-mentioned book. The pattern on the right is a factitious pattern, also of 163 pellets, which I constructed by modifying the other one to the least extent necessary to bring it into the 'poor' O and T category. To do this, I had to allow seven extra 5-in. voids as shown, and to increase the number of pellets in the inner 20-in. circle from the original 67 to 98. This was done suitably at random.

For the test, I chose a partridge, or, rather, its vulnerable area, as shown dotted in my sketch of the bird on the right. It makes a small target of about thirteen square inches. I applied this target 100 times, first to the good pattern and then to the poor one. To ensure a true random application, I divided the pattern circles into a large number of little numbered squares and drew correspondingly numbered counters out of a bag. The target was in each case dropped roughly over the square whose number had been drawn.

Expectations realised

The results entirely fulfilled my expectations. They may be summarised as follows:

	Good pattern	Poor pattern
Birds receiving no pellets	6	20
Birds receiving 1 or more	94	80
Birds receiving 2 or more	83	57
Birds receiving 3 or more	76	43
Birds receiving 4 or more	50	34
Birds receiving 5 or more	33	27
Birds receiving 6 or more	23	24
Birds receiving 8 or more	7	14
Birds receiving 10 or more	1	12
Birds receiving 12 or more	0	7

(As there were 100 tests in each case, the above figures may be read as percentages)

This table fairly exposes the three essential defects of inferior patterns—(1) the greater number of birds likely to escape through the gaps between the pellets (20 as opposed to 6 here); (2) the markedly fewer birds receiving the best number of pellets, having regard for their ultimate appearance on the

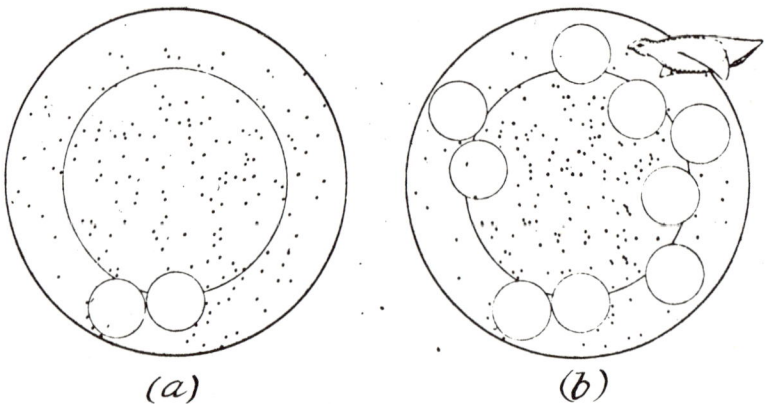

(a)   (b)

These two patterns contain the same number of pellets with the same overall spread, but (a) rates as being 'excellent' and (b) as 'poor'. The experiment described demonstrates that within wide limits pattern quality is more important than pellet count.

table (e.g. 34 as opposed to 50); and (3) the far higher number overdosed with lead (33 here as opposed to 8).

I am aware that these results are open to certain criticism. For example, the existence of a bird-sized void in a pattern does not necessarily represent an opportunity for one to escape, unless it is flying in the direction of the shot; but the comparison between the two patterns is nevertheless likely to remain a fair one. In short, the test fairly emphasises the advantages of the bespoke gun, or any other which is shot and regulated to give patterns of the required density and of good quality.

44   Your Best Pattern

The best kind of shotgun pattern for you, personally, in given circumstances, would obviously be one with a spread sufficiently wide to cover the largest aiming error you are normally likely to commit, according to your particular degree of skill, and sufficiently well garnished with pellets of adequate energy to assure a clean kill. It may be both interesting and helpful to follow up this line of enquiry.

But in so doing we must be practical; we cannot go straight out for a pattern that would guarantee an ordinary shooter 100 per cent kills to cartridges, because I can say at once that that would require an inordinate spread of the shot charge, which would have to be of excessive weight to maintain the necessary pattern density. So, too, would the gun, for the avoidance of unbearable recoil.

To find out what sort of pattern would enable a particular shooter to attain a more moderate and practical result, it is necessary to ascertain what are his typical aiming or pointing errors. For that, I can only offer myself for demonstration purposes, regardless of the risk of exposing the modesty of my pretensions as a shot.

So, I have taken an air rifle and have fired 100 *unaimed* shots with it at a fixed and level mark, 10 yards away. This was intended to show the sort of pointing errors I should be likely to make in shooting walked-up birds going straight away—a type of shot, incidentally, which I have never found so easy as it looks, presumably because I cannot get my swing going.

Each time, I brought the rifle up from the forward-and-down, or 'ready' position, and shot very quickly, as I should have had to do at wild and fast-flying partridges.

The air rifle, I should say, was a poor fit by shotgun standards, and for this and other reasons was not calculated to exhibit me in the character of a Walsingham or a de Grey. Still, it was fairly accurate, and it was not necessary in these circumstances to take account of its own contributory errors. So, let us take a look at the results I obtained. I have expressed them in terms of the number of pellets found between rings spaced at 1-in. intervals from the group centre. As 100 pellets in all were fired, the numbers found in any position are also the percentages of the total.

Ring	0–1	1–2	2–3	3–4	4–5	5–6	6–7	7–8 in.
Pellets in ring	2	8	12	25	13	7	7	5
Cumulative total	2	10	22	47	60	67	74	79

Interpretation

With these figures we can say straight away what sort of pattern a shooter of my standard would require in order to attain a given level of performance at the kind of shooting assumed. For example, the figures show that I got 79 per cent of my pellets within 8 in. of the centre of the target, so that if I had been using a shotgun a 16-in. spread would have covered the bulls-eye 79 per cent of the times I fired. The equivalent spread required at the good sporting range of 40 yds (instead of 10) would therefore be 16 × 4 or 64 in.

Working on these lines, I get the following figures of 40-yd spread for various standards of performance.

Kills to cartridges	20	30	40	50	60	70	80 per cent
Min. spread at 40 yds	23	27	30	34	40	51	65

So if, with my sort of pointing errors, I were so ambitious as to specify a pattern that would give me an 80 per cent performance at the sort of shooting contemplated, I should need a pattern 65 in. wide at 40 yds. And if we turn up the table of spread in the IMI *Shooter's Yearbook* or in my own *Shotguns and Cartridges* we find that even a true cylinder pattern has only a 58-in. spread at that range. Still, a 65-in. spread could be contrived, so we may as well carry on and consider what kind of charge I should need.

In the book just mentioned, I took 130 as the minimum pattern required for medium game. This, of course, means 130 pellets in the standard 30-in. circle; and to preserve the same density in my 65-in. pattern would require 610 pellets. The total charge, indeed, would need to be somewhat more, because we ought to allow at least another 5 per cent to cover the wild outer fringe. So, let us say that we should need 650 pellets altogether.

But 650 pellets of No. 6 would weigh a full 2⅜ oz., which is the load for a 4-in. 8-bore! This is a conclusion foreshadowed by my opening remarks.

Clearly, then, unless I could contrive to shoot much more accurately than I did in my experiment, I should need to pitch my requirements considerably lower when specifying a tailor-made pattern.

I am, I know, only an average shot; and Payne-Gallwey, out of his great experience, took a ratio of kills to cartridges of only 30 per cent as being appropriate to such a man. But to maintain such a ratio over an entire season, taking every kind of game and every shot fairly offered, and allowing for off-days, hangovers and hoodoos, requires a far higher standard of performance when shooting under favourable conditions. From my own experience, I should expect an average shooter to make 60 to 70 per cent at the kind of shooting I have in mind – say, 70 per cent as it was repetitive and from a fixed position.

A happy conclusion

Referring once again to my last table, it will be seen that, for a 70 per cent performance, I should need a 51-in. spread; and turning to the book, I find that this is the spread given for an improved cylinder pattern. This then, can be fairly taken as the pattern I need, and it is one which everyone knows can be filled adequately for all ordinary game shooting with an ounce to an ounce-and-an-eighth of No. 6 shot. So, by this independent enquiry, I am led to the same conclusion that thousands of others have reached by the sheer weight of practical experience.

But it should be recognised that if an average shot wants something better than average performance, he can have it – on terms. He can increase his shot charge, and *spread it proportionately more* over the map. Or he can increase his spread without increasing his charge, in which case he must restrict his shooting to somewhat shorter distances. This is often the unrecognised secret of much success, for most game is shot at medium range.

But what the average shooter cannot do is to command success by using *maximum* charges with *minimum* spread. This indeed is the killing combination for long-range work, *provided, and only provided,* that the shooter is sufficiently skilled to make good use of it, which often does not follow. It is a certain source of disappointment in the hands of the average man for use at short and medium distances.

45 Suspect Patterns

Accounts reach me from time to time of guns throwing extra-dense patterns perhaps between 80 and 90 per cent. Sometimes these patterns are attributed to a special load concocted by a home-loader, or to an unorthodox component in the cartridge. At other times, they are represented as arising from some special merit in the boring of the gun. More often than not – far more often than not – these accounts come from America, where the extra-dense pattern still seems to arouse more enthusiasm than it generally deserves.

Usually, when writing about pattern density and choke, I stress the undue demands that tight patterns make on the marksmanship of the shooter, and trot out my favourite old hobby-horse about the best degree of choke being the least degree consistent with the requirements of the class of sport concerned.

That remains true; but there is another aspect of the extra-dense pattern that needs consideration. It concerns the sacrifice that may have been made to achieve it. As pressure and velocity are reduced, patterns tend to close up, and an extra-dense pattern may mean no more than that velocity, and therefore penetration at a distance, is less than it should be for best results.

In one of my old shooting books – I think it is Blaine, but I have been unable to trace the reference – there is an account of how guns were sometimes sold to innocents on the strength of their allegedly marvellous shooting, as demonstrated by their ability to throw the entire charge into a hat at twenty paces, or whatever it may have been. This, of course, was in the muzzle-loading days, before the invention of choke; and the extra-dense pattern was achieved simply by reducing the powder charge, and thereby the muzzle velocity.

How this comes about may be fairly represented by my two drawings. The top one shows three pellets of a shot charge in flight, *a* being a truly round

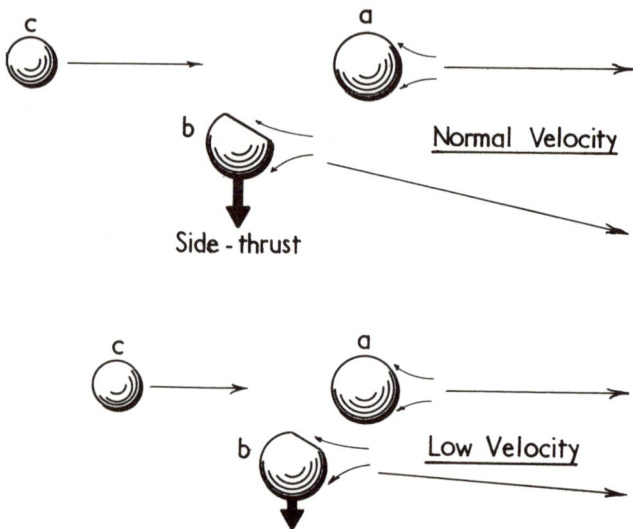

Behaviour of typical pellets in normal and low velocity charges compared.

pellet and *b* a damaged one, having a flat which it acquired by abrasion or compressive deformation in the barrel. The third pellet *c* is one that is slightly under size. The truly round pellet *a* is heading for the central part of the pattern, but the damaged one *b* is not acted on symmetrically by the air resistance, and thus experiences a side-thrust, as indicated, which has the effect of deflecting it from its proper course. The undersized pellet *c* is lagging because of its comparative lightness and inferior ranging power.

The lower drawing shows what happens when the pressure and velocity are reduced. The truly round pellet flies straight for the mark, as before, but the damaged one is affected in two ways. First, it has suffered less damage in the barrel; and since the air resistance now acts on it more symmetrically, it experiences less side-thrust. Secondly, the side-thrust is further reduced by its reduced speed — more than proportionately so, in fact, because air resistance varies as the square of the velocity. In consequence, it is less deflected from its proper direction, and will therefore contribute in due course to the making of a denser pattern.

A longer string

The spacing of the pellets lengthwise should also be noted. In the low velocity charge, represented by the lower drawing, the pellets are shown less widely separated than they are in the other case. This is because, in accordance with well-known principles, the stringing out of a shot charge in flight decreases as the velocity is reduced. High velocity loads must suffer *some* loss of practical efficiency on this account, however slight.

The main point I want to make, arising out of all this, is that the home-loader or amateur gun-doctor who achieves extra-dense patterns should not be too ready to congratulate himself. Quite apart from the practical difficulty of achieving the standard of marksmanship necessary to make good use of such patterns, they may be nothing more than an indication that the ballistics are on the low side. Similarly, one should treat with reserve any published accounts of wonderful patterns that are not accompanied by acceptable evidence of velocity.

There is also the corollary that anyone who forsakes standard for high velocity cartridges is giving hostages to fortune. The gain in velocity, by itself, is unlikely to be of any significance; but there may be a significant change in the performance of the gun.

46 *Pattern Appearance v. Efficiency*

For *comparing* the performance of shotguns, it is obviously necessary that we should have a standard procedure – hence the practice of shooting into a 30-in. circle at 40 yds. But for *demonstrating* their performance – that is to say, their suitability for performing a given task – this procedure is much open to question. The overall suitability and efficiency of a gun in the hands of a particular shooter is undoubtedly best determined by using it for the kind of sport for which it is principally intended. Provided that the shooter is an experienced man, who knows the sort of performance of which he should be capable, and provided that the trial period is long enough to yield an indicative result, no other test is necessary.

A few months ago, I went with a doctor friend to lend him my support in buying a second-hand gun, which he duly acquired. He took it straight away into service, and soon came back with entirely satisfactory accounts of its performance in the field. Moreover, the gun was thoroughly compatible with his personal needs and preferences in the way of weight, fit, balance, etc. Since, therefore, my friend was a mature sportsman, and one unlikely to be beguiled into premature and unwarranted enthusiasm, I took it that the gun had reasonably established itself as a success, which more prolonged service was likely to confirm.

So when he came back to me some while later with further good accounts of the gun, and expressing curiosity as to the sort of patterns it must be throwing to give him the results that he was getting, I did what I could to dissuade him from pursuing the matter. 'Why bother?' I said. 'You wouldn't propose to carry out a diagnostic operation on one of your patients to find out what it is that makes him so fit and well'. A patterning test is, after all, usually nothing more than an attempt to find out how a gun is likely to perform in the field, and is entirely superseded in due course by the record of such performance.

The matter goes further than that. I have known several cases of shooters whose confidence in their guns, fully justified by their field record, has been seriously undermined by ill-advised patterning tests. This applies with particular force to tests made on open-bored barrels – that is, true or improved cylinders – at 40 yds. What is worse, is when such tests are made on paper, and especially slightly crumpled paper or newspaper, when all the pellet marks cannot be seen at a glance. Then, indeed, the shooter will be lucky if he is not in some degree dismayed. 'Is *that* the sort of pattern I have been shooting with?' he may well say to himself. This loss of confidence can so readily come about, and can be so serious, that another friend of mine, who is in the gun trade, is much averse to demonstrating the shooting of an open-bored gun at 40 yds, especially to a prospective buyer of little experience. He contends that it would be far more realistic to test the gun – or rather, to demonstrate it – at a distance within the range-bracket of common usage, say, 30 yds. I agree.

I know a man who goes further. He is not concerned with yards, feet and inches. He sets up a small target on familiar shooting ground, and then retires to what his experience tells him is a thoroughly representative shooting distance. If the gun makes patterns of the right quality and density at that range, he is satisfied that it will not let him down. This could hardly be regarded as a test procedure, but it has some strictly practical merit.

The main point in all this was well brought home in the case of a correspondent who wrote to me some time ago complaining of the performance of a new 12-bore gun. In support of his complaint, he sent me a pattern made by the right barrel, which was supposed to be bored improved cylinder. The pattern was, to use his own words, 'as full of holes as an old dish clout'. It had been made by a Grand Prix cartridge loaded with $1\frac{1}{16}$ oz of No. 6 – nominally 287 pellets.

I do not positively remember the actual pellet count in the 30-in. circle, but I am fairly certain that it was 137, or 48 per cent of the total charge, as against the 50 per cent conventionally associated with I.C. boring. There was nothing wrong with that: a well-distributed pattern of 137 would be ideal for most of the general rough shooting for which the gun was required.

As for the holes in it, I found on applying my 5-in. circular gauge, which is the standard size of vacant patch that I use when assessing patterns, that there were seven such holes – seven places without a pellet, representing nearly a fifth of the effective pattern area, through which a partridge, grouse or even a hen pheasant could escape without being struck in a vital spot.

That, at least, was clearly my correspondent's impression; but it was a false impression, as I hope to show. But first, I should say that the degree of patchiness revealed was strictly normal for a pattern of 137, and implied nothing amiss. It is not until there are about 300 pellets in the 30-in. circle that one is entitled to expect complete freedom from open patches of the size described.

If, then, an ordinary 12-bore, bored improved cylinder, and loaded with a normal charge of No. 6, can be *expected* to throw patterns 'as full of holes as an old dish clout', how is it that gunmakers invariably recommend this boring for general rough shooting or driving in this country? The answer, like the gun, is double-barrelled.

First, the most successful gun is the one that performs best, not at 40 yds, but in the range-bracket within which most shots are taken, which is probably 20 to 30 yds. The patterns made at these distances are very different from the 40-yd patterns.

Secondly, patterns are misleading in that they do not show the length of the charge in flight, which may run into 3 or 4 yds at full range. A clear hole in a pattern should thus be regarded as an open, pellet-free tunnel right through the charge from front to back. Clearly, for a bird or other target to pass clean through this tunnel without risk of receiving a hit, it must either be stationary or travelling along a line parallel to the line of flight of the charge. If there is any sideways movement – if the bird is crossing or quartering – it will run into the side of the tunnel, and is likely to be struck. So, the presence of a number of bird-size holes in a pattern does not imply the existence of a corresponding number of chances of birds escaping scot free, even though caught well within the pattern circle.

That is why the practical efficiency of the patterns from open-bored guns is so often better than their appearance on the pattern plate would suggest. That, also, is why it may be unwise to enquire too closely into the sort of patterns a gun is throwing when its performance in the field is entirely satisfactory.

47 Funny Figures

I use the word 'funny' here in the sense of curious; and the 'figures' I have in mind are arithmetical figures, and not some of the less aesthetic revelations of the bathing beach. But since arithmetic is not a popular subject, or even one of the inescapable scholastic disciplines nowadays, I had better make it clear straightaway that my subject is shooting, and not any kind of calculation.

As we look around us, we see many things which are associated without being in any way related – or so it would appear. And yet, when we look more closely, we may find that they are indeed related, and so closely that the relationship can be expressed tightly in figures. Very funny sometimes, and sometimes very useful.

For example, we fire a shotgun at a target. The pellets make an untidy splatter of marks, the overall spread of which is largely determined by the choke. An experienced man may look at this splatter, and pronounce that it is a good, normal pattern. The main connotation of the word 'pattern' is a certain orderliness, but there is nothing orderly about this mess. But wait! – let us draw a circle to enclose the bulk of it, excluding the obvious stragglers, and count the pellet marks. Having done that, we can apply the laws of chance (known on high days and holidays as the Theory of Probability) to calculate, often with uncanny accuracy, certain things about that pattern which are highly relevant to successful shooting. We can predict the degree of central concentration it is likely to have, and the number of holes or voids or vacant patches of a certain size that we shall find. This may be merely funny,

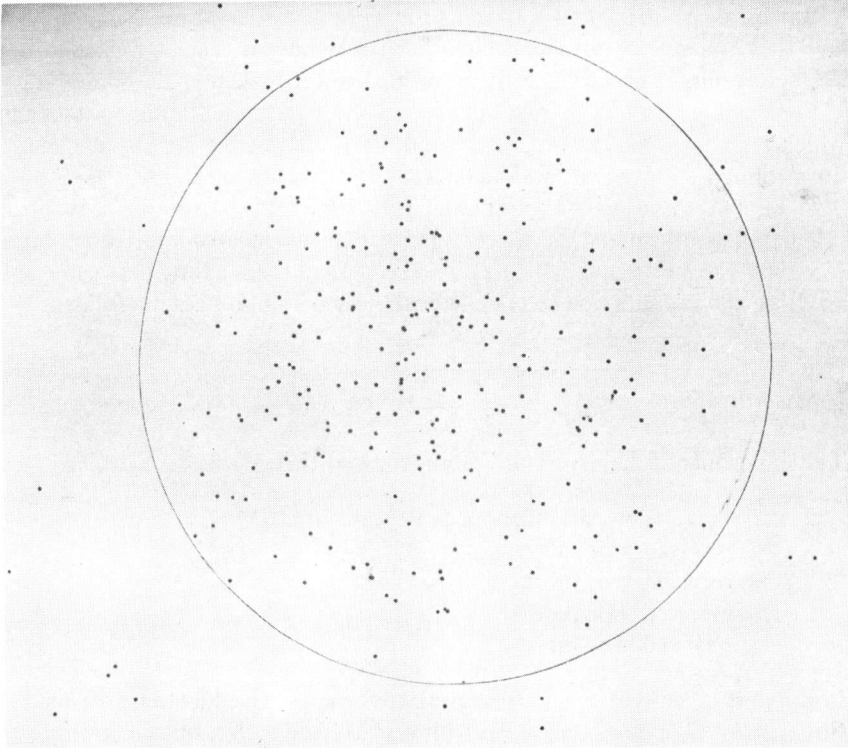

A typical shotgun pattern – 'an untidy splatter of marks'.

in the present sense, but it is most useful in reverse, by enabling us to establish certain standards by which to judge the probable effectiveness of our patterns in the field. I must refer readers whose curiosity is aroused, and who would like more information, to the latest (third) edition of *Shotguns and Cartridges*.

How many hits?

Every experienced shooter knows that birds may occasionally be killed by a single fluke pellet; but he equally knows that, for consistent results, there must be a certain minimum number of hits. The appropriate number for each type of game bird has been given by Burrard, who, following in the path of Journée and Metz-Noblat, worked out the pattern density necessary to ensure its attainment, *on average*.

But birds are not killed by average hits: only by actual ones, and it is a fact that the actual number inflicted by a good pattern, giving adequate average results, will vary greatly from bird to bird taken at the same range.

For example, in *Gough Thomas's Gun Book* I described an experiment in which a transparent cut-out, representing the vulnerable area of a mallard, was dropped 100 times at random on a good pattern giving an average number of 6 hits. But the actual number of hits varied from 1 to 12. My prior calculations indicated that there was an even chance of individual birds receiving 4 to 8 hits, and a 100 to 1 chance of all of them falling between 0 and 12. Both these predictions were curiously exact. Funnier results follow.

Odd coincidences

The experiment I have just described showed that —

> All 'birds' received 1 or more pellets
> 95% received 2 or more
> 81% received 3 or more
> 72% received 4 or more
> 58% received 5 or more

It is widely taken that a mallard requires five penetrative hits to be reasonably sure of a kill—or, say, four in its vulnerable regions. So, on the strength of the foregoing results, 72 per cent of kills could have been expected from the good, normal pattern chosen. Now the remarkable experiments in duck shooting carried out by the American Bureau of Sport Fisheries and Wildlife and reported in its Transactions of 1969* realised 71 per cent actually killed in comparable circumstances — 71 per cent against my theoretical 72 per cent. Is that simply to be dismissed as an odd coincidence, or is it evidence that my little experiment had a wider significance than I imagined? Perhaps it had, for the results were also strikingly paralleled by the French experiments in pigeon shooting which I reported in the 26 June 1975 issue of the *Shooting Times*.

What can I make of these funny figures that will help the shooting man in the field, and not merely titillate his curiosity? This, at least, I think for certain – that the smaller and therefore more numerous the pellets in the charge, the more certain and consistent the kills, always provided that the pellets have adequate striking energy or penetrative power at the range under consideration.

---

* *Shotguns and Cartridges* (3rd edn.) pp. 198-201.

Personal skills

Journée came up with some curious figures on the subject of human skills. The good General had been studying the varying degrees of proficiency exhibited by musketry recruits in the French Army, and he found a consistent relationship between the average and the best. The latter had just about twice the skill of the former, as determined by their aiming errors. What was more surprising, is that the same relation held good over the whole range of measurable physical activities. Journée was so impressed by this that he contemplated the existence of a corresponding natural law operative in the intellectual and moral spheres as well as in the physical.

In shooting with the shotgun, he found that the probable angular aiming error of the average shooter is about 1 degree, or 25 in. at 40 yds. The most skilled Monte Carlo pigeon shooters, however, had an average error of only 35 minutes of an arc, or 15 in. at the same distance – just about half the others, and representing twice the skill once again.

Now we come to what is to me the funniest figure of all. My predominant personal error, as experimentally determined, under conditions representing, as closely as possible, quick, instinctive shooting at wild, going-away birds, and as described on pages 226–7 of *Gough Thomas's Gun Book*, worked out at this identical figure of 15 in. at 40 yds.

Let my candid friends and shooting companions explain that away as best they can. I am content to contemplate it with unquestioning serenity.

48   Boring for 200 Straight

As compared with a rifle, a shotgun is a weapon of vast and manifold imprecision. The rifle is required to throw its single projectile to distances measurable in hundreds of yards, and with an error from round to round of, say, only 1/500th part of the range. The shotgun, on the other hand, and in a contrast that is almost ludicrous, is required to throw its pellets a mere 40 yds or so, and with a permitted error, even with a fully choked barrel, of about 1/70th part of the range. The comparison is open to criticism, but it serves to introduce my theme.

If we are prepared to extend this enormous degree of tolerance to a shotgun, why, it might be asked, is there all this fuss about the boring of barrels? Surely, any kind of plain tube would do, given the strength to resist the pressure? It could hardly fail to blow out the pellets in the kind of cloud that seems to be acceptable; or it could be pinched in a bit at the muzzle if a somewhat denser cloud were required.

No doubt shotguns have been, and are still being made in conformity with this sceptical (or cynical) philosophy; but it remains a fact that the practical effectiveness of a gun in the field is much influenced by the precise form of the bore, and even by the nature of its surface; and that, in the search for the best possible results, practically every conceivable variation from the plain, smooth-surfaced, cylindrical tube has been tried. I have been prompted to write this article by the consideration that, even at this late stage, experimentation in barrel boring is still going on, with a view to the further improvement of patterns for particular purposes.

The ideal

The ideal pattern – the one that would give the most successful and consistent performance – is, of course, one of appropriate spread, in which the pellets are distributed with geometrical uniformity, and which all arrive at the target simultaneously; and the best patterns are those approaching most closely to this ideal, adequate velocity at maximum range being understood. But best patterns can only be made with high-grade shot. Given that, and the possibility of loading it to the best advantage, it is to the boring of the barrel that we must look for results.

It appears to be widely believed that, in the pre-choke era, barrels were inevitably bored as true cylinders. So many of them may have been, but even in the flintlock days, the best gunmakers had started introducing subtle variations. The best known was the so-called friction-and-relief boring, described by Hawker, in which the bore undergoes a progressive constriction for about a third of its length; then remains constant for another third; and finally undergoes a progressive enlargement. The purpose of this system is almost explained by the name: it was to detain the charge until the powder had become thoroughly inflamed, and thereafter to promote its continued acceleration towards the muzzle by the reduction of friction as the pressure fell.

When choke was introduced, it soon proliferated into a number of forms. Some of them became established and well-known, and it is not necessary here to describe them. Others were in the nature of freakish variants, the purpose of which was obscure. One of these described by Greener, which is of special significance in the present context, was a kind of double choke. There was a constriction in the form of a ridge at about four inches from the muzzle, followed by a return to the original bore diameter, which was maintained right up to normal choke at the muzzle end.

The main bore associated with any kind or degree of choke is nowadays usually a true cylinder, but even in fairly recent times there have been considerable variations from this simple form. One in particular – the tapered entrance from the chamber cone to the main bore – appears to have been a legacy from the black powder days.

Variations in practice were not confined to the form of the bore, but also to its surface. It was held by some gunmakers in the past that roughness in the bore is a merit, and guns were sometimes deliberately roughened to improve the shooting. There is no mystery about any success that this practice may appear to have attained. I can only say now that the best quality patterns, though not necessarily those of most suitable density, are almost certainly made by high-grade shot when the individual pellets are discharged, undamaged, in a direction parallel to the bore axis, and with the lowest practicable muzzle pressure. This points to a long-barrelled true cylinder.

Favourable conditions

The practical conditions most nearly approaching the foregoing are (1) thoroughly efficient gas-sealing wadding, with maximum cushioning effect consistent with other factors: (2) the smoothest possible transition from the cartridge case to the bore; (3) the lowest breech pressure consistent with the attainment of the required velocity; (4) hard shot to help (3) in avoiding compressive deformation of the rearward pellets, and maybe cold-welding among them; (5) the smoothest bore, to avoid abrasion of the outer pellets; (6) a long barrel to reduce muzzle pressure; and (7) the least possible choke constriction consistent with attaining the required pattern density. A protective shot-cup, of course, reduces or eliminates abrasion, and plated shot inhibits cold-welding. It should be especially noted that choke has the incidental merit of breaking up, or tending to break up, any aggregations of pellets that have been cold-welded by high breech pressure, or fused together by gas escapes past the wadding.

Modern skeet guns

In the previous (1970) edition of *Shotguns and Cartridges* I described what was then to me a new system of boring. 'Some modern guns intended for skeet shooting', I said, 'have a kind of negative choke – an exaggerated conical or parallel enlargement of the bore at the muzzle which is claimed to improve the quality of the patterns and possibly to increase their spread.'

In the August 1972 issue of the American magazine, *Field and Stream*, there was a notice of a new skeet gun so bored. This is the Mauser 620, which, so far as I know, has not yet appeared in this country. It has the much exaggerated parallel enlargement I described for about four inches at the muzzle, preceded by – and here is the most interesting point – an internal ridge, as described by Greener over seventy years ago. There is also a very slight degree of choke at the end of the enlarged bore.

This boring is believed to be substantially the same as that used by the Russian Olympic gold medallist Eugeny Petrov when he broke 200 targets straight at Phoenix in 1970. It must give patterns of very wide spread and superior quality — but how it does so is to some degree a matter for conjecture.

My own belief is that the ridge could be valuable in breaking up any compacted portions of the shot charge, which would thereafter be realigned in the enlarged cylindrical bore, and finally brought under the influence of such slight degree of positive or negative choke as might be found expedient. An interesting development—or revival.

49   Pitting - an Anomaly

One of the occupational risks of writing a weekly magazine feature is that of being betrayed into a major inconsistency, which a reader with a long memory is sure to spot. The other day, I was charged with such an inconsistency on the subject of pitted barrels.

It appears that, in the course of the articles I write for the *Shooting Times* and in correspondence with readers, I have said or implied that guns with barrels in this condition might shoot better than those without these detestable blemishes. On the other hand, and in various contexts, I have urged the case for reducing friction between the shot charge and the bore, and have stressed the virtue of the protective shot-cup as a means to this end. I have praised the French practice of polishing the bores longitudinally, and have called attention to the superior merit of guns that have been 'shot-smoothed' by long service. How then, I was asked, can I reconcile these conflicting notions?

Let me say straight away that I was by no means embarrassed by this charge of inconsistency, which disappears on examination. Readers suffering perpetual irritation from the presence of pitting in their barrels may find some relief in following the argument.

The subject of pitting arises continually in my correspondence. Readers want to know whether it is dangerous, whether it affects the shooting of a gun, and whether a particular specimen is worth sleeving. A curious thing about these enquiries is that the majority of them, and I would guess a large majority, are concerned with what is described as 'slight pitting.'

Accordingly, my reply commonly takes the form of saying that if the pitting is indeed slight, the question of danger does not arise, nor does the necessity for sleeving. As for the shooting qualities, I say that they are unlikely to be affected; and then, if my correspondent seems to be worrying unduly on this point, I may add that some guns even seem to shoot better for slight pitting, and may mention the historical fact that guns have occasionally been deliberately roughened in the bore, in the belief that the shooting is thereby improved. In conclusion, I point out that slight pitting can usually be removed by lapping, though the best treatment is probably to be strong minded, and ignore it.

This comforting assurance about the shooting of pitted barrels admittedly runs counter to the ideal usually held up of a gun so made and so loaded that the pellets leave the muzzle free from all compressive or abrasive damage. Pitting must damage some of them to some extent – indeed, since about half the pellets of a normal game charge in a 12-bore gun are in contact with the barrel wall, a corresponding proportion are doomed to suffer abrasive damage to an extent proportional to the roughness of the surface.

According to all accepted theory, these damaged pellets, because of their loss, both of substance and of true rotundity, will not fly so fast or so truly as the undamaged ones. The pattern will therefore be more scattered, and the average striking energy will be reduced. But wait a moment! The pattern will be more scattered – true; but will the average striking energy be reduced? Bearing in mind that any roughness in the bore will tend to detain the shot charge, it may promote a more thorough and efficient combustion of the powder, and thus in the end actually enhance the muzzle velocity, to an extent that will do at least something to compensate for the greater rate at which the damaged pellets lose their initial energy.

This, of course, is the theory behind the deliberate roughening of shotgun barrels. It may have had some efficacy in the black powder days and in the particular circumstances in which it was practised; but I do not believe it to be a factor of any significance in the shooting of a modern gun with the slight degree of pitting contemplated. The more scattered pattern, however, remains for consideration.

The true test

So, to dispose of the charge of inconsistency, I have to show how a gun with pitted barrels, throwing a pattern more scattered than it otherwise would do, and delivering its pellets with a lower average energy, can possibly shoot better than it would in its virgin state. It should not be difficult.

It should be recognised that by 'shooting better', the average sportsman in this country is not referring to the density of the patterns revealed in tests at the gunmaker's plate, but to the gun's performance in the field. Here, the only true criterion is the game put into the bag, or, if you like, the kills-cartridges ratio. And since most game in driving or rough shooting is taken at distances not exceeding 30 yds or so, at which even an improved cylinder throws a pattern that is tighter and denser than is necessary, it follows at once that anything tending to scatter the pattern, provided that the quality of the distribution does not suffer unduly, will make for more success – at least, for more success in hitting.

As for killing, it must be realised that, within the range bracket contemplated, there are abundant reserves of pellet energy. A sound pellet of No. 6 at 30 yds has an energy of nearly 2 ft-lbs, which is twice the minimum required for medium game birds. A damaged pellet with as little as half this energy, would still, therefore, contribute usefully to the pattern.

So, a gun slightly pitted, and throwing, maybe, slightly wider patterns than it otherwise would do, may yet prove the better gun for work at moderate range. But the ideal is still the immaculate bore, throwing patterns of the best possible quality, of the highest attainable pellet energy, and of the right spread for the work in hand. As we press for longer and longer reach, the nearer we can get to that ideal the better.

Section 6

BALLISTICS

'Since there can be nothing more frustrating than swinging well and truly on birds, only to see them sail on, time and again, in unruffled contempt, the basic facts of shotgun potential need restating from time to time.'

50 *Safe but Not Suitable*

'What is the most powerful cartridge I can use in my gun?' That is one of the more familiar enquiries I receive. The enquirer then gives me particulars of his gun and its proof status and usually mentions the cartridge and load on which he has his eye. With the introduction of the Eley Magnum cartridges – the $2\frac{3}{4}$-in. loaded with $1\frac{1}{2}$ oz, and the 3-in. loaded with $1\frac{5}{8}$ – these enquiries have often struck a more urgent note. Thus, a correspondent (more critical and prudent than many) prefixes his enquiry with a quotation from the 1970 edition of *The Shooter's Year Book*, which says, with reference to these cartridges, that they must be used only in suitable guns, 'i.e. $2\frac{3}{4}$-in. cartridges in guns with $2\frac{3}{4}$-in. or 3-in. chambers, proof marked for at least $1\frac{1}{2}$ oz and/or marked for a service pressure of at least $3\frac{1}{2}$ tons per square inch. (Guns with European proof marks – 900 kg per sq. cm. proof pressure).' He goes on to say that his gun, an Ugartechea 12-bore with $2\frac{3}{4}$-in. chambers, is certified as having been proved at 900 kg, and asks would it not therefore be considered suitable for firing the $2\frac{3}{4}$-in. Eley Magnum? He adds a word of doubt. 'I always thought', he says, 'that a magnum cartridge needs a magnum gun.'

My enquirer is right, of course. I always have said that a light gun needs a light load, and, conversely, a magnum gun is needed to fire a magnum load. Here, then, it is necessary to make a sharp distinction between safe and suitable. The safety of a gun is primarily determined by its proof status – by the pressure, that is to say, which it survived without damage in the course of proof. But proof has limitations: it affords no guarantee in perpetuity of the durability of the gun in service, nor does it imply that the recoil will be acceptable to the average user when firing loads giving the maximum permissible service pressure. If a gun is regularly used with heavier loads than those appropriate to its mechanical robustness it will undergo accelerated deterioration: it may literally be shaken to pieces. Proof, after all, is a once-for-all test; but just as a man may over-tax his constitution on an isolated occasion without permanent damage, so may a gun survive a proof pressure from any subsequent approach to which it needs to be carefully safeguarded.

Proper criteria

Recoil is, fortunately for many guns, a more inescapable monitor of suitability. You can overload a willing donkey and get away with it, but if you overload your gun it will kick you, and serve you right. What a man may suffer in the way of recoil is subject to a number of extrinsic factors, such as the fit of the gun and the properties of the powder he uses, but there is a broad criterion of what the average man can stand. Burrard has expressed it in terms of the velocity with which the gun recoils, but that is not really a satisfactory standard because the weight of the gun is obviously an important factor.

A better and more comprehensive standard is afforded by the energy of recoil – that is, the kinetic energy, or energy of movement – which the shooter is called on to absorb. It can be taken that a shooter of average constitution, firing a fair number of cartridges in the course of a day, will tolerate a recoil energy of about 24ft-lbs. This ties in with Burrard's figure when applied to a 6¾ lb. gun. Journée puts the limit of acceptability at 4 m-kg, which is equivalent to 29 ft-lbs, and says that 5 m-kg (36 ft-lbs) would be considered painful by our average man.

But when we apply these criteria to the recoil that would be experienced when firing magnum cartridges in guns that might be considered suitable, when judged narrowly on the Eley statement quoted, we get a mental taste of what an imprudent shooter might suffer. I do not know what is the weight of the Ugartechea gun mentioned by my original enquirer, but my latest AYA 25-in. sidelock will afford a good example. It weighs 6 lb 5 oz, has 2¾-in. chambers and, according to the proof certificate, was tested by firing *four proof cartridges through each barrel* developing a pressure of 900 kg/sq. cm. A clear case for firing the 2¾-in. magnum, would you say? Let us work out the recoil energy and see ... It comes out at well over 38 ft-lbs, or between 5 and 6 m-kg. According to Journée, that falls between the painful and the utterly intolerable.

Misuse and abuse

I must clearly, therefore, abandon any ambition I may have entertained of being able to use the Eley 2¾-in. magnum in my AYA, and content myself with my familiar Impax or Grand Prix. It may, indeed, be *safe* to fire the magnum cartridge, but of its utter unsuitability there can be no possible doubt. Nor, really, has there ever been any. We do not have to work out recoil energies: the old rule that there should be 6 lb of gun to every ounce of shot gives a good rough guide, and according to that a gun to fire the 1½ oz magnum should weigh at least 9 lbs.

Although I have chosen this magnum enquiry to illustrate my point concerning the need to distinguish between what may be safe and what is suitable, there is really no need, or very little need, to warn shooters against using magnum cartridges in game guns; at least, not the sort of game guns considered. One shot should be a sufficient warning.

But the real danger lies in the use of heavy-load cartridges, such as the

Alphamax, in guns never intended for anything more than ordinary game loads. The shooter, especially if he is a tough lightweight, may decide that he can stand the recoil, but his gun, if it could speak, might express strong views to the contrary. I am afraid that there must be many fine English 2½-in. chambered game guns which have been exported to America and there re-chambered to 2¾-in., since when they have been regularly used with 1¼ oz duck loads. They may still be safe, despite the re-chambering without re-proof, but they are assuredly being hustled along to a premature end.

It should be noted that the addition of weight to the stock, whether in the form of a 'recoil reducer' or otherwise, or the use of a generous recoil pad, may protect the shooter from recoil, but they do nothing to protect the gun.

51 Wildfowling and the Cube Law

As sure as ever my house-martins make their preparations for departure, I detect a note of frustration in my correspondence. It arises chiefly from some of the new entry of shooters and wildfowlers who are not doing quite so well as they expected. In consequence they come to me with questions directed to finding out the best way of increasing the range and power of their guns, which seem to be curiously inadequate. Sometimes they are contemplating a different gun – one of larger bore, or with longer chambers, or with more choke, or of greater barrel length. Sometimes they want to know what is the most powerful proprietary cartridge they can fire in a gun of given proof status; and sometimes it is a home-loading question with the same end in view. Many of these may be appropriate questions in individual circumstances, but many, I am sure, arise from the fact that the enquirer has not yet got on terms with his gun, and has not yet arrived at a proper realisation of the short range of any shotgun. Lacking such realisation, he may be trying to shoot birds that are hopelessly out of range; or if he is not doing that he may be entertaining expectations of improvement that stand no chance of being translated into practice. Since there can be nothing more frustrating than swinging well and truly on birds, only to see them sail on, time and again, in unruffled contempt, the basic facts of shotgun potential need restating from time to time. I will try to do so with such new side-lights as I can contrive.

Basic needs

The basic requirements for successful and consistent performance with a shotgun, which no ordinary degree of skill can evade, are simply patterns of adequate quality and density, made by pellets of sufficient penetrative power. It does not matter a rap what kind of gun such patterns are thrown by — whether by a normal large-bore or a magnum small-bore. Provided the bird is fairly struck by such a pattern, it will come down.

Experience accumulated over many generations has established what sort of patterns, and what degree of penetrative power, are required for successful use against the various kinds of game. It also enables us to distinguish between what I may call ethical and sportsmanlike shooting and shooting that is neither. The one makes it reasonably certain that a truly aimed shot will bring the game to bag, whilst the other relies on the sort of flukes that can occasionally be brought off by the wide-open patterns made by unduly large shot. Young shooters should never be tempted from the straight and narrow path of good sportsmanship by accounts of fantastic shots pulled off by the use of shot of a size much larger than that commonly recommended for a given duty, for such accounts, if complete, would invariably include a far larger proportion of misses — or what is worse, of birds going off wounded by a single pellet in some non-vulnerable part of their anatomy.

Limitation of range

It must be recognised that, unlike a rifle bullet, which loses killing power simply by the loss of velocity incurred by its passage through the air, a charge of shot suffers a double loss of potential — partly by the loss of velocity of individual pellets, as in the case of the rifle bullet, and partly by their progressive dispersal. What is more, the rate of dispersal of the pellets increases with distance. For this reason, it is impossible to make a shoulder gun with a range much in excess of, say, 70 yds.

It is quite easy to demonstrate the truth of this if only we accept what I defined just now as the basic requirements for successful and consistent performance. All we need are the simple tables published in *The Shooter's Year Book* or my own *Shotguns and Cartridges*. From these we select a pellet size that will give us the required margin of penetrative power (or striking energy) for our purpose at a particular range. For simplicity, let us take 2 ft-lbs. Then assume that we need a minimum pattern of 80 pellets in the 30-in. circle, which is what we ought to have for wildfowling. If we take it that we shall be using a fully-choked gun, we can then see, or quickly work out, what proportion of the total charge this 80 pellets will represent, and can thus arrive at the weight of the charge. By so doing, we also arrive at the weight of the gun, which, to resist the recoil, must be in due proportion. For an exercise of this character, we can say that the gun should have 96 times the weight of the charge.

Now let us take another and longer range, and select a pellet capable of preserving the necessary 2 ft-lbs of energy at that range. It will, of course, be a larger pellet, and the minimum of 80 required will weigh proportionately more. Also, there will have to be more of them in the total charge, because it will now be more dispersed. And if we work out a sufficient number of cases on these lines, we shall arrive at the astonishing conclusion *that the weight of the charge, and therefore that of the gun, necessary for throwing a pattern of given density and pellet energy goes up as the cube of the range.*

Theory and practice

The practical operation of this 'cube law' (it is really only an approximate rule) is masked (a) by the excess power and weight possessed by our guns for close range work; (b) by our cashing in on reserves of pellet energy for moderate increases above normal range; and (c) by shooters accepting enhanced recoil for such increases. But as we demand still greater reach, the cube law bears down with full force, and we quickly find ourselves with a specification for a piece of artillery – in short, a punt-gun. These imposing weapons commonly weigh from 50 to 250 lbs, and fire anything from ½ to 2½ lbs of shot. And their range? Stanley Duncan, that eminent practitioner, recommends that it be taken as about 100 yds. Yet some shooters aspire to this with a 12-bore! They should test their guns for pattern at that range.

A point that most young or otherwise inexperienced shooters fail to recognise is the really superior standard of marksmanship required for long-range work with the shotgun. This is because leads require to be increased disproportionately as the range lengthens beyond about 35 yds. A duck crossing at 60 yds requires much more than twice the lead of one crossing at half the distance – the figure is about 2½ times, and few can achieve these abnormal leads without regular practice. It is better to recognise that there is a great deal of wildfowling that can be successfully undertaken with an ordinary, familiar game gun and standard game cartridges loaded with No. 4 or No. 3 shot. Such an outfit, combined with better use of approach tactics, and the avoidance of unduly long shots, can, in many circumstances, make for better sport than an unfamiliar, heavily choked, wildfowling magnum, well suited though it may be for the sea-wall.

An American view

In this connection, I have been much interested in a book sent me by a kind American correspondent – *American Wild Fowl Shooting*, by J. W. Long, published in New York in 1879.

Mr Long and his contemporaries, including the famous Fred Kimble, shot fantastic numbers of duck, and their ideas on guns and loads for this purpose command high respect. Mr Kimble, for example, is on record as having shot 1365 duck in the course of 17 days' shooting in 1872. ('His ammunition gave out nearly every day.') For this sort of work, the author recommends, as being used 'by the most successful duck hunters of my acquaintance', the following:

For a 10-gauge, 4 to 5½ drams of powder, 1 to 1¼ oz of shot.
For a 9-gauge, 4½ to 6 drams of powder, 1 to 1⅜ oz of shot.
For an 8-gauge, 5 to 7 drams of powder, 1⅛ to 1½ oz of shot.

Here indeed is matter for comment; but, to stick to my theme, all I need do is to draw the attention of my magnum-hungry correspondents to the light shot charges which these highly experienced American shooters of a century ago considered sufficient for their sport. A 12-bore charge of 1⅛ oz of No. 4 in a good, fully choked gun, held straight, will kill duck at 50 yds with fair reliability. Every eighth-ounce added beyond that increases the range by a mere couple of yards, until at about 60 yds pattern degeneration becomes so rapid that the practical limit for a gun of this gauge has been reached – and at a cost out of all proportion to the gain.

52   Shock v. Penetration

Practical sportsmen of undeniable experience appear in print from time to time to denounce all unnecessary fuss about shot sizes. A man armed with an ordinary 12-bore, they say, with one barrel open-bored and the other choked, and loaded with No. 6 shot, is well equipped to cope with any ordinary kind of winged game in this country. I must say that I largely agree.

I was brought to this point of view on the interchangeability of shot by early experience. I was snipe shooting, say, and was dutifully loaded with No. 8, when up from the bog would get a mallard or a large cock pheasant, only to fall dead, as though struck by lightning, rather than by my snipe shot. Experiences of this kind could be multiplied endlessly, and would appear to demonstrate the original proposition. Yet they would fail to expose its weakness or provide any indication of the marginal areas in which it pays to devote some special attention to shot size.

The apparent interchangeability of shot arises from two causes. First is the fact that, within considerable limits, the shock of a large number of small pellet strikes have the same traumatic effect – the same power, that is to say, to arrest a bird and bring about its immediate death – as the penetrative power of larger pellets, one or more of which may reach a vital organ.

Secondly, it must be recognised that most shooting is done at distances within which the shotgun has considerable reserves of killing power, as derived from the density of the patterns and the penetrative power of the shot. Within such distances, shot size ceases to be critical. Unduly large shot, which at full range would be too scattered, may thus make patterns of adequate density. Conversely, unduly small shot, which at full range would fail on penetrative power, may have more than enough to reach the vital parts of the game concerned.

But as we try to extend our reach, these ballistic reserves, on whichever side they may lie, progressively diminish, so that the maximum range *for consistent results* can only be attained by a balanced load, in which pattern and penetrative power jointly achieve the most effective combination. There is no room here for the wrong size of shot. If it is too big, killing will depend on accidental hits rather than on good marksmanship. And if it is too small, no degree of marksmanship will compensate for its lack of penetrative power.

Adjusting the balance

Yet there remains my first point — that, to a certain extent, shock may kill independently of the penetration of vital organs. This suggests the possibility that the best-balanced load for full range work may be one using shot of a smaller size than would otherwise appear desirable. It would involve exchanging some penetration for denser patterns and an increase in the average number of hits; but the exchange could be advantageous if the shock element were thereby increased. It is not easy to get to practical grips with this suggestion and to extract from it some useful conclusion that shooters can take straight into the field, more especially in the face of indications that the No. 6 shot for everything school of philosophy is already partly committed to the shock principle.

Still, there is reliable evidence available concerning the pellet energies needed to produce wounds of increasingly severe character in birds and animals. In his rare third edition, Journée quotes numerous experiments, the results of which have been reduced to simple arithmetical rules. He has divided wounds into several classes of severity, ranging from those of a purely superficial character to others that amount to blowing a bird to tatters. The only kind we need consider here are those he describes as Class B and Class C.

Class C wounds are the kind we would need to inflict if we insisted on our pellets having enough energy to develop full penetrative power. They would pierce the heaviest muscular tissue, break the largest bones and generally cause, or be capable of causing, immediately fatal injuries.

But the significant thing, bearing in mind that Journée's conclusions are based on practical experiments, is that the pellet energies he gives as being necessary to inflict wounds of this description are much in excess of those we normally have available. For example, a cock pheasant weighing 3 lbs would, according to him, need about 3·3 ft-lbs, which is rather more than a high-velocity pellet of No. 6 retains at 20 yds. So it would seem that the average pheasant killed stone dead at 30 to 40 yds with this size of shot must owe its death partly to the shock of the multiple injuries it is likely to suffer. The wounds caused by individual pellets are thus more likely to conform to Journée's Class B. These pellets 'penetrate deeply enough into the soft parts; they smash through the smaller bones and crack or bruise the big ones; and although they hardly ever stop the game in its tracks, they can cause death in due course.' The minimum pellet energy associated with wounds such as this, in the case of a 3 lb pheasant, works out at 1·6 ft-lbs.

An authoritative view

Here reality looms large. A standard velocity pellet of No. 6 retains this energy up to nearly 40 yds; and if we can contrive to strike the bird with three, four or more pellets, then the total traumatic effect – that is, multiple wounds plus shock – would assuredly bring about a clean kill.

So far so good: we have discovered what we already knew – that No. 6 will kill pheasants (and birds of similar weight) up to full sporting range. But we have also arrived at clear indications that it partly relies on the shock of multiple injuries to do so. The question therefore remains whether, in this typical case, we can arrive at an even better balanced load for full range work. Is it not possible that we could deal better with back-end pheasants by going over to No. 7 rather than to the more popular No. 5?

Here I am on more speculative ground. Before the last war, I was for many years a devotee of No. 7 shot, which seemed to suit my guns and certainly inspired my confidence. But far better evidence of this sort is provided by Sir Ralph Payne-Gallwey in his book *High Pheasants in Theory and Practice*. In it, he says, 'If we wish to kill our game, we have to kill it in the best way we can, and small shot, such as No. 7 . . . gives us the greatest chance of doing so, as it is more likely to hit in vital places than a large size.' In weighing this evidence, we must remember that Sir Ralph probably saw, and helped to shoot, as many high pheasants in the palmy days of shooting as any man in England. Also, he was of a very inquiring turn of mind, and questioned other shooters on their equipment and technique, as well as making many experiments and carrying out post-mortems on dead birds. In saying what he did about No. 7 shot, he was discussing 'really high' birds. Elsewhere, he makes a specific recommendation as follows: 'Even for birds of exceptional height, or from 38 to near 40 yards, I should pin my faith to 1 oz. of No. 7 and 34 grains of EC or the equivalent . . .'

Other applications

When I started this article I had hoped to discuss the interchangeability of shot in broader terms than I have succeeded in doing in the space available. Shock *versus* penetration in game shooting is only one aspect of the subject, which can be invoked in aid of problems arising in other ways, and in other fields of sport. A trap gun, for example, may give patterns of good quality but insufficient density. Instead of having it re-regulated in an endeavour to reduce the spread, it may be advantageous simply to switch to a smaller size of shot – say, No. 7 to No. 8. To a non-handicap shooter of quick reactions but imperfect accuracy, this might make for a notably better performance.

53   Sidelights on Velocity

'Someone was trying to tell me that high-velocity cartridges have less penetration than ordinary ones. Is that possible?'

The shooter who put that question to me at the Game Fair had a reason for asking. It appears that he had taken to a Continental self-loader, and had abandoned the ordinary Grand Prix cartridges he had previously used in favour of the high-velocity version, as giving more reliable operation with his weapon. Yet this new gun and the higher velocity cartridge did not seem to kill so well as the standard-velocity kind in his original gun, and he was therefore trying to find out why.

There may, of course, have been many reasons why his performance had fallen off with his new gun, any of them capable of creating the impression that his new cartridges lacked the killing power of the old. The gun could be throwing tighter patterns – too tight for his standard of accuracy – whereby he might be failing to take his birds with the dense, central concentration of pellets. Or it may not fit him so well as the old one did, which could have the same effect. Or the patterns could be too open to be capable of killing at the same distance as those from his old gun, or of inferior quality. All these are merely the bread-and-butter considerations that arise when attempting to compare the performance of a given shooter with two different guns.

But the suggestion conveyed by this shooter's opening question is of another order, and one that cannot be dismissed outright.

Two points at once arise. The first is that certain projectiles penetrate certain substances less effectively as their velocity is increased above an optimum figure. The celebrated Victorian gunmaker, J. D. Dougall, in his book *Shooting: its Appliances, Practice and Purpose*, published in 1875, quotes experiments in which conical leaden bullets, fired at clay, penetrated progressively deeper as the velocity was reduced, down to a certain limit. Thus, at 40 yds, the penetration with a given charge was 1 ft; at 100 yds, it was 2 ft; and at 200 yds it was 3½ ft. Indeed, it was commonplace among big game hunters in the days of black powder rifles firing spherical ball, or un-jacketed bullets of hardened lead, that excess velocity could reduce penetra-tive power; and the modern user of ·22 rifles must often have noticed, as I have, that the 40 grain solid bullet from the ordinary or standard LR cartridge penetrates softwood more deeply than does the same bullet from the HV cartridge.

There is no mystery in this. The capacity of a projectile to penetrate a resistant substance depends on its retaining its form. If, in the early stages of its penetration, it undergoes serious deformation, its capacity for further penetration will be proportionately reduced. A high striking velocity, by promoting this early deformation, may thus operate against penetration.

But whether this principle is ever of any significance in the case of small shot, fired at birds or small ground game, and within the normal limits of shotgun ballistics, is very much open to doubt. My own penetration tests, carried out with a rack of well separated cards, indicate that penetration is approximately proportional to striking energy, other things being constant. So, failing better evidence than my own experience affords, I would say that the answer to my Game Fair questioner is that high-velocity cartridges do not have less penetration than ordinary ones, but rather the contrary.

In that case, it might be suggested, the advantage lies with the high-velocity cartridge, and that we all ought to go in for high-velocity loads. Many of us evidently do: last season I went into a market town gun shop and asked for some ordinary Grand Prix – the standard velocity kind, loaded with 1 1/16 oz of shot. 'I'm sorry,' the shopman said, 'we've only got the 1⅛ oz high velocity kind. We don't keep the other – there's no demand for it.' Yet there must be many disadvantages of high velocity – the disproportionately en-hanced recoil, and the high degree of probability that the patterns will be inferior to those of the normal load; also that these disadvantages are not offset by any significant reduction in the forward lead required by a crossing bird.

But apart from these disadvantages, which I should have thought have been sufficiently well publicised in the past, there is a broad principle in-volved here which is by no means well or generally understood. It is the second of the two points I referred to, and may be broadly stated thus: If a gun is loaded with progressively increased charges, driven in each case at a muzzle velocity calculated to produce the maximum tolerable recoil, the total energy of the charge will not increase steadily as the velocity is increased, but will reach a maximum value, after which it will decline. Since, therefore, a bird of given size at a given distance will, taking one shot with another, intercept the same proportion of the total charge, and since penetration and killing power are proportional to striking energy, it follows that there will be one charge that is likely to be most effective in the field. As indicated, this will not necessarily be the charge launched with the highest velocity.

Verdict of experience

It is instructive to see how this works out in practical terms. Let us consider an ordinary 6½ lb game gun firing charges of No. 6 shot, and assume that the shooter fires a fair number of cartridges, so that he cannot stand abnormal recoil. A total recoil energy of 24 ft-lbs would be a fair limit to assume; and this would be produced in each case by the following charges and muzzle velocities:

Shot charge (oz)		$\frac{7}{8}$	1	$1\frac{1}{16}$	$1\frac{1}{8}$	$1\frac{3}{16}$	$1\frac{1}{4}$
Muzzle velocity (ft/sec)	1580	1390	1320	1250	1185	1125

From these figures we can work out the values of the total charge energy at a given range; and in the diagram below I have shown what they would be at the limiting range for the choke barrel, when the high-velocity load might be expected to come into its own. I have taken this as being 50 yds.

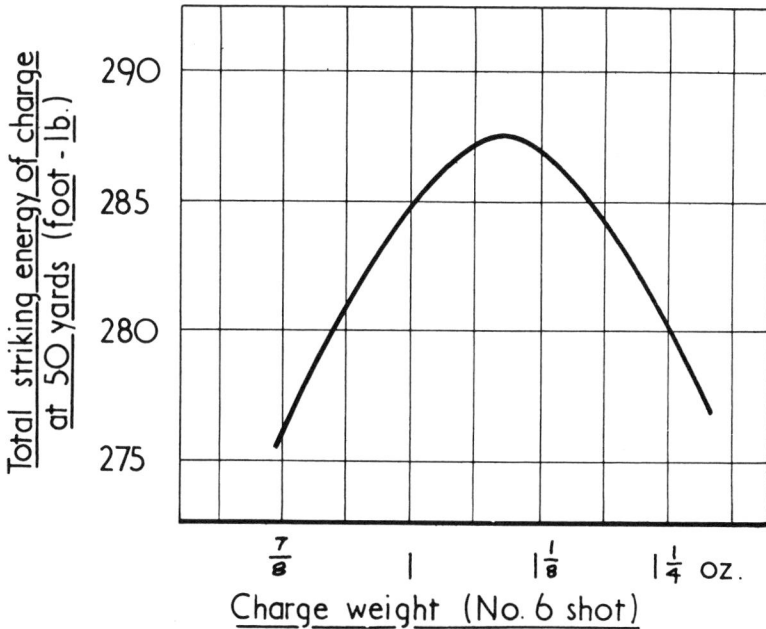

THE HEAVIEST BLOW   For a given maximum recoil in a 6½ lb. game gun the standard cartridge has the highest striking energy at full range.

It will be seen, however, that the heaviest blow would be struck by a full
$1\frac{1}{16}$ oz load launched with a muzzle velocity of a trifle under 1300 ft per
second. This is just about the prescription for a normal, standard-velocity,
Grand Prix cartridge.

As a result in no way preconditioned, this is sufficiently striking. Yet it is
not really surprising – it means no more than that our standard loads, arrived
at, as they have been, by generations of shooters firing untold millions of
cartridges, represent about the best available in their particular fields of
application.

So, to come back to where I started, even if high velocity loads penetrate
better than others, it does not necessarily pay to use them.

54   British and American Pressures

A correspondent from North Carolina asks, 'Would you consider writing on
the confusing subject of pressures, as it relates to the American published
figure of 10 000 lbs, more or less, for normal modern cartridges.' He uses
English guns and makes it clear that he is comparing this figure with the
service or working pressure of $3\frac{1}{4}$ tons (about 7300 lbs) stipulated by our
normal proof for 12-bore $2\frac{3}{4}$-in. chambered guns.

This reopens a subject I raised several years ago, when I warned users of
imported magnum or semi-magnum cartridges of the possibility that they
were submitting their guns to pressures for which they had never been designed. In consequence, several of the cartridges in question were tested at
the Birmingham Proof House, with the result that the Gun Trade Association issued a warning to retailers, reminding them of their responsibilities in
this connection under the Sale of Goods Act.

On the face of it, the situation seemed clear. If American cartridges are
normally loaded to pressures of around 10 000 lbs, as they are commonly
stated to be, we have only to reduce this figure to English tons to get the
impression that the excess over the official British service pressure is potentially serious: 10 000 lbs is, indeed, nearly $4\frac{1}{2}$ tons. (Perhaps I should remind
American readers that the English ton is 2240 lbs, not 2000.)

But the impression is not generally valid, as my correspondent suspects,
for, as he says, British cartridges feel fully as lively as standard American
field loads. Where, then, has our simple division sum gone wrong?

The answer is that it has certainly gone wrong in one place, and may have
gone wrong in two. The second possibility is the simpler, and so I will deal
with it first.

It does not by any means follow that all American field loads develop
pressures of 10 000 lbs or more. The 25 normal tested field loads for $2\frac{3}{4}$-in.

12-bores listed in the latest issue of the *Lyman Shotshell Handbook* have an average pressure of about 9150 lbs, whilst several of them, not to quote the lowest, are in the region of 8500. So, even on a direct arithmetical comparison, these latter cartridges would not develop anything like 4½ tons, but only a trifle over 3¾.

But the major error in this matter arises in quite a different way, which has nothing to do with arithmetic. It is caused by the fact that the pressures measured by British and American methods are not true or absolute pressures: they are merely indications provided by imperfect but highly practical apparatus for evaluating pressures for the purpose of manufacturing control. What is more, Britain, America and the Continental countries use different apparatus, which would give, or could be expected to give, three different results from precisely the same load. It is as if three men making certain articles were working with inaccurate rulers, all different. Provided that they did not start making comparisons, all would be well. The fact that their measurements were inaccurate in relation to official standards of length would not prevent their making several articles of exactly the same size, and detecting any discrepancy between them; but they would not agree on the dimensions of a particular component.

The crusher gauge

For the everyday purposes of science and engineering, there is no difficulty in measuring the absolute pressures of fluids or gases with the appropriate degree of accuracy. The maid-of-all-work for this purpose is the common Bourdon or Schaeffer pressure gauge, of which most garages have a specimen for registering tyre pressures. In any case, there will be one on the compressed air storage tank.

But the difficulty in measuring the maximum pressure at any point in a gun barrel arises chiefly from the fact that the pressure is highly transient, and if any ordinary kind of pressure gauge, adapted to withstand the high pressures concerned, were used, the inertia of the moving parts would prevent a true reading being observed or recorded.

So, to meet the requirements of routine ammunition testing, the crusher gauge has been developed. The test barrel is drilled with one or more transverse holes at the point or points at which it is desired to register the maximum pressure, and in each hole there is a little piston or plunger which communicates the pressure to a crusher of soft metal – usually lead or copper. The crusher takes the form of a small, stubby cylinder of standard dimensions which is squeezed against a fixed head by the pressure acting on the piston; and the extent of the squeeze is taken as a measure of the pressure. My drawing on page 168 shows the principle of the thing.

But before the gauge can be used, it has to be calibrated. In other words, the relationship between the amount of squeeze and the pressure has to be established. For this purpose, crushers are subjected to a range of deadweight loads, and the corresponding amount of squeeze in each case is recorded. The results are then set out in a table, called a 'tarage table', from which the pressure corresponding to any degree of squeeze can be read off.

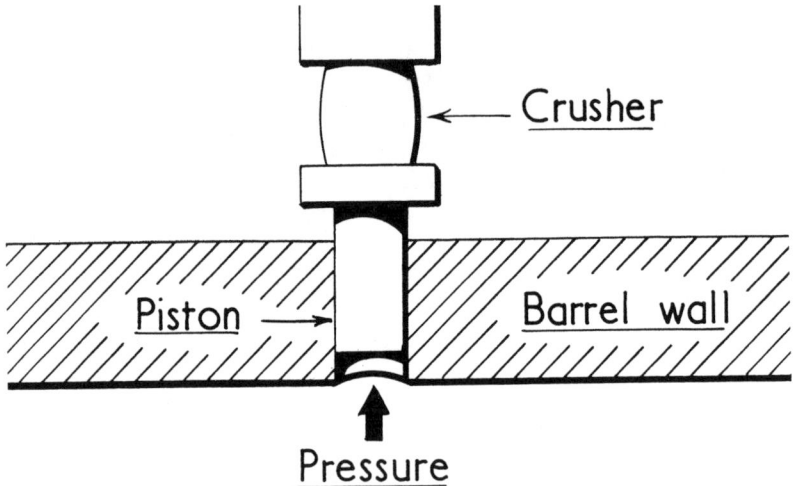

MEASURING PRESSURE IN A GUN BARREL The gas pressure acting on the piston shown squeezes the soft metal crusher. The degree of crushing furnishes a measure of the pressure.

But now comes the imperfection of the method, and the source of the errors involved, as well as the anomalies arising in attempting to compare the results of different forms of pressure gauge. Owing to the internal friction of the metal of the crusher, and to other sources of error, the amount of squeeze produced by a given transient pressure in a gun barrel will not be the same as that produced by a steady pressure of the same amount. The results are also affected by the diameter and weight of the pistons employed; and again, they may be translated into different pressures if different tarage tables are used.

For these reasons, it is thoroughly well recognised that the crusher gauge does not register absolute pressures: indeed, the results are now preferably referred to, not in terms of pounds or tons per square inch, but rather as 'Lead Units of Pressure' (L.U.P.) or 'Copper Units of Pressure' (C.U.P.). Still, as already indicated, the crusher gauge is an eminently practical tool for routine ammunition testing. It does not, however, establish a common language between two operators, such as the British and the American gun and ammunition trades, who do not use identical gauges or the same tarage table.

A rule of thumb

If, therefore, we want to compare British and American cartridges we must do what we did on the previous occasion I mentioned, and test them both in the same apparatus, and under the same conditions.

Some notable and reciprocal experiments have been made here and in the U.S.A., and as a practical indication of the results, I consider it safe to say that, over the common range of shotgun cartridges, it may be taken that American pressures in pounds per square inch, divided by 2800, will give a result near enough for practical purposes to what the same cartridges would develop in the British apparatus.

Thus, a 10 000 lb American cartridge corresponds closely to a British one of $3\frac{1}{2}$ tons, which is our standard service or working pressure for a 3-in. 12-bore. Similarly, 9000 lbs would correspond to about $3\frac{1}{4}$ tons ($2\frac{3}{4}$-in. 12-bore), and 8500 lbs to 3 tons ($2\frac{1}{2}$-in. 12-bore).

The indications, therefore, are that some American cartridges may be quite suitable for use in British guns, but in the absence of any appropriate indication on the carton, it is impossible to say which.

55 *Burning Questions*

A correspondent has been dipping into some American reloading literature, and has been puzzled by some of the idiom employed. 'What,' he asks, 'is a muzzle flash, and what is a "blooper"?' He goes on, 'Muzzle-flash sounds easy – I take it to be the flash we always see from the muzzle when shooting in poor light. But what is the apparently unfavourable significance attached to it? And in what way is it linked up with "bloopers", which seem to be associated with it?' There are some points of special interest here.

Muzzle-flash in this context is a somewhat ambiguous expression. It can, indeed, refer to three different things. There is the common or garden flash which can be seen at the muzzle of a gun every time it is fired in darkness or half-light. Then there is the exaggerated version of the common muzzle-flash, which may be seen every time with a particular load. This, I have no doubt, is the kind of muzzle-flash to which the American writer was referring – it is the kind described by the French as 'long-fire'. Finally there is the unusually bright flash which occurs only rarely, and is not necessarily associated with any particular load or cartridge. It may appear at the ejection port of a repeater, and has been known to distress left-handed shooters. The long-fire and the bright flash are obviously the ones we have to consider.

Causes and effects

If everything has been correctly arranged in a shotgun, the cap effectively inflames the powder, whereupon the strength of the crimp or other closure, combined with the inertia of the load and the friction it encounters in its passage through the bore, ensures the development of a pressure and temperature sufficient to consume it more or less completely over the barrel-length employed. In such case, the only muzzle-flash we see is the glow of the hot gases as they emerge.

But if anything has fallen short – if the cap is too weak thoroughly to inflame the powder; if the crimp fails to offer the necessary initial constraint; and if the load is too light or the barrel too short, then, by the time the charge issues from the muzzle, combustion of the powder will not be complete. As a result, the charge will be followed by an outrush of gas, bearing along with it a mass of still-burning powder grains. This, it may be readily imagined, will produce a muzzle-flash of the exaggerated sort which the American writer had in mind, and which the French, more distinctively, describe as *longs feux*. They are manifestations of the incomplete combustion of the powder charge, and are likely to be accompanied by inferior ballistics. In bad cases, the cartridges may markedly lack killing-power, and recoil may be noticeably light.

The 'blooper' takes on from there. The word is one of those delightful onomatopoeic expressions which accurately indicate the sound of the thing concerned. When the shortcomings just mentioned are sufficiently marked, there may be a complete breakdown of the normal process of combustion first described. In consequence, the gun may merely vomit its charge with a 'bloop' instead of a proper report, and the pellets may fall almost at the shooter's feet. Sometimes the wads may stay in the barrel—a dangerous possibility if the gun is reloaded regardless, and one that reinforces the familiar warning that the bores should always be inspected on the occurrence of any unusual sound in discharge, or any abnormal feeling of recoil.

Some years ago, there was a spate of this trouble with a certain foreign cartridge, of which I myself had some experience. Several cases were brought to my notice in which wads had remained in the gun, though, so far as I know, there were no accidents. The trouble would appear to have been caused by weak caps, whereby the powder was never properly inflamed, and gross amounts of unburnt residue were left in the barrel.

The subject of the bright, occasional flash, which I had to leave while pursuing the trail of the blooper, is more involved. It is explained by the fact that the muzzle gases discharged from a gun contain, or usually contain, or may contain certain amounts of free hydrogen, which, on mingling with the surrounding air, give an explosive mixture. It does not, however, follow that this mixture will be ignited, but it can be – for example, by a still-burning powder grain. If it is, there will be a flash quite different from that normally seen.

I cannot say that I have ever observed one of these bright, secondary muzzle flashes. I have, of course, seen many of the ordinary kind when shooting in half-light, but just as they are invisible in full daylight, so may the others be. It is also possible that, with the concentration on the target demanded in game shooting, a bright secondary flash would pass unnoticed by the shooter, even if it were capable of being observed by an onlooker.

But the possibilities are clearly indicated by some experiments carried out several years ago by Eley. I had had complaints of excessive flash from the ejection ports of self-loaders (not necessarily with Eley cartridges), and they may have provoked the investigation concerned. What Eley did was to arrange an ignition device alongside the ejection port of a self-loader, together with a camera, so that the ejection of each cartridge could be photographed. Most of the photographs came out clearly; but every now and then the picture was completely blotted out by a flash, indicating the firing of an explosive mixture of emergent gas.

Large-scale confirmation

In an interesting article in the May 1974 issue of the *American Rifleman*, Nils Kvale, of the Swedish Norma Projektifil concern, says that powder manufacturers nowadays incorporate a damping medium in their powders, whereby the secondary flash is not the problem it used to be. It appears that the secondary flash is well known to artillerists, and that it can be instigated by friction between the emergent masses of gas when the two or three big guns of a battleship, mounted in a single turret, are fired simultaneously.

56 *The Cap Must Fit*

When a fire has been properly laid, with paper, dry sticks and coal that is not too big or too small, all that is necessary to get it going is to apply a match to one place, when the natural inflammability of the materials will bring about their prompt ignition.

It was much the same with all guns right up to the latest phase of development of the flintlock. Owing to the high degree of inflammability of black powder, all that was basically necessary was to set light to the charge – somehow, somewhere – whereafter combustion ensued with reasonable efficiency provided that one or two other requirements were satisfied. These were (1) a shotload heavy enough to delay discharge until all the powder was consumed; (2) a barrel length adequate for this same purpose; and (3) powder of a suitable grain size, bearing in mind that the larger the grain the slower the rate of burning.

But even in the flintlock days it was recognised that there could be strong advantage in improving the ignition of the powder, and that if only the charge could be more quickly and thoroughly ignited, barrel length could be cut down without impairing its complete combustion. This idea reached its culmination in Henry Nock's patent breech, which was introduced in 1785 or thereabouts, and to which earlier reference has been made. When the powder was poured into a gun fitted with this kind of breech, a small portion of it fell through a constriction into an antechamber; and it was the powder in this antechamber, not the main bulk, which was ignited by the flash from the pan when the priming was fired by the sparks from the flint.

To ensure the efficient combustion of the powder in flint guns prior to the introduction of Henry Nock's patent breech in 1785, barrels of 40 or more inches in length were necessary, as in this old keeper's Queen Anne-style gun.

The effect was remarkable. The burning of the powder in the antechamber caused a jet of hot flame to shoot from the constriction right through the main charge, which was thereby thoroughly and instantly ignited. Pressure, and with it temperature, rose faster and higher than it did in guns with the old type of breech, and combustion was proportionately accelerated. It accordingly became feasible to reduce barrel length drastically – perhaps by as much as a foot – without affecting the shooting, and the sporting gun thereupon assumed what were substantially modern proportions.

Viewed in retrospect, the Nock type of breech (illustrated at (c) on p. 127) can be seen as a partial anticipation of the percussion principle. It set aside a small proportion of the main charge essentially for ignition purposes, in somewhat the same way as the percussion gun uses a special explosive to perform that function. It is a principle which assumed a new and heightened importance as we entered the era of smokeless powders.

The first and most conspicuous difference between these powders and the old black powder is that, unlike the latter, they are not highly inflammable, but quite the reverse. They are like a fire laid without paper, and need to be shot through with a strong, hot flame if they are to inflame and burn with the speed and completeness necessary in a gun. No longer is it even remotely feasible simply to set them alight – somehow, somewhere.

And not only are smokeless powders slow to ignite, but different brands vary considerably in their ignitability. This brings out at once the need to match cap and powder for the best results. If the cap, for instance, is too strong for the powder, the latter will ignite so rapidly as to give rise to an excessive breech pressure without any commensurate gain in velocity. Experiments carried out by the French Ammunition Association (SFM) and quoted by Journée in his 1949 edition show this very clearly. They took a 12-bore load of 35 grains of the French Poudre T and 1¼ oz of shot and fired it with caps containing progressively increased amounts of fulminate or detonating compound, that is, from 30 to 50 milligrams. The resulting pressures and muzzle velocities were as follows:

Weight of fulminate (milligrams)	Pressure (tons/sq. in.)	Muzzle velocity (feet/sec.)
30	1·90	1110
35	3·00	1200
40	3·25	1220
45	3·60	1220
50	3·75	1300
Total % increase:	95	17

(The figures have been slightly rounded-off in converting from metric to English units.)

The essential cap

From these results alone it is apparent that that insufficiently regarded little component, the cap, is in fact one of vital significance, and that home-loaders cannot afford to depart in this matter from the recommendations of the cartridge manufacturers. A hint of the possibilities is conveyed by an American cap advertisement which claims 74–76 milligrams of detonating compound as against the 62–64 milligrams stated to be used by a famous competitor. But what happens when the former caps are used by a reloader in conjunction with the powder and cases of the latter manufacturer is left to conjecture.

Reference to cases brings out two further points affecting the performance of a given cap. When a cap is struck and detonated, it explodes with such extreme rapidity that a transient high pressure is set up in the cap chamber, which may be, and I believe normally is, much higher than the maximum breech pressure subsequently developed in the gun. This high transient pressure finds relief through the flash-hole in the cap chamber; and the size of this hole has a considerable bearing on the efficient ignition of the main charge. Thus, the flash-hole in the Eley case suits the Eley cap, but not necessarily if it has become enlarged or if some other cap is substituted.

Again, the efficiency of ignition is affected by the base-wad – that is to say, by the shape of the powder chamber in the cartridge case. A given load in a conical-based case can give a maximum breech pressure 20 per cent or more above that loaded into a flat-based case using the same cap. This points to the need for the home-loader not to mix his used cases if he aims to produce consistent ammunition.

Elusive perfection

A matter that is of less importance now than it was in the days of the old corrosive caps is the strength of the striker blow. The performance of the older caps was especially variable when the striker blow was weak, but I am assured by manufacturers that the modern non-corrosive or styphnate cap is far less sensitive to variations in the force with which it is detonated. In other words, if it goes off, it goes off properly.

Much more could be written on this subject, but I have said enough to convey something of the difficulty of getting everything just right in the modern smokeless cartridge. Indeed, it seems that not all the large manufacturers can do this all the time. A few years ago, I had several complaints, and some direct experience, of extremely inefficient combustion in some well-known foreign cartridges, resulting in a gross amount of unburnt residue and occasional failures to expel the wadding – a dangerous possibility to which I have already referred. This was probably ignition trouble. Something of the same sort has recently happened with another foreign cartridge, which I hope was duly rectified.

But I owe it to our own old firm to say that in fifty years, whatever minor complaints I may have had to make (and for the life of me I cannot think of more than three), I have never had an Eley cartridge that did not go off properly, with every indication of satisfactory combustion.

57 *The Powder Must Burn*

In the previous chapter I tried to show how important is the part played by the cap or primer in the correct and efficient functioning of the modern cartridge. As compared with black powder, smokeless powder is both reluctant to ignite and slow to burn unless suitable conditions are realised; and failing their realisation, ballistics are likely to suffer and performance to fall below acceptable levels.

But although the cap has the important duty of inflaming the powder charge, it cannot by itself ensure efficient combustion, and I think, therefore, that it would be useful to consider some of the other factors involved. Every shooter has an interest in this matter, because the most carefully regulated charges can be ineffective unless the powder is properly burnt, and its potential chemical energy duly converted into striking energy. Besides, imperfect combustion can be anything from a nuisance to a danger. One of its consequences is much unburnt residue in the barrel, which can fall back and clog the breech mechanism; and in really bad cases there is a risk that the wadding column may not be expelled – a danger much accentuated in really cold weather.

The efficient burning of a given charge of powder is dependent on its attaining a certain pressure and temperature after it has been ignited, and this in turn is dependent on adequate resistance being opposed to the hot gases as they are evolved. If they are allowed to expand prematurely, either through the wadding being too soft or elastic, or to the shot charge being too light, or to the crimp being weak, the pressure and temperature will never rise to the level necessary for complete combustion; and instead of the maximum being attained within an inch or so of the standing breech, it may not occur until the shot charge is well on its way down the barrel. These conditions, separately or in combination, are the cause of 'muzzle flashes', when, especially in fading light, a long flame may be seen issuing from the gun. Although in these circumstances the maximum pressure at the breech end of the barrel will be below its proper value, the pressure at the muzzle may be well above normal, and patterns will almost certainly be 'blown'.

A risk for home-loaders

There is a point here on which home-loaders can run into danger. If by the use of an unsatisfactory combination of cap and powder, a given load is found to be giving an inadequate velocity, it might be considered safe to increase the powder charge. But if the low velocity were due to conditions such as those just described, or to the use of an unduly slow-burning powder, the effect of adding more of it might be to raise the pressure peak, already occurring where the barrel wall is much thinner than it is at the breech, above the safe level, or even to cause a burst. I cannot recall an instance of this happening, but I believe it to be well within the bounds of possibility.

In discussing the things that may give rise to inefficient combustion of the powder charge, I seem in danger of obscuring the contrary possibilities, whereby pressures may be raised unduly, perhaps above the safety limit. They are possibilities of which the home-loader in particular should be constantly aware, but it is not my present purpose to consider them. I can only say now that what may appear to be insignificant changes in quantities or components or methods of charging can have unforeseeable and disproportionate effects, and that the only safe course is to stick closely to the book. The liberties we used to take with black powder are quite inadmissible with smokeless.

58   The Shot for the Job

A West Country acquaintance asks a curious question. 'Several years ago,' he says, 'when you first published particulars of how to make your own shot on the short-drop principle, I tried my hand at it, with fair success. In fact I used the home-made shot in my hand-loads for quite a time. Then I suppose, I lost interest, and went back to factory shot. A year or two later, something – I don't know what it was: perhaps it was the price increase or one of those economy urges – but something made me start making my own shot again, and I carried on with it for another year or two. Now I'm back on factory shot.

'The funny thing,' he continued, 'is that on looking back over the record, I'm pretty certain that I have done better with my home-made shot than I have with the factory product. I know that my wife's home-made bread makes the scorched-dough factory bread look very poor stuff, but I can't see anything like that in the case of my shot. Admittedly, it doesn't even look so good as the boughten kind, and yet, as I say, I seem to have shot better with it. Can you explain it?'

In reply to my questions, it appeared that, apart from the change of shot, there had been very little change in the conditions surrounding my friend's sport. He shoots game and pigeon chiefly, and over the same territory, and has used the same gun throughout – a medium quality English boxlock, believed to have 'a bit of choke' in the right barrel and rather more than a bit in the left.

I have never seen the gun concerned, but I have a specimen of the shot in front of me now. It is good of its kind, but not really outstanding. It appears to have been graded to about No. 5; and although on casual inspection it is little inferior to factory shot, it is noticeable that it has no corresponding tendency to roll freely around the flat tin lid in which it is confined. Closer scrutiny reveals the reason: all the pellets are roughly the shape of a Coburg loaf, with a rounded top and a flattened bottom. Some of them have a little dimple in the underside, which, in association with the general shape, is caused, I believe, by running the shot at the lowest possible temperature (in itself, a good thing), but with rather too short a drop to the water.

Is it possible then, that there is some special magic in the distinctive shape of these pellets – some ballistic virtue which the more perfectly spherical

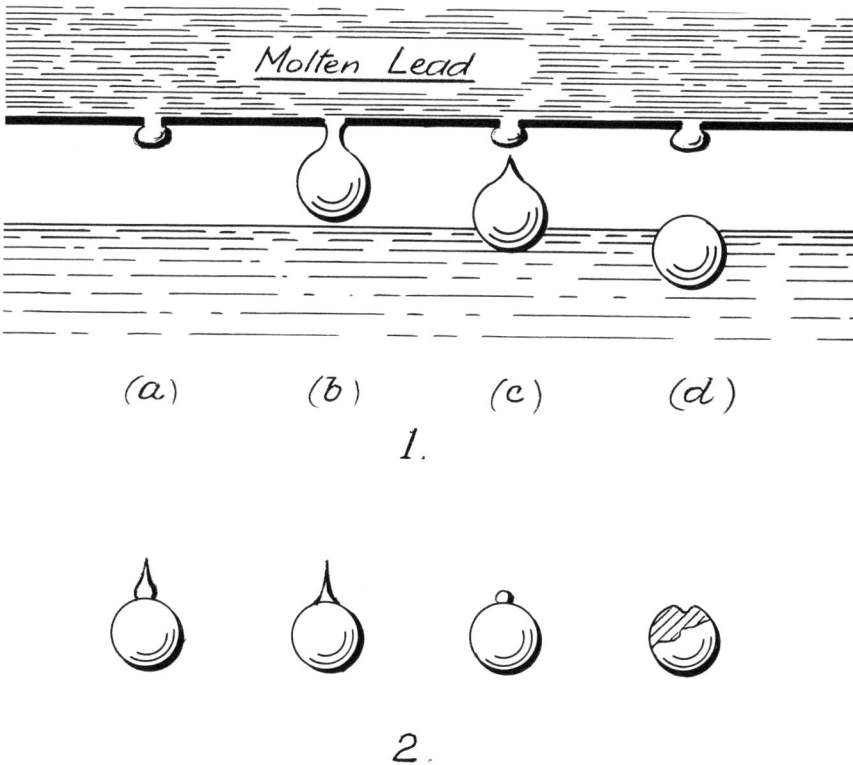

Molten Lead

(a)   (b)   (c)   (d)

1.

2.

THE FORMATION OF HOME-MADE SHOT USING THE SHORT-DROP PROCESS.
1. (a) Molten lead emerging from the reservoir; (b) droplet nearly fully formed before touching water; (c) detached but with molten tail while lower part is solidified; and (d) tail collapsed into still-molten upper part of pellet.
2. Typical abnormal pellets.

factory shot does not possess? That, I consider, is an unnecessary hypothesis. Assuming the correctness of the original observation – that these pellets give a somewhat better performance than their more symmetrical factory-made counterparts – there is an easy explanation. It is simply that they do not fly so truly, and therefore make a more open pattern – one, that is to say, of wider spread – and that, in the range bracket within which my friend does most of his shooting, the wider spread may be noticeably more advantageous.

An eye to conditions

Shooting writers, myself included, are perhaps over-inclined to consider the spread of the shot charge as being solely a function of the effective degree of choke, and to overlook the influence of the shot itself. Yet we do not fail to stress the importance of high-quality shot, and its preservation from damage in its course up the barrel, if the best results of which a given gun is capable are to be achieved. In so doing we are in danger of identifying 'best results' with 'best results at maximum range,' and forgetting that most field shooting in this country is done at moderate distances. We are also in danger of over-looking some contrary indications.

One of them is the way in which shooters are occasionally astonished and delighted by their success with an old gun which, in addition to having no perceptible degree of choke, has badly pitted barrels, so that about half the shot charge is severely abraded. Another is the market that exists among knowing shooters on the Continent for cartridges loaded with what might be called pre-ruined shot – in other words, the *plomb carré* or 'square' shot of the FN *Dispersante* cartridges. My good American friend, Roger Barlow, subjects some of the shot he intends to use on quail in his South Carolina woods to a preliminary battering. These are all ways of making 'fliers' – those allegedly useless, low-energy pellets found on the outer fringe of patterns. But the parasitic flier at 40 to 50 yds is a working pellet at 20 or 30, and rakes in birds which a closer, more orderly pattern might miss. If most birds are taken within the latter bracket, the case for perfect shot is weakened, and the opportunity for something inferior improved.

It is all a matter of selecting the right tools for the job – the fully choked gun with best-quality shot, and every protective device for long-range work, and the open-bored gun with maximum spread for work at close range. My friend's gun, with its 'bit of choke' and his home-made shot, are probably well adapted to what they are called on to do.

59 Shot Stringing

One of my Continental correspondents has appealed to me for moral support in resisting what he regards as the heretical views of one of his compatriots, a writer, who maintains that a long shot-string is advantageous, in that it is capable of bringing to bag birds that might otherwise be missed in front.

This is not a new doctrine: it has been argued here and elsewhere. The noted French small-bore magnum specialist, M. Kerné, conceding that the long shot column within the bore of these guns tends to cause abnormal stringing of the charge in flight, represents this as being an advantage with crossing shots, presumably for the reason stated, but otherwise of no significance. '*Elle ne peut, au contraire,*' he says, '*que présenter un avantage dans le tir de traversard ; dans le tir devant soi, aucune importance . . .*'

But although it must be admitted that birds are occasionally missed in front – more often, indeed, than was once commonly admitted – and although it must be allowed that a bird so missed with the bulk of the charge can yet fly into the tail portion of a long shot-string, it by no means follows that the long string is advantageous. Argument on the subject is perennial, and so it is worth examining in some detail.

First, it would be well to take a look at a typical shot-string. When a charge of shot leaves the muzzle of a gun, it not only spreads laterally but also draws out lengthwise, so that at full range there may be 10 to 15 ft or more between the leading pellets and the laggards. So, if we want a mental picture of the size and shape of the envelope necessary to contain an ordinary game charge at, say, 40 yds, we should imagine something like a stumpy sausage, about 40 to 50 in. in diameter, according to whether it was fired from a choke or a cylinder, and perhaps 10 to 12 ft long (see page 180).

To complete the picture, we must further imagine that the pellets within this sausage-shaped envelope are chiefly concentrated at the forward end. Half the pellets would be in the front 3 to 4 ft; three-quarters of them would be in the front 5 ft; whilst the last 3 ft would contain only about one-tenth of the total. This, I must emphasise, is only a typical picture of a 12-bore game charge – say, 1 to $1\frac{1}{8}$ oz of No. 6 shot.

Energy distribution

So much for the distribution of the pellets in space at full range. But there is a further aspect of distribution – the distribution of energy among the individual pellets, which determines their penetration and killing power. In the typical shot-string, not only is the bulk of the charge concentrated forward, but there is an even greater concentration of energy. Since all the pellets left

the gun together, with a common velocity, it follows that the pellets in the
rear of the shot-string could only have come to occupy that position in consequence of their travelling slower than the others. This reduced rate of
travel could in turn have come about from the fact that the pellets in a given
charge are not all absolutely uniform in size to start with, nor are they all
absolutely round; and even if they were, they would not all be launched in
that state, for some of them have been abraded or distorted in their passage
through the bore of the gun.

The effect of all this in the typical game charge we have been considering
is that the first 3 or 4 ft of the shot-string would not only contain about half
the total pellets, but it would also carry with it more than half the total energy.

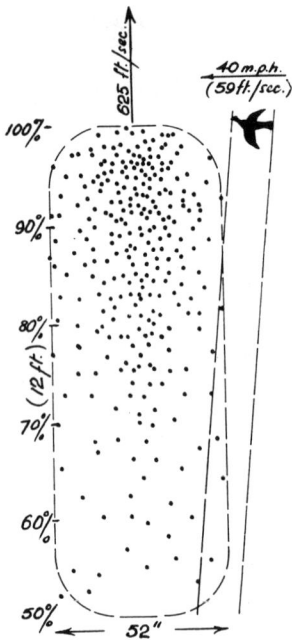

EFFECT OF STRINGING OF SHOT   Bird, missed in
front, runs into the weak tail of the shot string.

Opinions and arguments

Before attempting to show the significance of all this in relation to the point
under consideration, which is whether the long shot-string is actually advantageous, it might be well to break off to say that my facts, as stated, were
derived from R. W. Griffiths's celebrated experiments on the stringing of
shot, carried out as long ago as 1887. What Griffiths did, in essence, was to fire
at a stationary target of thin paper, having behind it another target which was

moving at a known velocity. By comparing the two patterns thus obtained, it was possible to say in what order the pellets reached the target, and what were the intervals separating them. In *The Modern Shotgun*, Burrard describes Griffiths's experiments in detail, and comments instructively on them. But there is one point on which I consider Burrard to have been misleading. Regarding pellet energy, he says that at 40 yds 95 per cent of the shot charge is effective, and that the ineffective 5 per cent is found only at the tail of the string. In my opinion, this tends to give the impression that a bird running into any part of the string save the extreme tail would be adequately dealt with, which is not the case, if only because the pellets are so thinly scattered to the rear. Also Burrard bases his statement on the arbitrary minimum standard of effectiveness, and has insufficient regard for the game-getting merit associated with the progressive increase of pellet energy towards the front of the string. The vital facts for my present argument are that the tail part — say the rear half — contains probably less than a quarter of the total pellets and that their individual energy may be anything from 20 to 50 per cent less than that of the leaders, dependent on their position.

Conclusions

With these considerations in mind, we can see what happens to a bird that is missed in front, but caught by the rearward part of the charge. The diagram on page 180 shows to scale a typical shot-string at 40 yds, as thrown by an improved cylinder 12-bore loaded with $1\frac{1}{16}$ oz of No. 6 shot. The pellets marked correctly indicate the lengthwise distribution to be expected, and the percentage figures give the proportionate pellet energies at different levels.

The bird shown is of about the size of a pigeon, and is supposed to be crossing at 40 m.p.h. It is taken as having been missed forward, just sufficiently for it to escape the front part of the shot-string. In these circumstances it would run the gauntlet of that part of the string enclosed within the sloping parallel lines. As will be seen, this is a part thinly occupied by relatively low-energy pellets, and the chances are that if the bird were not missed altogether, it would only be pricked or wounded. The case against a long shot-string is strengthened if, instead of considering a game charge at 40 yds. we take a wildfowling charge at more extended range.

It is further strengthened by the consideration that the long string is evidence of imperfection — it is caused by imperfect and imperfectly graded pellets, as well as by pellets that have suffered damage in the gun. As shot, cartridges and guns are improved, shot-strings close up, and more high-energy pellets are concentrated forwards, where, taking one shot with another, they are most effective.

60   *A Curious Superstition*

An Essex wildfowler takes it as an assured fact that the effective range of a shotgun fired over water is less than when it is fired over dry land, and asks me to say why.

I am no stranger to this belief, which may well be old enough to rank as a piece of shooting folk-lore, and I have previously had it stowed away in my mind along with other and similar beliefs, which impute a loss of power to guns fired under a variety of unfamiliar conditions. Alpine shooters will tell you, for example, that guns fired over a chasm or deep ravine will not carry so far as when fired over ground in the ordinary way.

Coming back to the original proposition, critically regarded, it seems nonsense. At the same time, I must admit that my own experience has sometimes seemed to endorse it; so I believe there may be a few grains of truth scattered about here which may pay for the gleaning.

When alleged facts of this sort are offered for consumption, unsupported by any practical tests or other evidence, they are open to immediate suspicion as being subjective, and I believe that there is indeed one common explanation – or partial explanation – of this sort in the particular cases mentioned. It is simply that in such circumstances there is abnormal difficulty in estimating range. This is especially so when shooting over water, when one is deprived of all the incidental aids to range estimation provided by intervening objects.

Years ago, most of my wildfowling was done afloat, and I often had the double disadvantage of being deprived of all such aid, and also of shooting from an abnormally low position. One gets the same thing, I notice, when shooting pigeon from a deep ditch hide, with no view of the surface of the ground. Perhaps the worst of these situations is met with when punting up creeks between steep mud banks, cutting off all view around. Then, when fowl have appeared against the sky, perhaps after being flushed from around a bend by the sound of my approach (or conceivably by telepathic warning of the nearness of an enemy), I have often badly misjudged their range. As for shooting over airy spaces, I can offer no comment from my own experience, though I should think that the same difficulty in estimating range would apply.

The point of all this, of course, is that for good, consistent shooting there must be good, consistent estimation of range – at least to the extent of recognizing when birds are fairly within shot. If, when shooting over open water, there is a tendency to under-estimate range, as there may well be, performance must suffer, and the gun may seem to have lost something of its normal reach.

But, it may be objected, if this is a true explanation, it would apply equally well to all birds taken well up in the air, and clear of all ground objects. Perhaps it does, and perhaps the general standard of performance at such birds suffers somewhat accordingly. But there are mitigating circumstances. The height of tall pheasants, for example, can often be inferred from the height of the trees over which they have been driven; and if the shooter is badly out in his reckoning he usually has a chance of getting his eye in, with a few ranging shots.

A possible explanation

But my Essex wildfowler, I suspect, would not think this broad explanation good enough. Indeed, I am sure that he is convinced of there being some ballistical factor involved.

Of course, there is the fact that the shooters who, for generations past, have done most shooting over water will be those who, more than any others, have shot most with damp ammunition – exclusively black powder for the greater part of the time. And since black powder is much affected by damp, collective experience may have made a genuine observation here without recognizing the true cause. This may be only a featherweight speculation, but what follows is not.

Some of the best wildfowling, often, as a matter of course, involving shooting over water, is experienced under the most wintry conditions, with high barometer and low temperature, and it is not generally recognised that these conditions can open up patterns to a marked degree. Thus, a gun which passed its patterning test at a Birmingham maker's plate at 400 ft above sea level under summer conditions, with the barometer at, say, 28.5 in. and the thermometer at 75 degrees, and which threw a pattern of 75 per cent with certain ammunition, would definitely not put up the same performance at sea level, with the glass standing at 30 in., and the temperature down to freezing.

On the scanty data available, I should expect to lose about 10 points per cent of pattern density for every 30 degrees drop in temperature, so that, under the conditions assumed, the pattern might come down to about 60 per cent. This, I should make clear, is nothing to do with the coldness of the air, as such, but rather its increased density as the temperature falls, and the scattering effect of this denser air on the patterns. The air density would be further increased under the conditions assumed by the rise in the barometer, and by the change of site from Birmingham to sea level. The former might reduce the pattern to 56 per cent, and the latter might knock off yet another point.

So that, I think, really gives my enquirer something to bite on. If he can relate his observation of reduced gun-power to increased air density, as brought about by cold and/or a rising glass, rather than to the fact of shooting over water, he is entitled to regard it as a genuine one. For the rest, I can only regard it as a false impression, arising out of the difficulty of judging distances over water.

The converse problem

This relationship between air density and pattern density works, of course, both ways, and I wish now that I had asked our Olympic gold medallist, Robert Braithwaite, to check what patterns his Browning gun made when he was shooting in Mexico. At 7000-odd ft, it will certainly have made markedly tighter patterns than those to which he is accustomed, and unless he took steps to adapt it to the situation, it could have made things difficult for him. I remember concluding, and may have mentioned here, that when I was shooting ptarmigan in Wester Ross at the modest elevation of around 3000 ft, my improved cylinder barrel was almost certainly making half-choke patterns.

Since there is relatively little shooting done at over, say, 2000 ft in this country, the relation between patterns and altitude appears to have escaped notice, but in its converse aspect, as applying possibly to my Essex wildfowler, and all others who rely most on their guns under wintry conditions, I feel that it is something we ought to know more about.

Now, if I lived, say, at Llanberis, I should be strongly tempted to embark on the Snowdon Railway with my portable pattern plate, and to do a careful series of tests, both at the top of that noble mountain and at the bottom, recording the temperature, barometric pressure and humidity at both stations. Such tests, properly performed and recorded, would provide data from which some unfamiliar country in shotgun performance could be very pleasantly and profitably explored.

61   Short-Range Devices

When I wrote recently about the ideal gun for all ranges, I was thinking chiefly about our lack of a gun suited to the occasions when we know that most or all of our shots will have to be taken at short distances, as, for example, shooting bolted rabbits, or woodcock or other game in close woodland. There are even covert shoots where one knows that there is no hope (or fear) of really high birds, and that a gun capable of making good 25 yd patterns would be the most efficient weapon. I believe that pride, as well as the eternal search for guns of maximum reach, tends to blind us to the large amount of short-range work we are called upon to do in the course of a season's well mixed

A CASE FOR MAXIMUM SPREAD   For shooting quail in the South Carolina pine woods, Roger Barlow uses a Bretton O/U with slow-rifled barrel throwing patterns as shown in the illustration on p.188.

shooting. That may be why we in this country are content to have no guns or ammunition adapted to this large and important sector of our sport.

As I pointed out before, the Continental sportsman is better served: he has his spreader cartridges and his barrels rifled with a very slow twist, and specially designed to give high-quality patterns of wide spread. These latter in particular, used with the small sizes of shot for which they are intended, should be enough to ensure a preponderance of Frenchmen among the members of the Bol's Woodcock Club; for I believe it to be true that French gunmakers are the leading manufacturers and advocates of the slow-rifled shot barrel for close-range shooting. A familiar combination is a *canon rayé* or rifled barrel on the right and a half choke on the left, so that, with a double-triggered gun, the sportsman is well equipped for anything on offer from about 15 to 45 yds, subject only to his submitting to the bother of loading his choke barrel with shot of a size more suited to its capacity.

The police view

The mere fact of writing previously stirred me to some further activity on this subject. I have thought how easy it would be – or should be – to import one of the French rifled barrels; or failing that, to have an existing barrel rifled here; or even to rifle it oneself. The only snags would appear to be those arising out of rules and regulations – chiefly the Firearms Act.

I accordingly had a talk with our Deputy Chief Constable on the possibility of a shot barrel of this kind being accepted as a smooth-bore. I made the point that such a barrel is essentially a shot-spreading device, and would therefore be less lethal than one of the ordinary kind if the gun to which it was fitted ever fell into criminal hands. The Deputy was as sympathetic and helpful as I have always found the police to be. He grasped the practicalities of the situation and asked for twenty-four hours for consideration.

But when he came back to me, it was with an adverse decision. The Act, he explained, was quite specific in its distinction between rifled arms and smooth-bores, and left no scope or loophole for the kind of interpretation I sought. In his view, therefore, and that of his advisers, any gun incorporating a *canon rayé* would of necessity have to be treated as a rifled firearm and subjected to Firearm Certificate procedure. This, of course, would be a nuisance, but not necessarily a bar to the acquisition of such a gun by a *bona fide* applicant. Still, it was a check, and turned my thoughts in another direction — that of reviewing the various tricks and devices for increasing in a controlled manner the lateral dispersion of shots from a smooth-bore. Also, I wanted to satisfy myself that there was nothing that was being overlooked in this neglected field — no old and abandoned idea that it might pay to revive in the light of modern resources; and no new idea that one might conceive as being practical and worth immediate trial. I believe I have hit on one example in each of these categories.

The Courtier principle

There are, of course, some half-dozen different kinds of spreader, scatter or brush cartridges. They are all well established and are sufficiently well-known to need no further reference here. But there is one that never seems to have crossed the Channel, though it was once in commercial production in France; and there seems to be some possibility that it could advantageously be revived in plastic form. This was the Courtier cartridge — briefly, a cartridge designed to shoot a bullet or slug from a smooth-bored barrel with the accuracy of a rifle. It was a paper cartridge with a thin brass lining, from which projected helical ridges or lands, engaging with corresponding grooves in the bullet. The bullet therefore left the cartridge with a spin, which partially survived the passage of the bore. The result was an accuracy about twice that of the ordinary solid ball.

But there were serious disadvantages, apart from cost. Ballistics had to be kept to a low level for reasonable results; and the torsional reaction of the bullet on the case appears to have had the effect of grinding the latter into the chamber, so that it was extremely hard to extract. Altogether, the Courtier cartridge must be accounted a failure. As far as I can see, it was never tried as a shot-dispersing device.

The Galand cartridge

This was left to a Paris gunmaker named Galand, who in 1898 patented and duly manufactured a modified Courtier cartridge intended for short-range shotgun shooting of the kind we are considering. Galand called his cartridge the *épervier*, which I thought was French for sparrowhawk, though I find that it also means casting-net – a descriptive term in the circumstances. It was made in two sorts. The first had a twist of about 12 in., and gave a spread of over 50 in. at 22 yds. The second had a twist of 25 in., and gave a spread at the same distance of 35 in. *The spread appears to have been irrespective of the degree of choke in the barrel*, the spin being the dominant influence on the charge.

The Galand cartridge was sold for a considerable period, and evidently enjoyed a measure of success; but it inherited to some degree the extraction difficulty of the Courtier, and this may well have been the cause of its disappearance.

A case for revival?

But now it seems to me that our modern plastic cases might offer some scope for a revival of the Galand cartridge in a much simplified form.

One of the main objections to the production of ordinary spreader cartridges is, I gather, the fact that they do not lend themselves to straightforward machine production. However, it is possible that if a modern plastic case were impressed internally with a suitable rifling, it might be capable of functioning as well as the metal-lined Galand, and that its greater strength and resilience could make it immune from the extraction trouble that haunted the other. Such a case might well need special wadding, but it could be machine-loaded throughout, and I hope that some manufacturer may be induced to give the matter a trial. The suggestion would appear to fall more particularly in the Winchester Company's court, for it seems that their compression-formed cases could be produced, if required, in rifled form, without any additional operation.

What would appear at first glance to be the ideal solution to the short-range shooting problem is the ordinary small-bore adapter with the addition of slow-rifling to the normally smooth bore. With such rifling to promote orderly and controlled dispersion, even the detestable 3-in. ·410 loaded with ⅝ oz of No. 9, might be induced to make good killing 30-in. patterns for woodcock at 20 to 25 yds, at which distance these small pellets would have ample penetrative power. However, this is not good enough, because an unencumbered improved cylinder 12-bore could make just as large a pattern, and one just as dense, with a normal game charge of No. 6, and a better one with No. 7 or 8. So, to cash in on this idea would need a substantially larger charge and a greater spread. This would need a $2\frac{3}{4}$-in. 12/20 adapter and an ounce charge.

The feasibility of such an adapter is unfortunately much in doubt, and I must leave further consideration of the idea to the specialist firms who manufacture these accessories.

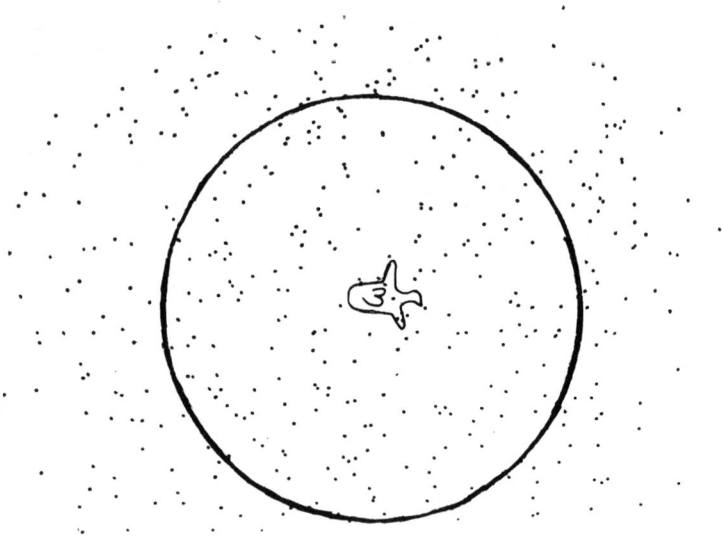

PATTERN FOR CLOSE-RANGE SHOOTING   Typical pattern thrown at 18 yards by slow-twist rifled barrel of Bretton 12-bore firing $1\frac{1}{8}$ oz. of No. 8 shot.

Section 7

CHOKE

'Choke boring, both in its inception and its execution, is a thoroughly empirical business . . . and may, even now, harbour some unknown and unsuspected factors.'

62 How Choke Works

A Yorkshire correspondent writes, 'May I ask you to explain in one of your articles how choke works? This is a question to which a scientific answer is long overdue. Fred Kimble, if he was the inventor, used empirical methods to attain the desired result, so avoiding the issue of explanation a hundred years ago. Surely at this stage we can state in proper terms what happens in a choke.'

Before I try to give the explanation required, I must say a word about Fred Kimble. Choke boring is one of those inventions in every way likely to have been made intuitively. The first man to have squirted water under pressure from a hose probably discovered that by pinching the end of it he could concentrate the stream of water and accelerate the reduced jet emerging from the opening thus restricted. It needed no heaven-sent inspiration to suspect that something of the same sort could be done to the charge of shot issuing from the muzzle of a gun; nor did it require any lengthy or costly experimenting to put the suspicion to a practical test. So, I am quite prepared to believe, along with most patriotic Americans, that Fred Kimble, in the early 1870s, did independently invent choke, and that others before him (including at least one American) did the same. But as a patriotic Englishman, I must put in a word for William Rochester Pape, the well-known gunmaker of Newcastle-on-Tyne, who had fully mastered the principle several years before Kimble, and first patented it. Pape's patent (British Patent No. 1501) was in fact dated 29 May 1866, and if we want to attach a name to the invention, Pape's is about the best we can find. But Kimble in America and Greener in England have the best claim to be regarded as the fathers of choke boring in their respective countries, for they most conspicuously urged and demonstrated its advantages, which Pape never seems to have done.

Twin principles

I believe that there are two principles at work in the action of choke. The first emerges clearly from the investigations of one M. Tresca at the French *Conservatoire des Arts et Métiers*, who studied the effects of forcing plastic substances, including shot charges, through constricted orifices. My sketch on page 192 shows one of his experimental results. It clearly indicates that plastic material being forced through the throat of a die undergoes an acceleration, which, in the case of a charge of shot, means that the forward part of the charge gains very slightly on the rearward part. This longitudinal separation, easily visible in flash photographs taken just as the charge is leaving the muzzle of a choke-bored gun, is probably enhanced by the slight check experienced by

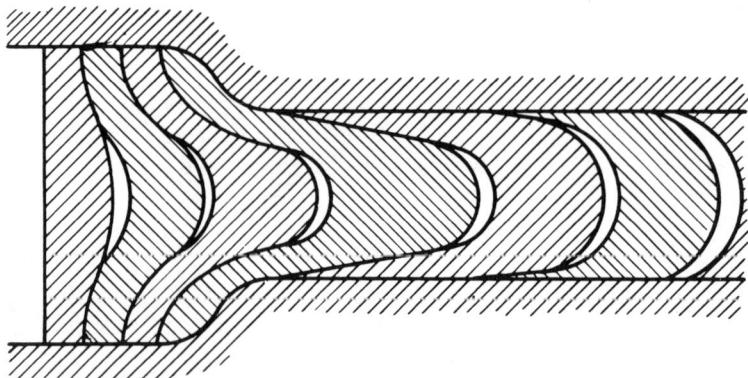

Effect of forcing a plastic substance through a constricted orifice.

the wad column and the rearward pellets as they approach the choke. The net result is shown in exaggerated form at (a) in my second sketch shown below.

The second principle is dependent on the first. Given the degree of charge-separation described, the outer and more forward pellets are free to be deflected slightly inwards by the slope of the choke, as indicated at (b). Flash photographs show that, in consequence, the overall diameter of the front part of the charge, after a few inches of flight, is actually less than the bore diameter, whereas the compacted rearward portion begins to disperse immediately it is free from the constraint of the muzzle.

Contrasting cylinder

The appearance of a similar charge a few inches from the muzzle of a true cylinder is strikingly different. Freed from the support of the barrel, and

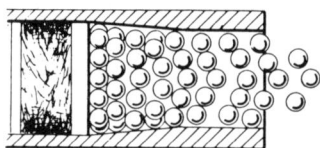

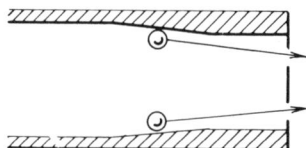

(a)   (b)

THE DUAL EFFECT OF CHOKE   (a) exaggerated view of acceleration of shot charge. (b) inward deflection of outside pellets.

punching its way into the resistant air, it quickly begins to assume a flattened or mushroom shape; and whereas at 3 or 4 ft the charge from the choke still retains its forward concentration, that from the cylinder has already undergone a marked dispersal. I think it would be true to say that the difference between choke and cylinder patterns is not so much due to the concentrating process that takes place in the choke as it is to the prevention of this early dispersal, whereby the air gains immediate access to the centre of the charge from the cylinder gun, and goes riving and sundering among the pellets and scattering them, literally, to the wind – though not necessarily or always to the shooter's disadvantage.

An empirical business

Whether or not this explanation of the action of choke conforms to my correspondent's conception of 'proper terms', I do not know, though I suspect it may not. But the truth is that choke boring, both in its inception and its execution, is a thoroughly empirical business, and that its effect on the shot charge may, even now, harbour some unknown and unsuspected factors. In the nature of things, it is very hard to know exactly what goes on in the ten-thousandth of a second, more or less, for which the charge is under the control of the choke, even though flash photography now gives us some astonishingly sharp and clear pictures of the mass of pellets *after* they have left the muzzle. But so far as I know, we are still without sure explanations of a number of choke anomalies. Why, for example, can pattern density sometimes be improved by *reducing* the choke constriction? And conversely, why do some guns, carrying but a moderate degree of choke, throw patterns of a density beyond all expectation? And how is it that Oberfell and Thompson got patterns of better quality and greater density from choke tubes that had been deliberately roughened than they did from the same tubes in their original smooth state? When we can explain these things, and perhaps some others, in terms of our basic conceptions of choke-action, we may be in a position to claim that we really understand choke at last. Then, perhaps, we shall be able to bore guns out of hand to comply with a predetermined performance specification.

63   Mysteries of Choke (I)

On reading my previous chapter on 'How Choke Works', I am glad to see that I avoided giving the impression that we know everything about the subject. Indeed, for all our wonderful modern flash photographs of pellets emerging from the muzzles of choked and cylinder barrels, we are, as I said, still without sure explanations of some of the things that happen to a charge of shot when it passes through the choke.

I now want to draw attention to an aspect of choke-action that has been neglected or overlooked by all the authorities I have ever read, and also to mention one of its principal effects. In a subsequent chapter, I will try to consider how this action may be involved in some curious features occasionally observed in choke patterns.

Degrees of compression

First, a quick look at what happens to a charge of shot in its progress up the barrel. Note that all the pellets, as they reach the choke, are travelling at the same speed. This means that every individual one, assuming a perfect charge, has been acted on by the same propulsive force for the same period of time. (Mathematicians, please keep out of this. I know what you are going to say, but it would only cause confusion.)

But the gas pressure does not act on all the pellets – it only acts through the wad on the rearward layer, and this layer, having absorbed its due share of the total pressure, passes what is left on to the next layer, and so on. The foremost layer, having nothing to pass on, merely absorbs enough to give it the same acceleration as the rest.

This is not scientific language, but I think it makes the action fairly clear. The effect is that all the pellets in the charge, except those right in front, are squeezed and to some extent crushed. One has only to imagine a tightly packed crowd being forced out of a narrow street by a bull-dozer, to get a good impression of what takes place. The people nearest to the bull-dozer, with all the weight of the crowd before them, will obviously be crushed worst – the others progressively less so.

In a shotgun, the degree of crushing suffered by the rearward pellets is formidable. An ordinary 12-bore game charge may contain, say, eight layers of 40 pellets each; and but for the cushioning effect of the wad, which can be much or little, the rearmost layer would be subjected to a maximum crushing force of seven-eighths of the peak pressure. The next would suffer six-eighths and the next five-eighths, and so on. This would mean that *each single pellet* in the rear layer would be crushed with a force of some 60 lbs. (Imagine a weight of over half a hundredweight sitting on top of a single pellet of No. 6!) And even if the wad were so effective as to cushion this force to a level average throughout the length of the barrel, each rearmost pellet would still be subjected to a crushing force of about 20 lbs.

My sketch is intended to represent what goes on in terms of this squeezing, and thus in the deformation and consolidation of the pellets. It is, of course,

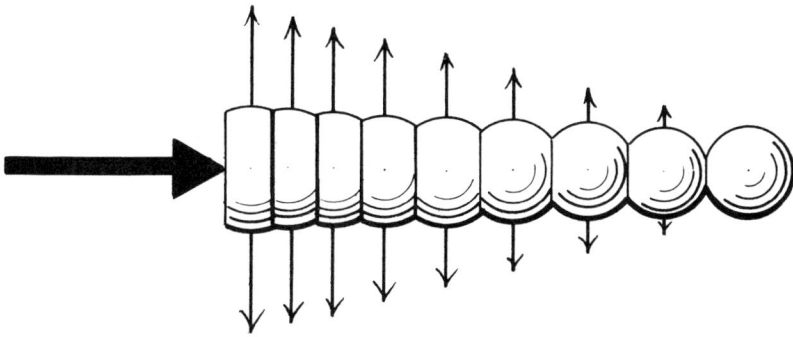

EFFECT ON A COLUMN OF PELLETS OF A POWERFUL ACCELERATING FORCE   The rearward pellets undergo the most crushing and squeezing, the more forward ones progressively less.

exaggerated. It also indicates by means of arrows how the lateral squeezing of the charge varies along its length, and how it is that the rearmost pellets suffer worst, by compressive deformation and by abrasion against the barrel wall.

This brings me straight to the aspect of choke-action that appears to have been neglected or overlooked. It even escaped the attention of the great Journée, whom Burrard was content merely to quote. Both of these authorities give illustrations in their books which I suggest, with due deference, convey a highly misleading picture of what takes place (below). Treating the shot charge as a whole, they show how it undergoes acceleration in the choke, and how the outer pellets receive an inward impulse from its conical surface. The pellets (according to them) being nicely separated, *all* the outer ones are free to respond to the impulse, and to shape a course directed more towards the centre of the target than they otherwise would do.

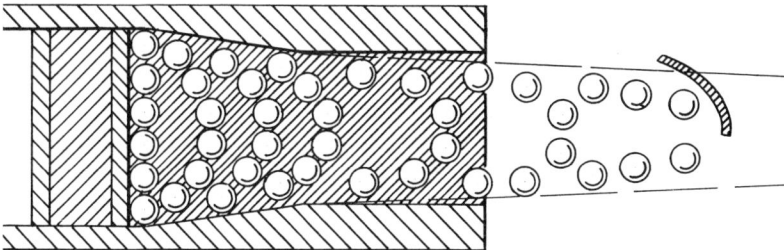

PASSAGE OF SHOT PELLETS THROUGH CHOKE – AFTER JOURNÉE   The excessive elongation of the charge is misleading and contrary to the evidence of flash photographs.

A variable response

In my view, however, it is impossible to understand choke-action without recognising that the forward and rearward portions of the charge respond differently to the muzzle constriction. Flash photographs confirm that some degree of acceleration does, in fact, take place, and that the forward pellets are indeed directed inwards, so that the emerging charge has an overall diameter slightly less than that of the bore (below). But not the rearward portion. Having been heavily squeezed and to some degree consolidated by the crushing forces to which it has been subjected, its outer pellets are not free to respond to the inward-acting impulse of the choke. Rather, the compacted mass is compressed by the choke constriction, whereafter it emerges in an unregulated manner as determined by a number of adventitious factors, including the degree of choke, the sharpness or gradualness of the constriction, the size of the pellets and the way they stack, their hardness, the shape of the wad, whether the pellets are 'black', and therefore prone to cold-welding, or plated and free from any such tendency, etc.

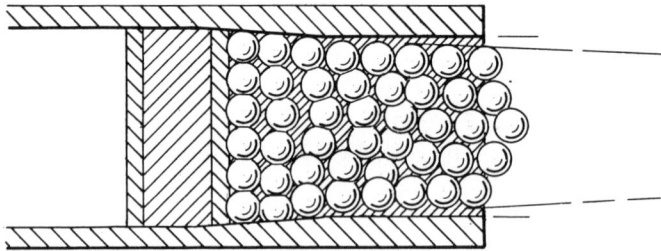

NEARER TO THE TRUTH   The forward pellets have become slightly separated by acceleration in the choke and are free to respond to it, but the rearward ones are more consolidated, and are merely crushed in the mass by the constriction.

In the light of all these considerations, I think it would be realistic to regard every pattern thrown by a heavily choked barrel as being, in a sense, two patterns, one superimposed on the other – the first being a controlled and concentrated pattern made by the forward portion of the charge, and the second a more dispersed and erratic version made by the rearward portion. The latter, comprising most of the damaged pellets, would contribute most of the 'fliers', and would occupy the tail end of the shot-string in flight. The pellets of this second pattern would thus have a lower average striking energy than the others.

This conception ties in very well with the known fact that the patterns thrown by heavily choked barrels show a marked central concentration from which those produced by true or improved cylinders are free. If, in the stand-ard 30-in. circle, we draw a smaller one comprising half the total area, we may expect to find no more than half the pellets in it if the gun is a cylinder. But if it is a full choke, 60 to 65 per cent of the pellets may be included. This is why I always say that, over the greater part of the pattern circle, the perfor-mance of the open-bored barrel at full range approaches that of the choke much more nearly than the commonly quoted pattern percentages suggest.

64   Mysteries of Choke (II)

In my last chapter I suggested that for a proper understanding of what happens in a choke-bored gun, it is necessary to consider separately the front and the rear parts of the shot charge, on which the choke constriction appears to act somewhat differently. I said, with what I hope was due deference, that this aspect of choke-action seems to have been neglected or overlooked by our leading authorities, but that it is capable of explaining some of the curious and imperfectly understood things that happen with choke-bored guns.

A choked gun barrel is a pipe with a constricted nozzle; and since a charge of shot behaves to some extent like a liquid, it is easy to understand that the broad effect of the choke is to accelerate and concentrate the charge.

Dual action

But the effect of the choke extends far beyond the muzzle of the gun. The reason is that the conical portion, which leads up to the final constriction, imparts an inward-acting impulse to all pellets coming into contact with it; and *if they are free to respond to it*, they are thereby directed more to the centre of the pattern. The leading pellets undoubtedly *are* free: they have undergone some degree of acceleration in the choke, and if not actually separated are at least loosely packed. But it is a different story with the rearward pellets. They have been subjected to far higher pressures in their course up the barrel, and are thereby deformed and compacted. As they pass through the choke they are squeezed in the mass, and when they emerge may be seen from flash photographs to behave differently from those well in front of them. The forward pellets, under the influence of the choke, continue to converge, so that at some little distance from the muzzle they form a mass of smaller diameter than that of the constricted bore from which they emerged. But not the rearward ones. They start diverging immediately.

So, in pursuance of this conception of the dual nature of the choke action, I suggested that the pattern thrown by a choke barrel could be regarded as being in effect two patterns – one, a dense, controlled pattern made by the forward pellets, and the other, a more open and erratic one, superimposed upon it, and made by those to the rear. This explains the greater degree of central concentration found in choke patterns as opposed to those thrown by cylinders – a demerit in the former, since the ideal is one that is uniformly distributed over the whole of the circle.

A thought for the wad

Some little-understood aspects of choke performance now begin to show in a clearer light, and some suggestions emerge whereby patterns may conceivably be improved.

It had long been known that concave wads – felt wads, that is to say, with a cup-shaped depression facing forwards – tend to give denser patterns than those with a flat front, particularly with the smaller sizes of shot. I believe that the Australians are notably fond of wads of this kind, and for the reason stated.

The explanation would appear to be that the rearward pellets instead of approaching the choke in flat, compacted layers, do so in a bowed or dished formation, which yields to the choke by becoming more dished, and not by being squeezed in the mass. The pellets thus to some extent escape further deformation, and submit to the centralizing impulse of the conical surface more after the manner of the forward ones.

I notice that, in all the modern plastic wads that I have had an opportunity of examining, the bottom of the shot-cup is a flat surface; but I suggest that where patterns of maximum density and quality are necessary, it might pay to modify this detail, and to adopt a concave bottom.

Roughened barrels

A thing that has long puzzled me is the suggestion that pitted barrels shoot 'harder' than those with virgin surfaces. The belief that they do so is old-established, and many attempts have been made to improve the shooting of guns by deliberately roughening the bores. This cannot have failed to increase pellet damage, and according to all sound, modern doctrine, will have reduced pattern density. But this, of course, may have enabled many shooters to put more game in the bag, and given them the impression that their guns are shooting harder. The increased resistance to the passage of the shot charge up the barrel, by raising the temperature and pressure of combustion, may indeed have improved the ballistics, but not, one would say, *not* pattern density.

And yet we have the disturbing experiments of Oberfell and Thompson, who found that by deliberately roughening the surface of choke tubes, they did, in fact, increase both the density and quality of their patterns.

Perhaps we now have the explanation. If the compacted rearward layers of pellets, as they pass through the choke, are not submitted to a smooth, progressive constriction, but are thoroughly shaken up, whether by pitting or by Oberfell and Thompson's corrugations, one can readily imagine that their cohesion will be broken, and that the individual pellets will become more free to submit to the choke cone's inward impulse. They may suffer more damage from this treatment, but by becoming more amenable to the choke's guidance, may fly truer for all that.

Sparing the antimony

One of the approaches to patterns of the highest quality and density is, of course, through the use of especially hardened shot, whereby the compressive deformation of the rearward pellets is reduced. But shot is hardened by alloying the lead with antimony, which, I understand, is becoming very scarce and costly.

Bearing in mind the different conditions to which the front and rear parts of the shot charge are subjected, there would appear to be some scope for the suggestion that the charge should be loaded in two stages: the first with pellets of high antimonial content, and the second with those of lower. There would, indeed, seem to be no justification, apart from the exigencies of practical manufacture, for the use of hardened shot in the forward layers in any circumstances.

65 What Is My Choke?

One of the questions I am most frequently asked is, 'How much choke does my gun carry?' The correspondents who ask me this question invariably include a sketch or description of the proof and other marks on the gun, from which, if it is of Continental manufacture, I can often say what was the degree of muzzle constriction *at the time of proof*.

But in offering that information, I am conscious that it may be of little use to my questioner. It depends on what he really wants to know, and why he wants to know it. If he is one of those shooters whose confidence in the use of his weapon depends on his knowledge of, or belief in, the tightness of the patterns it throws, he may be fully reassured by knowing that the muzzle constriction conforms to the degree normally associated with full choke.

American shooters, we are told, often test their guns with a dime, or 10 cent piece. This small silver coin, when freshly minted, has a diameter of about ·703 in., which probably reduces after moderate wear to ·700 in. If, therefore, a gun is bored to the standard 12-bore dimension of ·729 in., and the muzzle will not accept a dime, it is taken that the gun carries at least 30 mils or thousandths of an inch, or 'points' of choke. With modern ammunition that may indeed be enough to ensure the delivery of full choke patterns. But if the gun is overbored by 10 mils, say, the same muzzle diameter will represent 40 points of choke, which, though it corresponds to the old full choke standard, may represent an over-choke with plastic ammunition; and over-chokes often give patterns that are less dense than those thrown by chokes of more moderate degree. The difference can be conspicuous.

Three points thus emerge. The first is that the degree of choke, regarded merely as the overall constriction in the bore of a gun, cannot be ascertained by measuring the diameter at the muzzle only: it is, in fact, determined by the difference between the diameter at 9 in. from the breech and that at the muzzle. The second point is that pattern density is not necessarily proportional to the degree of choke, even when correctly determined in this manner.

This conclusion is not relevant only to the shooter who wants to be assured of the tightness of his patterns: it applies equally to the opposite case. Readers often come to me with a tale of woe – of how their performance has deteriorated since they started shooting with a new gun. Sometimes they recognize that their degree of skill, combined with the range-bracket within which most of their game is taken, is best suited by an open-bored gun, or, at least, a gun with an open-bored right barrel; and they have come to suspect that they are getting patterns much tighter than the nominal boring or the advertised specification of the gun would imply. So they ask me what degree of choke the gun actually carries.

It cannot be too widely understood that there is only one way to find out how a gun behaves with a given load or cartridge, and that is to test it, and test it properly. Inferences based on the measured degree of choke can be highly misleading. If a gun has been bought second-hand, there is no longer even any assurance that the degree of choke is the same as that stamped on the barrels as existing at the time of proof. The previous owner may have had the gun opened out.

Measurement and tests

To bring out the practical significance of these points, I have measured and tested two typical medium quality Continental 12-bores, both of which were stamped with the diameter of the bore at breech and muzzle at the time of proof.

Gun No. 1, a second-hand specimen, had a right barrel which was stamped 18·5/18·2, signifying a constriction of 0·3 millimetres. To convert this to 'points' of choke, we multiply by 1000 and divide by 25·4, getting 12 points. This implies something slightly tighter than quarter-choke, which is nominally associated with 55 per cent patterns.

By actual measurement, however, this barrel gauged ·729/·722 in., indicating a constriction of only 7 points, implying improved cylinder boring and 50 per cent patterns.

By test with Grand Prix cartridges (1 1⁄16 oz of No. 6) this barrel duly gave good and consistent patterns averaging 49 per cent over eight shots. This was, in fact, very satisfactory improved cylinder performance – not quarter-choke, as the stamped dimensions implied.

The left barrel revealed a larger anomaly. Thus, the stamped dimensions were 18·5/17·9, a difference of 0·6 millimetres, or 24 points of choke. Actual measurement gave ·729/·707 in., or 22 points – nearly the same. This would normally be accepted as half-choke boring, which is down in the book as affording 60 per cent patterns. But on test with the same cartridge, this barrel gave full choke patterns of 71 per cent, and very good and consistent patterns at that.

Acceptable tolerance

In the light of the foregoing detail, the results obtained from Gun No. 2, believed new, may be tabulated as follows.

| | Choke | | Pattern | |
	Indicated	Measured	Nominal	Actual
Right	8 pts.	10 pts.	55%	48%
Left	20	18	Under 60%	66%

The third point that emerges immediately from the foregoing is that the constriction in a Continental gun, as sold, may not be the same as that measured at the time of proof. But there is no indication in any measurements I have ever made that there is anything out of order here. Continental proof authorities may well recognise that after a gun has been proved, the maker may wish to polish the bores, and that there may accordingly be some slight variation from the stamped dimensions, even in a new gun. Our own proof houses officially allow a three-thousandths tolerance of this kind in connection with chamber dimensions.

Things to recognise

But by far the more important conclusion is that, even with a cartridge not employing a modern plastic-skirted wad with protective shot cup, guns are capable of throwing patterns substantially denser than the overall degree of bore constriction might imply. The man who wants dense patterns should therefore recognise that he may be getting them, despite dimensional indications to the contrary. He should also recognise that if the dimensional indications favour the notion that he is getting super-dense patterns, they may be misleading. On the other hand, the man who needs open patterns should not be misled by the moderate choke constriction indicated or measured as existing in his gun. It may, as I say, be throwing far denser patterns than he realises, especially if he is using full plastic ammunition.

This last is one of the first things to be considered when there has been a marked falling off in performance consequent on the acquisition of a new gun. It often happens that a man has been shooting well for years with a gun that was never properly fitted to him; so that when he takes to a new one, which has been properly fitted, he reasonably expects to shoot even better. In such circumstances, it is a bitter disappointment for him to realise that he has, in fact, suffered a setback. Yet the whole explanation may lie in the increased density of his patterns.

There is a point here that should be particularly noted by users of repeaters or other single-barrelled weapons with a variable choke device. It is fatally easy to fall into the way of thinking that, by screwing up the ring more and more, one is getting denser and denser patterns. It may well happen that density increases for the first few clicks, but that thereafter there is little gain, with perhaps some decline in quality. Tests alone will establish the truth.

Section 8

RANGE

'The matter of range haunts the shotgun user—or, if it does not, then it should, subject to some latitude of interpretation of the word "haunts".'

66 *Estimating Range*

The matter of range haunts the shotgun user – or, if it does not, then it should, subject to some latitude of interpretation of that word, 'haunts'.

The reason is twofold. In the first place, the shotgun is a powerful weapon, and at very close range is capable of blowing small game to tatters. But then the energy of the charge is dissipated so quickly that at a relatively short distance it becomes harmless. What is more, the practical effectiveness of the charge diminishes even more rapidly than the total energy. This arises from the progressive spreading of the pellets, whereby the proportion capable of being brought to bear on a given target is rapidly reduced as the range extends.

This is not a matter for lamentation: seen large, it is a good thing, failing which shooting as a social amusement would be impossible. Even the solitary rough shooter would find himself under a grave handicap if he had to make anxious calculations of where his shot pellets were likely to land two or three hundred yards away. At the same time, it imposes on the shooter the need for maintaining an alert consciousness of the distance of his game, so that he may avoid, on the one hand, taking it too close for its fair appearance, in due course, on the table; and, on the other, too far to admit of a clean kill.

A remarkable comparison

It is both interesting and salutary to take a closer look at what all this means in practical terms. It can best be done by pictorial comparison with the performance of a rifle of similar power, as in the diagram on p. 206. An ordinary charge of 1⅛ oz of No. 6 shot fired from a 12-bore gun has a muzzle energy of about 1760 ft-lb. This is roughly the same as the muzzle energy of a bullet from a popular stalking rifle. The 160 grain bullet of the ·256 Mannlicher Schönauer cartridge, for example, has a nominal muzzle energy of 1880 ft-lb.

In the diagram, therefore, which shows energy in terms of range, the bullet and the charge of shot start at more or less the same place. But whereas the bullet, as represented by the top curve, retains more than half its original energy at 300 yds, the shot-charge, represented by the next curve (a) has lost this much at 20. At 50 yds, it has less than a quarter of its energy left.

What is more, if instead of considering the total energy of the shot-charge, we consider the proportion capable of being brought to bear by a fully choked gun on a game bird, with a vulnerable area of, say, 20 sq. in., we get the remarkable situation represented by the third curve (b). It shows that, of the original energy of 1760 ft-lb, only about 20 is available on the target at 30 yds. Beyond that distance, the amount is too small to be shown on a

diagram of the scale dictated by the rifle bullet. Calculation suggests, however, that at 50 yds, there is only a trifle more than 2 ft-lb available on target.

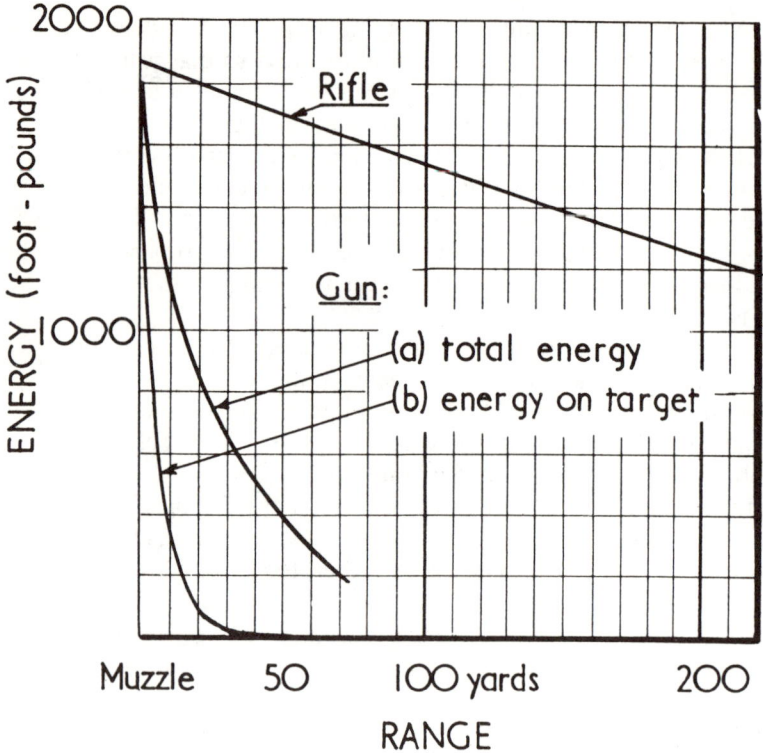

RIFLE AND SHOTGUN COMPARED   The loss of energy by the shot charge is relatively
so rapid that good range-estimation is clearly essential.

Looking at the diagram with a comprehending eye, one cannot fail to
get the impression that, as compared with the sustained deadliness of the
rifle bullet, the charge of shot is a mere puff of smoke. I would not press the
analogy to the point of belittling the devastating power of the shotgun at
close range, but it nevertheless has certain validity. Indeed, if only the size of
shot is small enough, it begins to approximate closely to the truth. Ordinary
dust shot cannot be relied on to penetrate common 20-mil cardboard at
10 yds; and I doubt if a charge of genuine lead dust (as opposed to so-called
dust shot, around three-hundredths of an inch in diameter) would even travel
that distance.
    A basic ballistical truth comes up here, and is well worth mentioning. *It
is that the distances travelled by different sizes of round shot for a given loss of*

velocity are proportional to their diameters. This, of course, offers immediate encouragement to devotees of the larger shot sizes, and it is undoubtedly true that very large shot will occasionally score kills at distances at which the more popular sizes would hardly penetrate skin-deep. Yet the loss of pattern involved imposes a reliance on flukes and acceptance of the possibility that the game concerned may go off merely wounded, however accurate the shooting. This is not sport. Nothing can relieve the regular sportsman of the responsibility for cultivating his judgment of distances, and his ability to decide instantly when a bird is far enough away to be shootable without spoiling it for the table, and yet not so far away as to be beyond the reasonable reach of his gun.

Useful practice

It is not easy. On my walks, I frequently stop and say, 'How far to that tree?' —and then, having made my estimate, I carefully pace the distance. The practice is undoubtedly useful, but results discourage complacency. A Hampshire correspondent writes, 'This morning, I put a decoy pigeon on a stick, and approached it from three different directions, each time marking

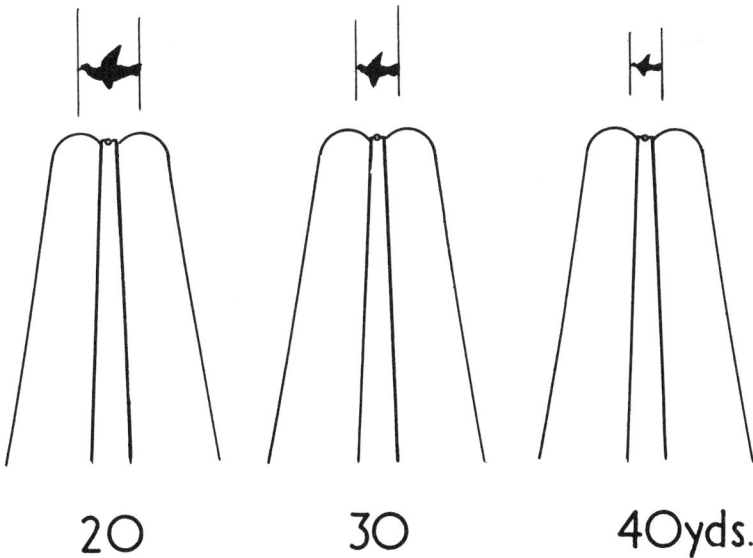

20   30   40yds.

A ROUGH AND READY RANGE-FINDER   The illustration shows the appearance of a wood pigeon at various distances in relation to the muzzle of a 28-inch 12-bore.

the place when I estimated I was 50, 45 and 40 yds away. I then measured the distances with a tape measure.

'At an estimated 50 yds, I was 41 yds away.

At an estimated 45 yds, I was 38 yds away.

At an estimated 40 yds, I was 38 yds away.

'I finally estimated when I was 50 yds away from an oak tree, and measured it to be 43 yds.'

But my correspondent was an experienced sportsman, and his estimates, if not impressively accurate, were at least conservative. The trouble comes when the inexperienced optimist imagines that 60 or 70 yds is still within his reach. And if it is not easy to estimate these distances on the ground, it is really difficult to estimate them in the air. The best guide I can think of is to use the muzzle of the gun as a basis for comparison. In my drawing on page 207, I have shown carefully to scale what a pigeon looks like in relation to the muzzle of a 12-bore with 28-in. barrels, when the gun is mounted so that the foresight is about 37 in. from the shooter's eye.

67   More About Range

The ability to judge distances is undoubtedly a prime qualification for anyone who wishes to use a shotgun in a sportsmanlike and effective manner; and, as the years roll by, I become increasingly impressed with the need for cultivating this ability at all stages of our experience, especially the earlier ones.

Even at shooting schools, the subject, I suspect, is much neglected. Beginners are taught the elements of safety, gun handling and the technique of lead-and-swing, follow-through and footwork. But how often, I wonder, are they impressed with the shortness of shotgun range, and the need for cultivating an intuitive appreciation of when a bird is within fair shooting distance and when it is not? Very infrequently, I would guess; and still less frequently are they put through any practice in distance judging, or subjected to any tests, or given any of the many tips that help in this important matter.

Yet there is a great deal that could be done in the course of normal instruction. The beginner, say, is practising at clays being thrown over a belt of trees, and his instructor could easily ask him to estimate the height of the trees, and their distance from the stand, and the height of the clays as they come over the shooter, and could correct him from his knowledge. From his intimate acquaintance with the features of the ground, the instructor could often say fairly accurately how far a particular clay was at the moment it was smashed (I am thinking now of walked-up and other low birds), and could ask his pupil to give his opinion. By these and similar means the beginner could be impressed with the importance of judging distances when shooting, and induced to form the habit of doing so on all convenient occasions. In time, this process becomes subconscious and, as it were, instinctive, and enables the mature shooter to decide, more quickly and better than most, whether a bird is too close, nicely shootable, or too far off.

I have little doubt of the reason for this neglect on the part of the shooting schools. It is simply that practice clays are thrown at readily shootable distances, and that, within these distances, range is of no significance where inanimate and inedible targets are concerned. This is because the lead or forward allowance required in such circumstances is substantially proportional to distance, so that the angle of lead, which is what the shooter really goes by, is practically constant for crossing birds of given speed.

Thus, if a target needed a lead of 2 ft at 10 yds, it would need 4 ft at 20 yds, and 6 ft at 30 yds. As will be seen from the sketch below, this represents a constant angle. The shooting school pupil is therefore under no necessity to form any estimate of the distance of the target. Provided he gives it the familiar angular lead, he can cope equally well at all ranges within his limited experience.

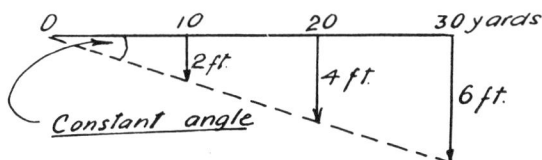

But when he takes the field, and has to deal with birds on offer at extended ranges, his familiar angular lead is no longer adequate. At such ranges, the slowing down of the shot charge becomes sufficiently marked to make it necessary to increase the angular lead, and it is then that the ability to judge distances becomes important. A bird that required a 4 ft lead at 20 yds, as in our first example, and 6 ft at 30 yds would need, not the proportionate 8 ft and 10 ft at 40 and 50 yds, but more like 9 ft and 12 ft. And a shooter with a heavily loaded and fully choked gun who might aspire to a 60-yd bird would need, not 12 ft (being twice the 6 ft allowance assumed for 30 yds) but about 16 ft.

So, even if the shooter has the exceptional skill necessary to step up his angular lead to the extent needed for successful long shots, he cannot apply it unless he has corresponding skill in judging distances. I am sure that I have many a time seen game birds fired at 50 or 60 yds away by good and considerate sportsmen who would be among the first to accept 40 yds as their limiting range. How often I have done the same thing myself I would prefer not to guess. Fortunately, it is seldom indeed that the birds concerned are any the worse for the experience.

An optical illusion

A point that comes up here is the exceptional difficulty of judging the distance of birds high up in the air, and away from any trees or landscape features against which they can be compared. Payne-Gallwey has drawn special attention to this point in connection with high pheasants, and has even committed himself to a graphic comparison indicating that such birds look only about half the size that they do when seen at the same distance horizontally. There is indeed a genuine optical illusion involved, for the explanation of which we are indebted to an eminent Belgian astronomer. He was seeking an explanation of the enormous disparity in apparent diameter between, say, a large, yellow summer moon rising above low trees, and the same moon seen high and brilliant in a frosty winter sky. The reason, he decided, was that we do not instinctively regard the sky as a hemispherical bowl, but as a much-flattened vault, which comes down relatively low above our heads. The reason for this conception is simply that, near the horizon, we see the sky passing behind landscape features which we know are far distant; whereas straight overhead there are no such features, but only clouds, which look, and usually are, far nearer than the remote hills, etc., on the horizon, which give the sky its horizontal scale.

In consequence, the moon, seen low down, presents to the eye the apparent diameter a-b in my sketch below; whereas when it is high overhead, this is reduced to c-d. This familiar illusion would appear to apply equally to high

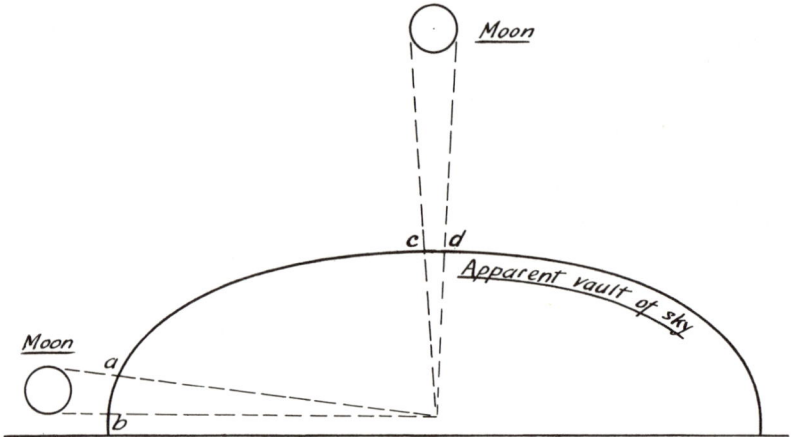

A FAMILIAR ILLUSION EXPLAINED   Birds, as well as the heavenly bodies, look smaller when high overhead.

and low birds, though I must confess myself incapable of extracting any comfort from the fact, except, possibly, that the 'archangels' are not always quite so difficult as they look.

More education needed

But what can be extracted from the foregoing is that all concerned with bringing on the young shooter – shooting school instructors, gun-club coaches, fathers, elder brothers, or what you will – should make more of their opportunities for cultivating their pupil's proficiency in judging distances, and his recognition of its importance to anyone who aspires to full competence with the gun.

And it is not only beginners. Mature shooters whose early education was neglected in this important department, as mine certainly was, are still open to self-improvement. I have made some suggestions to this end in the preceding chapter; and Major Roderick Willett, in an article in *The Field*, has offered some other hints of a very practical kind. One of them, I recall, is that only when the white patches on the neck of a wood pigeon are visible, is the bird fairly shootable.

Section 9

POINTABILITY

'The relationship between vision and the shotgun is one of the most fruitful topics . . .'

68   *What the Eye Sees*

The relationship between vision and the shotgun is surely one of the most fruitful topics on which my correspondents exercise themselves. Small wonder, then, that I find myself returning to it. It crops up in many guises – whether one should aim or not aim; whether this kind of gun is more pointable than that; whether the rib has any real value or function in shooting; whether or not the difficulty that some two-eyed shooters appear to have in using an O/U is pure fancy; and so on. Then there is the subject of the master eye, in all its ramifications; and the 'lazy eye'; and the question of what to advise a reader with a congenital squint, which caught me neatly off my balance.

Not so many years ago, I was a member of the no-nonsense school in these matters. 'When I forget my gun I hit: when I see it I miss,' I might have said, with rhetorical exaggeration. 'All you have to do,' I might have added, 'is to forget your gun entirely, to concentrate on your bird, and to swing right through it, pulling the trigger as you pass' – which remains good advice that I would like to act on more consistently than I do. But what it overlooks is that, however much one may concentrate on the bird, however much one may forget the gun, and however freely one may swing, the gun still has to be *directed* – somehow. It is not enough to swing it just anywhere: it has to be swung in close relationship to the path that is being followed by the target. 'Of course it has,' an expert shooter might say, 'one does it by instinct.' True, it might suffice; but though he may believe that he does not see his gun when he is shooting well, it is an undeniable fact that it comes into his field of view, and that he therefore cannot help seeing it, if only subconsciously; and I have latterly had no doubt that by what he thus sees, he is at least aided in the accurate direction of his weapon. If this were not so, he would be like a man shooting at glow-worms in the dark – entirely dependent on his natural powers of co-ordination.

Our imaginary expert might insist at this stage that that is exactly what he does depend on. In that event, one might reasonably ask him why he, of all men, is the one who attaches most importance to a well-fitting gun, which comes up so accurately and so readily right in line with his master eye. What, indeed, would master eye have to do with his shooting? He uses *both* his eyes, and his natural powers of co-ordination would be no less effective if his master eye were not aligned with his gun. There is no talk of master eye among those who follow sports involving no implement, in which there is total and unmistakable dependence on natural co-ordination.

So, we cannot resist the conclusion that in shooting there is at least some degree of subconscious aiming involved; and this opens the door wide to all the purveyors of theories about ribs, 'single sighting planes' and the like.

215

These same purveyors are a mixture. They include some with respectable theories about raising the subconscious visual impact of the gun to optimum level; some whose notions defy any critical evaluation except as confidence-boosters; and some who, by thoughtlessly repeating the slogan last quoted, unconsciously continue the propaganda of the American arms industry of the 1920s, which, it would seem, was designed to reconcile shooters in the U.S. forever to the mass-produced repeater with its single barrel.

An involuntary experiment

I have said much of this before in one context or another, but two fresh points come up. The first is that, ever since I deserted the no-nonsense school, I have wanted to make an experiment to see just how far a good instinctive shooter is, in fact, dependent on the subconscious view of his gun. To do this would involve some arrangements for making the gun invisible without impairing the visibility of the target – obviously not easy to contrive. But one of my American correspondents, a lawyer, to whom I am indebted for several keen and critical observations on shotguns and their ways, stumbled across a solution. I quote from his letter.

'With regard to your column in the *Shooting Times* of July 19 . . . the comments about the rib and its effects struck right home. For some time I have believed that Churchill was on the right track with his high, narrow rib, and having recently acquired one of his XXV's as well as having Westley Richards install such a rib on my old resleeved Purdey, I think it is beneficial.

'But a few weeks ago, when at Camp Perry, Ohio, for the National Matches, I was having my first experience with International Skeet. It so happened that we kept shooting through dusk, changing to white targets, which, with lights on, were very visible. BUT, as the light failed to the point when I could not see the front sight or rib, it was like navigation in fog without the benefit of compass. The only ones hit gave me the impression of pure accident. I know the pundits say, "If you see the rib you miss", but I was seeing the target clearly, without seeing the rib or the barrels, and missing every time.

'As the light failed further, so the artificial lights showed up the rib and foresight. Confidence came back, and my usual modest performance resumed. It was *most impressive*.'

The elevated-eye technique

My second point is a speculation. It arises on the technique of a certain school of Italians, who shoot with the master eye high above the standing breech –

maybe so high that the cheekbone and jaw, which normally lock over the comb, and locate the eye in a fixed position in relation to the rib, are out of contact with the gun altogether, though sometimes the eye is located by a comb of exceptional height.

This, in its more extreme manifestations, must be regarded as something intermediate between shooting from the hip and shooting in the ordinary style. It must require great accuracy in gun mounting so that the eye, deprived of its normal contact with the stock, occupies an invariable position in relation to the breech. It also requires, naturally enough, that the bird or target shall be taken floating well above the foresight.

The outstanding effect of this technique is to give the shooter a far better view of his gun than he ordinarily gets, whether consciously or subconsciously seen, and perhaps a better sense of its direction. It will also give him a totally unobstructed view of the target in all directions, which may be especially important in live pigeon trapshooting. It was noticed that the winning Italian team at the World Championship meeting at Mexico City in 1966 practised this elevated-eye technique with their double-triggered, side-by-side guns, though whether they, or any of them, abandoned comb-contact I do not know.

Even without such a demonstration, anything that the subtle and ingenious Italians have arrived at is worth attention, and I wonder what scope there may be for a graduated adaptation of this technique, according to the idiosyncrasies of the individual shooter. Does it follow that we are all best suited by having our guns fitted so that we just peep over the standing breech?

The question presents itself to me with special force at the moment, because, this season, I am concentrating on using a gun with a high, built-up comb, provided to cure low shooting. So, although I do not have to take my birds floating well above the foresight, I am getting a splendid bird's-eye view of my barrels, which, though a trifle disconcerting at first, is something that is growing on me. I think it safe to say that anyone with a low-shooting gun that has been cured in this way, or by straightening the stock, whereby he has a better view of his barrels and rib, may end up with a margin of advantage, even though that better view may be only for subconscious consumption.

69   Pointability of the O/U

I am sure that so long as I continue to write about shooting I shall be consulted by readers who, on going over from a side-by-side to an over-and-under gun, find that they can no longer shoot satisfactorily with both eyes open, as they have been accustomed to doing, and who feel impelled to close or dim the non-aiming eye.

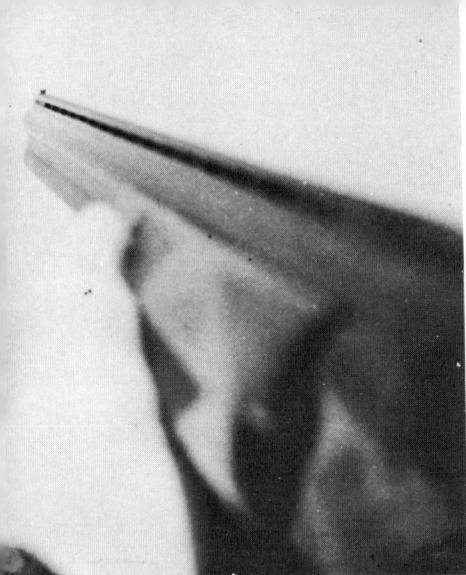

A STUDY IN O/U POINTABILITY Photographs show left- and right-eye views respectively of the gun just as it is coming into position for taking a shot. Note the dominance of the left eye picture, and the dependence of the right eye on a well-matted, non-reflective rib.

The loss of binocular vision is undoubtedly a disadvantage, especially to driven game shots and others who favour the follow-through style of shooting. Not only does it impair the faculty of judging distance, but it means that, when dealing with oncoming birds, the target is lost sight of at a certain stage, being blotted out by the gun. When shooting with both eyes open, on the other hand, the muzzle end of the gun seems to be transparent, and the target continues to be seen, *and in the right relation to the aiming eye and the rib.*

It is now several years since I arrived at what I felt sure was the true explanation of this curious experience, which I myself shared when trying to shoot with an O/U. I believe that when shooting with a side-by-side gun, the dominant visual impression is that received by the aiming eye – the two barrels, the rib, and more especially the two dark grooves that outline the rib. By contrast, the visual impact of the left-hand barrel, seen in side-view by the other eye, is relatively slight.

With an O/U, however, this situation is reversed. The aiming eye sees the rib, which may or may not make a good visual impression – a point to which I will return in a moment; but there can be no doubt that the dominant impression is that made on the non-aiming eye by the side view of the stacked barrels, topped, maybe, by a conspicuous raised and ventilated rib. Since there can be no doubt that we are all aided in pointing a gun by what we consciously or subconsciously see of it, it follows that, when shooting with both eyes open, the one that receives the dominant impression will tend to take charge. Unfortunately, with an O/U, this is the wrong eye.

Photographic evidence

In the two photographs on page 218 I have tried to recapture what the two eyes independently see of a normal O/U. In both cases the camera was focused on a spot just ahead of the foresight, which will be seen to have come out quite sharply. The breech end of the gun, of course, appears completely blurred; and this, together with everything else, is substantially as it would have been seen immediately preparatory to taking a shot.

The dominant impression is undoubtedly that made on the left eye by the side-view. At the same time, it must be allowed that the rib offers an admirably clear and firm guide to the aiming eye; and here comes what, to me, is a new point – or, at least, a new emphasis on an old one. The gun photographed was new: the barrels and rib were deeply blued, and the surface of the rib was the nearest thing I have seen in a mass-produced weapon to a proper file-cut rib. It had been knurled into a surface comprising a vast number of tiny, sharp-pointed pyramids, which prevented the light from the sky just ahead of the gun from being reflected back into the shooter's eye, as represented by the camera.

But few ribs on inexpensive guns are as well knurled as this; and even this one, when the tops of all those little pyramids have been blunted by wear, and made shiny by having their blueing worn off, will not look so dark and conspicuous as it does in the photograph. I have studied some knurled ribs that are almost as reflective as the plain hollow rib shown on p. 197 of *Gough Thomas's Gun Book*, which would have been literally invisible against a grey sky, had it not been for the two dark grooves on either side of it.

A lesson and a question

There is a lesson in this for me, and maybe for some others. It is that the nature of the surface of the rib is far more important in an O/U than it is in a side-by-side. The latter can be as shiny as it likes without losing its visual impact, which it derives from its bordering grooves. But once the former has become shiny it is largely useless as an aid to pointing – a function that the non-aiming eye increasingly tends to take over.

All this may be of little significance to the trapshooter. As he shoulders his gun preparatory to taking his shot, he deliberately aims it at a spot over the trap-house, and by so doing puts his gun expressly under the command of his aiming eye. The foresight and maybe the mid-sight are enough. But not in field shooting, and not in skeet. The lesson mentioned had, no doubt, been fully mastered by the designer of the Browning 'Broadway', which, with its wide rib and two deep, parallel grooves, secures to the O/U an inherent facility of the double.

Students of firearms history, incidentally, may wonder, as I have done, whether there is anything in this question of pointability that would help to explain the curious history of the O/U. It was, as is well known, the earliest form of double gun; and since it was as easy in the muzzle-loading days to make guns one way as it was the other, this choice of the O/U form could not have been dictated by the exigencies of manufacture, but rather by some considerations arising out of practical shooting.

These early O/Us, it must be remembered, were made for shooting deliberately aimed solid ball, and since shooters were normally accustomed to aiming along single barrels, the obvious thing to do with a second barrel was to tuck it away out of sight, where it would not interfere with the familiar view.

But when Henry Nock's patent breech of the 1780s enabled the barrels of flintlocks to be drastically shortened, so that double guns became a practical proposition for wing-shooting, the over-and-under principle was dropped. It was, in fact, dropped so decisively that, with the perfecting of side-by-side breechloaders, and the difficulty of designing breech-loading O/Us of corresponding efficiency, the prospect of the latter staging a revival seemed inconceivably remote. We know that when they were revived it was in an attempt to exploit a novelty, for commercial reasons. The long eclipse of the O/U, dating from the rise of shooting with the double gun, thus remains to be explained; and perhaps the explanation may be found in an early anticipation of the difficulty that many modern field shooters have discovered in adapting themselves to double guns made on this principle. Those who are still trying might do worse than take a critical look at their ribs.

70   Pointability on Trial

In the *Shooting Times* of 20 June 1970, Michael Kemp had an article that strongly attracted my attention. It was entitled, 'Hands not Eyes', and described the technique of a snipe shooter who shot successfully without putting the butt of his gun to his shoulder. In other words, he shot by natural co-ordination, and without any help from the conscious or subconscious aiming of his gun, as commonly understood.

I remember that a friend of mine, long ago, used to shoot rabbits bolting in covert very competently from the hip; and Roger Barlow, the well-known American writer, who insists that he is 'not a particularly good shot at either game or clays', nevertheless shot seven going-away targets straight in this manner. This, he tells me, was when he was working to demonstrate his thesis, 'we shoot where we look'.

There is really nothing astonishing about this. It is an entirely natural process, and is immediately recognisable as the one most frequently employed whenever a tool, implement or weapon has to be directed with precision against a fixed or moving object. The games player does not aim his bat, club, racquet or stick: he simply eyes the ball and leaves the rest to his hands. The carpenter does not aim his hammer at the nail: he just looks at the nail and hits it. Indeed, I wonder what would have happened if shotguns, from their very earliest appearance, had been perfectly adapted to wing shooting, and had been used for nothing else. Would we ever have mounted them at the shoulder in the familiar aiming posture? – or would we have done what would then have seemed to be the natural and normal thing, and pointed them by instinct? Nobody knows: the question is by no means self-answering.

Why then do we make all this fuss about the fitting of our guns? And why do some of our *best* shots make the *most* fuss, even though they are prepared to swear that they totally ignore the gun in the act of shooting – indeed, that they do not even see it?

The answer, which I have more than once pointed out in different con-texts, is that, however accurately a man may be able to shoot by natural co-ordination, he will shoot still better if he invokes the aid of his eye to aim the gun. The fact that the aiming is often – and best – done subconsciously does not detract from its value. Moreover, the value of the aid is two-fold: it not only raises the level of performance but it tends to stabilize it. Michael Kemp's snipe shooter, I noticed, occasionally went hopelessly off his form; and when this took place he had to slog on in the blind hope that it would return. The man who shoots normally from the shoulder also, of course, goes off his form; but he does not go so far off, and is likely to recover earlier. This is because the aiming of his gun, for all that it may be completely sub-conscious, provides him with a basis or datum or guide-line to which his purely muscular co-ordination is to some extent tied by the optical link.

This brings out the need for good gun fitting, because if the datum or guide-line is not true, it will be like a false beacon to a mariner.

An experiment

But just *how much* does subconscious aiming add to the accuracy of our performance? 'Obviously, quite a lot,' I once wrote. But that was only a guess, and I feel that it would be good to know the truth. It would put us in a better position to deal with a variety of questions concerned with raising the efficiency of the shooter and his gun. What we need, then, is a practical experi-ment.

It seems that the question could be fairly answered by a two-part experi-ment on the following lines. The first part would be carried out in more or less total darkness, so that the shooter would not be able to see his gun. He would be asked to take a number of snapshots at a tiny, fixed light-spot on a target at a convenient distance. He would shoot from the shoulder in the ordinary way, and the point of impact of each shot would be marked on the target. The gun should be a thoroughly familiar game gun.

The experiment would then be repeated in daylight, an ordinary aiming mark being used. From the results obtained, the average error for each phase could be worked out. On the understanding that in the daylight phase the shooter would shoot quickly and instinctively, taking no conscious notice of his gun, a comparison of the results would give a fair indication of the value of subconscious visual pointability to the particular shooter, and the extent of the field in which he might seek to profit from attention to gun-fit, type of rib, foresight, etc.

I need hardly say that the experiment could best be carried out with a spotlight projector in the barrel, which is switched on by the falling hammer.

SHOOTING BY NATURAL CO-ORDINATION   Roger Barlow, who insists that he is 'not a particularly good shot' breaks seven targets straight, shooting from the hip. But he breaks more when he shoots from the shoulder.

Some results

Since writing the foregoing, I have had an opportunity of performing such an experiment, using a spotlight projector kindly provided by ASI in one of my regular game guns. I fired 25 snapshots in darkness at a pinpoint of light from a distance of 9 yds, and then another 25 at the same target in daylight. The results are set out in the following table.

	In darkness	*In daylight*
	(natural co-ordination only)	(natural co-ordination plus subconscious aiming)
Average error		
(a) Actual	2·66 in.	1·33 in.
(b) Equivalent at 30 yds.	12 in. (approx.)	6 in. (approx.)

This result, though so pleasantly round, was arrived at by a painstaking analysis of the observations. *It indicates that a man of normal-to-good co-ordination, as I am by ordinary tests, is likely to have his average pointing error halved by his subconscious view of the aiming line of his gun.* Any shooter who imagines, therefore, that he shoots purely by instinct, and that the things that contribute to the visual pointability of a gun mean nothing to him, should start entertaining some doubts.

An incidental but interesting fact that emerges from the test carried out in darkness is that if I had been shooting live rounds, even from a fully choked gun, I should have covered the aiming mark with my pattern circle every time at 30 yds. (The normal spread at this distance is about 27 in.) In view of this, Roger Barlow's seven-straight targets shot from the hip are fully intelligible.

I ought not to close this account without a description of the gun I used, with special reference to its visual pointability. It was, in fact, an AYA XXV, with a Churchill-style rib and a bright silver or electrum foresight decidedly larger than those commonly fitted to best English guns. The sight is a flattened sphere, $\frac{1}{8}$-in. in diameter, and together with the deep, dark grooves outlining the narrow rib, makes the gun decidedly more pointable than it would be if it had a plain hollow rib and a more conventional foresight.

It would be reasonable to assume that these features had some influence on the results obtained in the daylight test, and that without them, the gain in accuracy would have been somewhat less.

Scope for further experiments

There, for the moment, my experimenting has stopped. But if I had the time to follow up this line of enquiry, I should be tempted to try the effect of various aids to pointability – different ribs, different surface finishes on ribs, larger and smaller foresights, mid-sights, and so on. I should expect to find that, as the visual pointability of the gun was stepped up, there would be a reduction in error *up to a point*; but after that, I should expect things to start going into reverse. Once the optimum point had been passed, anything that tended to make the gun more conspicuous in the shooter's field of view would attract conscious attention to it, to the detriment of concentration on the target, or, with the lead-and-swing method, on the appropriate point ahead of it.

RECOIL

'Shooters have long known that two apparently identical guns, firing the same load, can recoil quite differently.'

71   Reducing Recoil

An experienced sportsman came to me the other day asking what he could do to reduce the recoil of his gun, which he was beginning to feel unduly because of advancing years and the onset of some disability. There must be many shooters in the same position – indeed it is one in which most of us are likely to find ourselves if only we live and shoot long enough. There are also many young shooters, as I know full well, who are up against recoil trouble, arising out of their tendency to seek out the most heavily charged cartridges capable of being fired in their guns; so perhaps it would be helpful to take a look at the ways in which recoil can be reduced or its effects minimised.

It must be recognised at the outset that what we are concerned with here is recoil in its broadest sense, as conveying the overall effect of the recoiling gun on the shooter's muscular and nervous organisation – the total effect, in short, to which he is sensible. I call this the 'sensible' recoil to distinguish it from 'dynamic' recoil, which is the recoil measured in the ballistical laboratory, and which is expressed in precise terms, such as the distance by which a standard pendulum gun recoils when firing the load under investigation. Unfortunately, sensible recoil cannot be so expressed.

Dynamic recoil is important, if only because a large dynamic recoil usually means a large sensible recoil. But it is not all-important, because it can be tamed so as to produce relatively little effect on the shooter, as in the case of the gas-operated automatics. Also conditions can exist whereby a load giving but a moderate dynamic recoil can give rise to an objectionable sensible recoil. Again, dynamic recoil takes no account of the effect on the shooter's sense of hearing. Yet this makes a contribution to the general shock of recoil that cannot be ignored.

To get down to practical cases, the first kind to be considered is that of the shooter who has a gun that appears to suit him. All he asks is to be relieved of some of the recoil. If there are no indications of special recoil sensitivity or of the gun recoiling abnormally, the stock answer is to reduce the load. If the gun is an ordinary 12-bore, weighing upwards of 6 lbs, the shooter might be advised to consider the lighter factory loads for this calibre. For example, instead of the $1\frac{1}{16}$ or $1\frac{1}{8}$ oz Grand Prix, he might find sufficient relief by going over to the 1 oz Impax or even the $\frac{7}{8}$ oz Trainer – this last being a neglected cartridge among game shooters, but one capable of giving excellent results against driven game, or pigeon shot over decoys, or any other medium-sized birds taken at moderate range. It has the further merit of being economical. At 35 yds – a good sporting range – a Trainer cartridge in an improved cylinder should give nearly 180 pellets of No. 7 in the 30-in. circle and would thus deal effectively with most of the shots offered in the kind of sport considered.

The average wildfowler firing maximum charges does not often complain about recoil – he probably fires too few cartridges for that; but the youngster who would hardly venture out pigeon shooting with anything less than the $1\frac{3}{16}$ oz Maximum, which he fires, maybe, from a light single-barrelled gun, often gets off a good many shots, and suffers painfully in consequence. In his case, the stock remedy of some reduction in load is particularly applicable. He should recognise that the loss of effective range brought about by cutting down the shot charge by $\frac{1}{8}$ oz is only about 3 yds – *an amount too small to be appreciated in the air at normal shooting distances.* But it would usually cure his trouble – and (in 1976) save him 57p. a 100 on his cartridges into the bargain.

Importance of fit

But although this prescription of load-reduction may be effective, and may involve no appreciable loss of performance, there may be other things that should be looked into. The first is the fit of the gun. The fact that a shooter has got thoroughly used to a gun does not necessarily mean that it fits him, and there may be advantageous possibilities of modifying the stock in some way so as to reduce the effect of recoil. Bruised arm and cheek can certainly be caused by bad mounting or hold, but they can equally be caused, or at least aggravated, by a badly fitting stock. There seem to be some generally accepted principles here that are worth setting out. Thus:

1.   The straighter the stock a shooter can take, the better from the point of view of recoil. This applies both to bend and cast.
2.   The minimum bend to heel being determined (chiefly by the length of the shooter's neck and the slope of his shoulders), the bend to comb should be the maximum consistent with maintaining the correct height of the aiming eye above the breech.
3.   A level comb is better than a sloping one.
4.   If necessary, 2 and 3 above can be reconciled by a Monte Carlo or Greener Rational stock.
5.   The stock should be as long as the shooter can comfortably take.
6.   A broad, well-rounded butt is better than a narrow, angular one; and a soft rubber recoil-pad better than hard wood or horn.
7.   Bruised second finger is often caused by a stock that is too short. Failing that, it may be caused by an insufficiently firm or prematurely relaxed grip. A semi-pistol grip may help, or even a full one on a single-triggered gun. The trouble is minimised if the trigger guard has a well-sloped rearward curve. Incidentally, little rubber cushions are available for attaching to the guard at this point.

I said that these were generally accepted principles; but since expert gun fitters may differ as to what constitutes the proper stock for a given man, perhaps I should attach an appropriate reservation. They are at least points for critical regard when seeking to minimise recoil.

Heads and ears

So far, I have dealt chiefly with bruising, or the things that in bad cases can lead to bruising. These indeed are the things with which many shooters are principally concerned, particularly if there is some muscular trouble or arthritis in the offing. But other shooters, when they feel themselves beginning to suffer from recoil, feel it mainly in their heads. I do myself. This leads us into some more subtle considerations.

The first is the nature of the shock to the ears. This is chiefly due to muzzle blast, which is less with long barrels than with short. But some repeaters deliver a painful shock to the ears through metallic impact in the receiver, and I have cases of such headaches being caused by the firing of a single shot. And whilst dealing with repeaters and other single-barrelled guns, I should point out that although muzzle-brakes are effective in reducing dynamic recoil, they increase the effect of muzzle-blast on the shooter's ears, and in ear-sensitive cases this might even nullify the prospective benefit.

I have previously pointed out that the rate of rise of pressure in the gun, and therefore against the shooter's shoulder, can have a marked effect on sensible recoil. In consequence, the same shot load driven at the same velocity by two different powders can produce different values of sensible recoil. Contrary to what might be expected, it is the faster-burning powders that produce the least sensation, *other things being equal*. For the experimental evidence and a full explanation I must refer interested readers to my *Shotguns and Cartridges*. All I can add here is the suggestion that, in case of trouble, it is worth trying different brands of cartridges carrying the same load.

Shooters have long known that two apparently identical guns, firing the same load, can recoil quite differently. For example, a slight local enlargement of the bore just in front of the chamber cone can produce a very heavy sensible recoil. So can an exaggerated headspace clearance. In *Gough Thomas's Gun Book* I have quoted several cases, including that of a robust young shooter who found that ten normal cartridges in moderately rapid succession were as much as he could stand firing from an ordinary game gun. Yet, when he built up the heads of the cartridges with metal foil in accordance with my suggestion, the excessive recoil disappeared. The recoil of a given gun is therefore not necessarily typical of others of the same type and weight.

72 *Avoiding Punishment*

There must be more shooters in trouble with recoil than one would imagine.

For example, one of my Scottish correspondents was suffering from bruising on the angle of his jaw, where he had actually developed a painful cyst of extravasated blood called a hæmatocele. I recommended him to take medical advice with a view to having this removed, and thereafter to have his gun refitted on lines I suggested.

Another case arose as a comment on this one, and came from a Windsor correspondent, whose letter I quote.

'I had a similar problem at one time,' he says, 'and my family doctor advised me either to cure the trouble or give up shooting.

'The perfect cure, I found, was a matched, fitted and glued Monte Carlo cheek-piece, with a *forward* slope on the comb of at least 5 degrees from the line of sight. This compares with the average slope on a normal stock of 5 degrees *rearward*.

'The reversal of this angle is enough to cause the comb to drop away from the cheek under recoil, and enables me to shoot $2\frac{3}{4}$-in. magnums without a qualm, even with careless gun mounting under rough field conditions.'

This is a good point. It is well known that guns with deeply bent stocks are inclined to bruise the shooter's face, and it is usually assumed that this is because of their greater upward jump on recoil. But it is clear that, even if the gun comes straight back, the cheek-bone takes a blow from a normal stock, though not from one with a reverse slope on the comb. My sketch should make this clear.

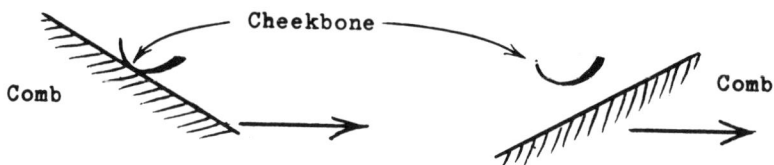

Cheekbone receives blow from comb with normal slope, but not when slope is reversed.

The principle concerned was, I believe, understood in the muzzle-loading days, and guns of that period may occasionally be seen with combs that slope upwards to the rear.

But it must be recognised here that my Scottish correspondent and the one from Windsor have been suffering from different complaints. The former had bruising on the angle of his jaw, which, in my opinion, could only come about from a side-blow, whereas the latter suffered bruising of the cheekbone, which required a vertical blow.

My sketch below should make the distinction clear. It shows that the human skull has a more or less right-angled recess, padded with flesh, into which the stock of a correctly fitted gun neatly fits. The horizontal part of this recess is formed by the malar projection or cheekbone. The vertical part is formed by the flank of the jaw. So, although my Windsor correspondent's prescription seems to be an admirable one for curing bruising of the face – that is, of the cheekbone – it is unlikely to cure bruising of the jaw. For that, I relied mainly on getting rid of the hæmatocele and adopting an American-style fitting, with rather more bend and no cast-off. The effect of this would be as shown in the illustration. The head would lean more over to the left; and although the stock would still be snugged into the face, the angle of the jaw would be more out of harm's way. It will not be overlooked that a strongly cast-off gun, coming straight back, will tend to bruise the jaw in the same way that a strongly bent one will tend to bruise the cheekbone.

A cure for recoil

My remaining case did not involve any question of fit, but merely of excessive recoil. It concerned one of the old BSA double 12-bores in the possession of an Irish sportsman, who found the recoil to be unduly severe with a normal charge. I suspected the trouble to be excessive headspace clearance, and recalled the case described on page 229, on the strength of which I put up to my

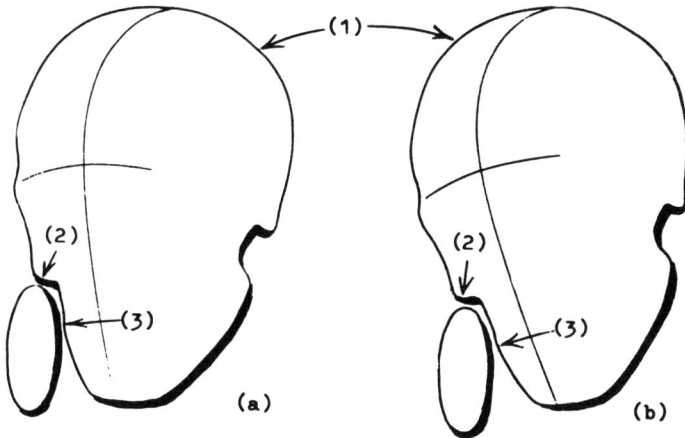

REDUCING IMPACT ON THE JAW BY AMERICAN STYLE FITTING   1. outline of skull; 2. malar or cheekbone; 3. flank of jaw.

Irish correspondent a suggestion for a permanent cure. This was simply to solder two thin discs or shims of steel, of appropriate thickness, to the standing breech. For experimental purposes, and to make sure that they cleared the opening arc, I suggested that they might be secured temporarily with Araldite. In case anyone interested is not familiar with this remarkable stuff, I would say that it is a synthetic resin adhesive, obtainable everywhere, with an astonishing capacity for sticking metal to metal, provided that the surfaces have been carefully degreased.

My correspondent duly reported:

'I fixed two 10/1000 inch discs, slightly less in diameter than the base of the cartridge, to the breech face, using Araldite. It was quite easy to locate them by dropping the tumblers and fitting the holes in the discs over the firing pins. I wiped the excess adhesive away very carefully and closed the breech on two empty cases.

'It required a very definite "clonk" to close the breech on my paper reloads, but the factory loaded, plastic Impax fitted beautifully, with no discernible clearance when the gun was shaken fore and aft.

'The result is most gratifying. The gun now shoots "as sweet as a nut". Shooting at "Coke" tins from the Webley launcher gave no sense of recoil at all.'

I must confess to being pleased with this trick, which seems to be highly successful in appropriate cases – so much so as to be worth some further consideration of the best way to perform it. I would apply a crinkled lead-foil crusher to the head of my familiar cartridge, and after closing the gun would 'mike' the thickness of the crusher to ascertain the maximum permissible thickness of the steel disc or shim, which I would make of corresponding gauge.

If the gun were fitted with disc-inset strikers, I should be inclined to hard-solder the shims to the striker discs, and would hope that there would be no possibility of any kind of dirt accumulating behind the shim and lifting it off the face of the breech. Pending the assurance of experience, soft solder might be safer, and would be the obvious choice for permanently attaching the shims to a plain breech face.

73   Automatic Shotguns and Recoil

Arising out of something I wrote on automatic shotguns, a shooter has come up with a question involving an attractive mixture of theory and practice concerning these weapons. He is the owner of a recoil-operated 12-bore – one of the long-recoil type, as exemplified by the original F.N. Browning five-shot, from which, following some ill-advised adjustment or lubrication or both, he had experienced punishing recoil. By the time he raised the matter with me, he had overcome his trouble, but it had left a very pointed question in his mind which he put to me for an answer. What he said in effect was this — 'I can understand that automatics can soften the effect of recoil, but if they fail to do that, how is it possible for them to recoil more than an ordinary gun? It seems that Newton's laws of motion aren't always true.'

This was by no means the first time in my experience that Newton has been called to account on some question of recoil. The particular law concerned is that which is usually interpreted by shooters as requiring that the weight of the gun multiplied by the speed of its recoil shall always be equal to the weight of the charge multiplied by the speed of its departure. If indeed this were always true, then it would seem that an ordinary gun with a fixed breech, firing a given charge, would have the greatest possible recoil for one of its weight. An automatic, in which some part of the recoil energy is absorbed in working the mechanism, can readily be imagined as recoiling less strongly; but if, under the worst possible conditions, none of the recoil energy were so absorbed, it would seem that the automatic would be back on all-fours with the ordinary gun. Where, then, does the extra recoil energy come from? A nice question.

Before attempting to answer it, we must take a look at the kind of gun concerned. Basically, it consists of two parts: a barrel and a receiver. The receiver is fitted with a stock at one end and a magazine tube at the other, and the barrel is arranged to slide on this tube, there being a strong spring to hold it in the forward position except in the act of firing, when the barrel recoils, working the breech mechanism in the process. The only other practical feature of which we need to take any cognizance for present purposes is a friction device, the purpose of which is to impede or limit the freedom with which the barrel can slide over the tube. In the case of the F. N. Browning mentioned there is a split and bevelled bronze friction ring and a steel ring bevelled on one face and plane on the other. By alternative assemblies a greater or lesser amount of friction can be introduced, according to whether standard or heavy-load cartridges are being used. The amount of friction can also be much influenced by the degree of lubrication — *so can the recoil*. Indeed, the makers of this particular weapon say that 'if the kick of the gun seems too violent, oil the tube less and use the friction ring. If the recoil is insufficient (as evidenced by failures to eject) take away the friction ring and oil the tube more abundantly.'

All this provides a good indication of where recoil energy is absorbed in long-recoil automatics, and of what my correspondent had been doing to increase the recoil of his gun; but it still does not explain how the recoil can possibly be more than that of an ordinary gun with a fixed breech. Yet it provides a clue; and the clue is to be found in the fact that the barrel recoils to some degree independently of the gun as a whole.

Momentum v. energy

It will be remembered that Newton's law above-mentioned requires that the weight multiplied by the speed of recoil of an ordinary gun shall be equal to the weight multiplied by the speed of the issuing charge. But weight multiplied by speed is momentum, not energy. So, when Newton's law requires that the momentum of the gun and the charge shall be the same, it must not be taken to mean that their energies are the same ... which is just as well, because if they were, a gun would do equal damage at both ends. Actually, the recoil energy of the gun is less than the energy of the charge in inverse proportion to their relative weights. So, if the charge weighs 1 oz and the gun weighs 100 oz, the recoil energy will be only $\frac{1}{100}$ of the energy of the charge as it leaves the muzzle.

But when we leave the fixed-breech gun and come to consider the recoil-operated automatic, we have a different picture. In the latter weapon, what starts to recoil as the charge is ignited is predominantly the barrel. Indeed, if it were not for the friction device and the recoil spring, the parts of the gun with which the shooter makes contact, namely, the stock, the receiver and the fore-end, would not commence to recoil at all. The barrel would merely slide freely back on the magazine tube until something stopped it, and it will be helpful to consider what would happen in that event.

Let us say, for the sake of simplicity, that the barrel weighs 3 lbs and the whole gun 6 lbs, the charge weighing 1 oz, as before. In that case, the recoil energy of the barrel would be, not $\frac{1}{100}$ of the charge energy, but twice that, or $\frac{1}{50}$. And if, when the barrel came up against its stop, it transmitted the whole of its energy to the receiver, *the gun would recoil with precisely twice the energy of a fixed breech gun of the same weight, firing the same load.*

Practical considerations

In practice, of course, things are never as bad as that. However much oil is put on the magazine tube, and however incorrectly or inappropriately the braking device is assembled, there will always be some friction. There will be more in the breech mechanism; and finally, when the barrel and the associated moving parts are arrested, their energy is never wholly transmitted: some part of it will always disappear as heat. But it remains a fact that, unless there is a due absorption by friction of the barrel's recoil energy, the amount finally transmitted to the gun, and thence to the shooter's shoulder, can substantially exceed what would be developed by a fixed-breech gun of the same weight. Incidentally, it will be noticed that, in arriving at this conclusion, we have done no violence to Sir Isaac Newton or his Laws of Motion.

Other applications

The principle explained accounts for other forms of unpleasantness occasionally to be observed in firearms. If, owing to excessive headspace clearance in a rifle, or to a shotgun being too deeply rimmed or off the face, the cartridge case gets a free run back to the head of the bolt, or to the standing breech, recoil may be much augmented. This is without invoking extreme cases in which the weapon is damaged. The point is that here, as in the recoil-operated shotgun, there is something which recoils independently of the gun as a whole; and being relatively very light it acquires a high kinetic energy, which, subject to losses, is duly delivered up to the gun. I have previously quoted several cases of excessive recoil in shotguns arising in this way.

Herein lies the explanation, or one of the explanations, of the reduced recoil of French sliding-breech guns of the Darne type. In these guns there is a compressive breech closure which positively takes up all clearance between the cartridge head and the breech face, whereby recoil is reduced to the minimum of which a fixed breech gun is capable.

TROUBLES, PROBLEMS AND DANGERS

'The thing that limits the safe life of any good, honestly-made gun is not the fair wear and tear it has had, but outstandingly the abuse or neglect it may have suffered.'

'Ah me! What perils do environ,
The man that meddles with cold iron.'
(Butler, *Hudibras*)

74 Accident!

Considering the number of shotguns in use, the extreme variations that exist in their quality and condition, and the inevitable proportion of ignorant and careless users, the accident rate is remarkably low. This may be seen as a tribute to the manufacturers of guns and ammunition, as well as to the vigilance of men's guardian angels.

Still, accidents happen; and just as the passengers on a liner are supposed to know their boat drill, so should shooters carry at the back of their minds the proper way to act if ever they have the misfortune to be involved in a gun accident, whether as a responsible agent, a victim, or merely as a witness.

Two broad categories of accident at once appear, according to whether or not fault is attributable to the gun or ammunition concerned. Where somebody has been hurt, the immediate concern is, of course, first-aid. I daresay that most of us, at one time or another, have been taught the elements of this subject – how to stop arterial bleeding and how to treat shock. But if we do not know, or have forgotten, we certainly ought to find out.

Insurance

Another matter for immediate concern arises on insurance. Every shooter, unless he is uncommonly imprudent, will be insured against third party claims. For all that, anyone who has had the misfortune to injure another should beware of the access of remorse which, especially in a man of generous spirit, may make him only too ready to take all the blame on himself. Sober reflection may make it clear that the injured party, or somebody or something else, contributed very materially to the accident; but by that time, the man primarily responsible may have gravely prejudiced his position, for which his insurance company would not thank him. Decent, gentlemanly feeling may indeed require expression of profound regret, but not necessarily an admission of liability, which will in any case be barred by the terms under which he freely accepted insurance.

During the last war, we had an official poster which said, 'Careless talk costs lives.' Here we might say, 'Careless words cost thousands', or may do, if a nasty case comes to court. Anything, for example, that the hapless shooter may have said that could be interpreted as indicating that he knew his gun to be defective, could be highly damaging.

Incidentally, I wonder how many owners of high-class guns are *adequately* covered for loss or damage. Two of my friends were, and were very glad of the fact when one of them had his gun burgled, and the other lost his barrels.

Safety in vigilance

Coming now to the gun and its ammunition, accidents may be actual or potential, and the importance of recognising the potential accident is worth special emphasis. It may save a life.

No abnormality in gun or cartridge can safely be ignored: no dent, bulge, crack or sign of weakness in barrels or action; no unusual report, or excessive recoil, or abnormal deposit in the bores; no failure or partial failure of the breech-locking, safety or trigger mechanisms but should be investigated.

Some of these potential accidents are hair-raising experiences. A man puts up his gun at a bird and pulls the trigger. Click! – nothing happens. Thinking that he has forgotten to reload, he relaxes and lowers the gun, and is about to open it when it goes off of its own accord – harmlessly, we may hope. Another, having fired his right barrel, attempts to fire his left. But the trigger will not budge, despite the hard tug he involuntarily gives it. When he looks, he finds that the safety catch is on, and thinks that he must have put it on inadvertently. So, unguardedly, he slips it off, whereupon his left barrel fires without his touching the trigger.

A wildfowler with a repeater, having finished shooting, pumps the gun dry, points it at the ground and pulls the trigger, whereupon it goes off, and blows a big hole in the earth at the feet of his companion, who happens to be his wife.

These are not imaginary cases, but each time there was a possibility – I would not like to put it higher than that – that the danger could have been foreseen and prevented.

The first incident was due to a hangfire – an insidious thing, because a modern shooter, using good cartridges, can shoot all his life without experiencing a single instance, and is almost certain to be unprepared for it when it happens. But in the case concerned, there had been four of them with a certain foreign cartridge, which, by the really excessive unburnt residue it left in the barrel, could have been recognised as probably having faulty ignition and being prone to hangfires.

If the shooter is sufficiently alert to recognise the possibility that he has a hangfire on his hands, and not to think, as most of us would, that he has forgotten to load, he should keep his gun firmly shouldered while he counts ten, and then lower it quickly down to his side before he opens it.

The second incident was due to two minor maladjustments in the safety mechanism. The first was a weak spring or the equivalent, which allowed the catch to be thrown back by the recoil of the first barrel; and the second was an undue clearance between the safety block and the trigger, which allowed the scar to be very nearly cleared of the bent by a strong pull. If the shooter had previously noticed this tendency on the part of the safety catch to throw back (it is a common trouble) he should have had it put right.

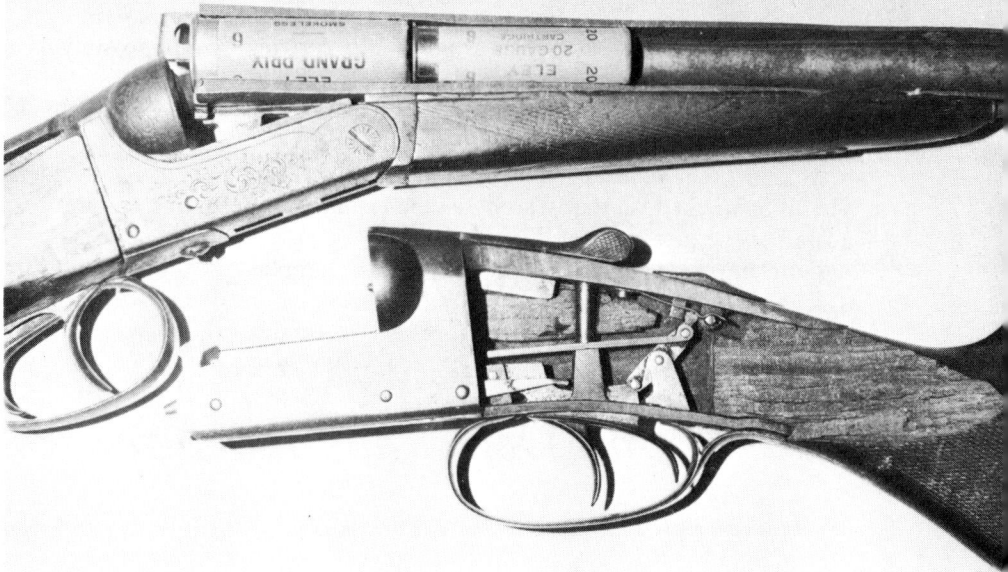

(*Top*) A 12-bore gun with barrel sectioned to show how a 20-gauge cartridge can be inadvertently loaded in front of a 12-gauge and remain lodged and unnoticed in front of the chamber. This is one of the commonest causes of serious gun accidents. (*Bottom*) The effect of firing an unduly heavily loaded cartridge in a boxlock gun. The head of the stock has been dangerously splintered.

The third incident was probably due to a worn, jammed or faulty extractor, which failed to withdraw the potentially fatal cartridge left in the chamber. It may have failed previously – I do not know – but if it had, the moral needs no underlining.

Prudent procedure

Where an accident has been caused by the bursting or other failure of the gun, an independent and authoritative report on the cause is desirable and may be necessary. For this purpose, the damaged gun, together with all parts that can be found, should preferably be impounded by an independent witness and sent just as they are to one of the Proof Houses, together with the remains of the fired cartridge and any others from the same box, as well as the box itself. On no account should the gun be cleaned.

The gun should be accompanied by a report giving all antecedent circumstances capable of affecting whether any obstruction, such as mud, snow, cleaning material or a component from a faulty cartridge, could possibly have entered, or been left in, the bore.

If the cartridges were home-loads, particulars of the charges used should be given, and representative samples sent.

A good point that has been made is that the exact spot of the accident should be marked, so that search may be resumed, if necessary, for any part missed at the first attempt.

If a claim for compensation is pending, the suppliers of the gun and cartridges should be notified of the circumstances, so that if they desire, they may inspect the exhibits while they are in the custody of the proof authority.

75   A Bad Defect and its Cure

An Irish correspondent came to me in trouble recently because his new gun — a well-known model by an English maker — was found to shoot low. This might not have mattered very much if it had been his only gun, because he might have learned always to shoot high enough to compensate for its defect. But it was not his only gun: he had others that did not shoot low, and so he rightly returned the gun to the makers for re-regulation. Unfortunately, whatever they did to it had little or no effect, and so I was reduced to advising him to have the stock straightened, or to add height to the comb by means of an indiarubber comb-raiser.

This incident, and others, have made me wonder whether gunmakers are normally prepared and equipped to alter the point of impact of the charge in relation to the point of aim. One at least of our more celebrated makers has frankly admitted that this is a matter to which nobody in the past appears to have paid much attention. I am sure that this is so, and it is significant that Burrard makes no reference to it that I can find in *The Modern Shotgun*. Nor do other authorities who might have been expected to do so.

For all that, accuracy in a shotgun is an important merit. True, owing to the statistical fact that far more birds are missed under than are missed over, it is advantageous to have a gun that throws its charge well up to the mark. But a low-shooting one, particularly if it is used turn-and-turn about with others free from this defect, can play the devil with performance. It is not simply a matter of missing, but also of reducing range and effectiveness through the consistent use of the upper, marginal part of the pattern instead of the denser, central region.

If, as it appears, the gun trade has been generally neglectful of acquiring tricks for correcting low shooting, it is probably because one of them — the straightening of the stock — is normally effective and acceptable to the shooter. This process, by raising the comb, raises the shooter's cheekbone, and with

it his eye; and since the eye is the gun's backsight, the effect is the same as that
of raising the backsight of a rifle.

But once again, if the shooter uses several guns, straightening the stock of
one of them to cure low shooting may not be entirely acceptable. One of its
side-effects is to give the shooter a more elevated view of his gun rib — maybe
an admirable and advantageous thing to a one-gun man, but a possible source
of a feeling of unfamiliarity and of being ill-fitted to another. Better for the
gunmaker to be prepared to alter the point of impact of the charge centre by
operating on the gun. This may be a much more subtle process.

Since the advent of the variable choke and changeable choke tubes, American gunmakers in particular have become accustomed to rectifying the low
shooting commonly brought about by such contrivances by the simple
expedient of giving the barrel a slight upward spring or set. This can also be
done with double guns provided that the barrels have been assembled by
hard soldering, as most Continental guns are. But in this country we have
good reasons for preferring to assemble our barrels by soft soldering, and I
can well imagine that a gunmaker would be reluctant to try springing barrels
put together in this way.

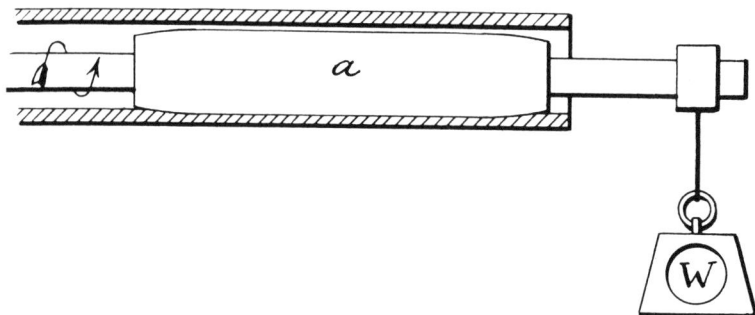

A REMEDY FOR LOW SHOOTING   Formation of an eccentric recess for regulating
point of impact of shot charge. The loosely fitting lead lap (*a*), dressed with oil
and emery, is pressed against one side only of the bore, as suggested by the
weight (*W*).

A more sophisticated trick, but one hardly applicable to a finished gun, is
to alter the distribution of metal in the barrel. This modifies the vibrations
that take place on firing, and can have a most pronounced effect on the point
of impact. For example, I have two guns — same make, same model and substantially identical. But one of them shoots nicely high and the other badly
low, and my performance with the low-shooter fully demonstrates the evil of
its peculiarity. Yet the only difference I have been able to detect between these
two guns is that, in striking up the barrels of the low shooter, the barrel

maker left appreciably more metal forward, so that the point of balance of these barrels is $\frac{1}{2}$ in. nearer to the muzzle than it is in the others. A trifling difference, maybe, but it cost me at least twenty pheasants before I spotted it.

Yet another trick is eccentric choking, which may be known to English gunmakers, though I have never seen an example of it except on a foreign gun. This was a jug, or recess, or Fairburn type of choke, *applied to the under-side of the bore only*. It looked as if it could have been done very easily by working with a *loosely fitted* lead lap, weighted or otherwise biased as indicated on page 243. The gun gave good, consistent patterns, delivered well high, though what it would have done without its eccentric jug-choke, I could only guess.

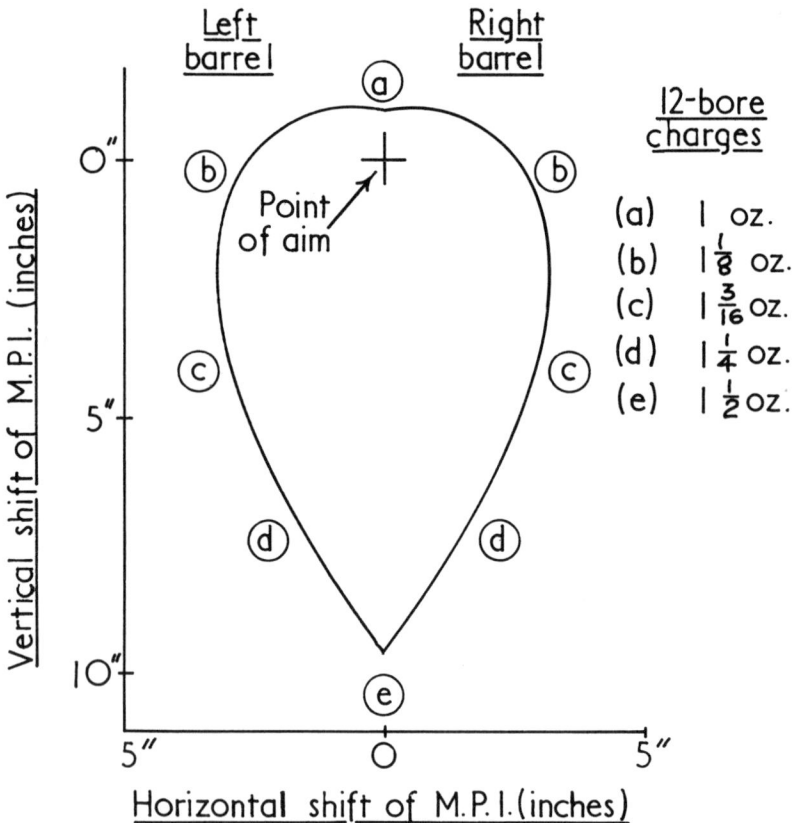

HOW HEAVY LOADS MAY AFFECT ACCURACY   Notional diagram indicating possible changes in mean point of impact of charge centre of a $2\frac{3}{4}$-inch 12-bore gun with various loads at 40 yards.

However, this is a simple and cheap operation to carry out on any gun, and its value as a regulating device deserves to be better appraised and its application better understood. Every shooter should know, not only *how* his gun shoots, but *where* it shoots, and he should not lightly suffer one that shoots low.

Incidentally, guns are best tested for point of impact at 20 yds., at which range the pattern centre is more easily identified than it is at 40.

Load v. accuracy

As previously mentioned, young aspirants often write to me asking what is the most powerful cartridge that they can safely fire in their guns, evidently in the belief that success in shooting is proportional to the weight of lead that they can throw into the sky. Not only do they fail to recognise how little extra range is conferred by magnum loads – only 2 or 3 yds for every extra $\frac{1}{8}$ oz – but how adversely the accuracy of shooting may be affected. They should realise that *every increase of load beyond a certain point causes a gun to shoot progressively lower, whereby the densest part of the pattern, by which a bird might otherwise be struck, may pass completely beneath it.*

This situation is represented by the diagram on page 244, which shows the variation that may be expected in the mean point of impact of various charges when fired from the same gun. There is nothing specific about this diagram – guns are highly variable in this connection – but it fairly shows the sort of behaviour of which every gun should be suspected failing proof by trial to the contrary.

76   Do Guns Tire?

A letter from a Buckinghamshire correspondent raises a question that worries many users and prospective buyers of old guns, as he testifies, and it is evidently one that can do with an airing.

'I read in a book on pigeon shooting a few days ago,' he says, 'that it was better to buy a cheap new gun than even a good second-hand one, the argument being that a new boxlock at around £100 was safer than one of the other kind.

'The author went on to say that there was a considerable number of old guns about which in his opinion were coming to the end of their life, and he fully expected to hear of a growing number of accidents due to failure of these guns in the not too distant future. I don't think the word "fatigue" was mentioned in the book, but that was obviously what was meant. I suppose that fatigue is as likely to set in in a gun barrel as in any other piece of metal, and as far as I know no gunmaker does a fatigue check on guns that come in to him for overhaul.

'What *is* the life of a best gun in normal circumstances and given good maintenance?'

Fatigue, so called, is, of course, a well-known phenomenon in metals. Also, some metals can in certain circumstances undergo degenerative changes quite spontaneously. But because of the tempting analogy between these things and human fatigue and ageing, they are the subject of much loose thinking and even looser expression. 'Metal,' says a well-known writer in one of his shooting books, 'tires with age and use, and becomes subject to fatigue.' That is putting things in the woolliest possible terms, and as a general statement is simply not true. For example, at breakfast this morning we were using some table implements that have been in daily use for the best part of 200 years. Were they tired or suffering from fatigue? I would defy anyone to prove it.

Fatigue in metals

One must first be clear as to what is meant by fatigue in this context. It can be defined as a condition induced in metals by repeated fluctuations or reversals of stress, whereby a specimen may fail at a load considerably lower than that which it is capable of steadily sustaining.

If we take a number of similar test-pieces from a particular sample of metal and subject them to long-continued stress-cycles, diminishing in intensity from one test-piece to another, we find what common sense would suggest – that the ones more highly stressed fail after fewer repetitions than the others. We also find what is most significant for our present purpose – that unless the stress exceeds a certain limit, called the fatigue limit, it is impossible to procure failure of the specimen, no matter how many times the stress cycle may be repeated. So, it is not age that induces fatigue in metal, nor is it use, as such, but only *repeated stressing above the fatigue limit*. If, therefore, a mechanical part is never stressed beyond this limit, and is preserved from other sources of deterioration, it may continue indefinitely in service without any increased risk of failure. It would be very nice if we could be assured that this applies to all parts of a good gun when preserved from abuse, but unfortunately there is no such assurance, for at least three reasons.

First, if a part is stressed *beyond* the fatigue limit for more than a certain number of times, the metal may suffer damage to its internal structure whereby it may subsequently fail *within* the fatigue limit.

Again, the fatigue limit can be much reduced by bad design of parts, for example, by abrupt changes in stressed sections; or by bad workmanship, such as a scratch or score across the surface of such a section. Thus, a barrel scored in the rib groove may pass proof, but may subsequently fail in service; and a spring, however well tempered, will soon snap if it has a file-mark on its outer edge.

And lastly, gun designers cannot know what are the fatigue limits of the various stress-bearing parts of a gun. There are no *in situ* tests for fatigue, and even formal tests on prepared steel test-pieces may require millions of stress-cycles to establish the fatigue limit with any certainty. The only fatigue tests possible with a gun are therefore the tests imposed by service – a point to which I will return.

Degenerative changes

I said just now that, in certain circumstances, some metals could undergo degenerative changes of their own accord – that is, by mere process of time. This is true of the medium-carbon steels such as are used for making gun barrels. The risk of a gun barrel failing through this cause may be extremely remote, but I know of no grounds on which it can be totally excluded.

The subject is a very technical one, but the broad principle can be easily explained.

We all know that it is possible to dissolve more sugar in hot water than it is in cold. Also that if we dissolve as much as possible in hot water, giving what is called a saturated solution, the solution will become super-saturated as it cools, and the surplus sugar will take the first opportunity of crystallizing out. Similarly, certain elements can exist in saturated solution in hot, fluid steel, and can give rise to a super-saturated solid when the steel is cold. In the course of time, these solutions break down with the precipitation of sub-microscopic particles of the dissolved elements, whereby the steel may suffer an increase in hardness and a big loss of impact strength.

This is what is called precipitation hardening. There are other and similar changes possible in gun steels, but it would give a false impression to enlarge on them. World-wide experience over generations justifies confidence that the processes, and, perhaps, the time involved between the making of the steel and the proving of the finished gun barrels fairly eliminated any risk of failure from these causes.

Indefinite life

One thing can be said with assurance, and that is that the prognostications of the author quoted by my correspondent are based on false premises. The guns in regular use today are of all ages, from the earliest central-fire hammer guns to the latest post-war productions. There is no dominant age-group approaching a dangerous senescence, and therefore no impending epidemic of failures. The number of guns of all ages and grades that fail in normal service, other than those that have suffered abuse or neglect, or improper repair, or some obstruction in the barrel, is utterly negligible, and the possibility of their so doing is well inside the margin of acceptable risk.

It must be recognized that the modern sporting gun is the product of a long, harsh and testing process of evolution, in the course of which materials, designs and dimensions have been proved to the limit. Further, among some of the oldest of the high quality guns still in service are many – I could probably say very many without risk of exaggeration – that, in their day, have fired more cartridges than the average shooter would fire in a century. The noted Boss gun used by Eley for routine cartridge testing fired, I believe, about $1\frac{1}{2}$ million cartridges without significant deterioration. This is as many as a fairly active modern game shooter would fire in, say, 500 to 1000 years! And this gun, be it noted, is no freak. It is simply a straight forward, best quality English game gun, such as might have been made by any one of a dozen makers of its period.

So, the answer to my correspondent's straight question is that the life of a best gun in normal circumstances, and given good maintenance, is indeterminate. The thing that limits the safe life of any good, honestly-made gun is not the fair wear and tear it has had, but outstandingly the abuse or neglect it may have suffered. It is an unfortunate fact that good guns last so long that they nearly always pass through several hands, and are very lucky if they escape neglect at some stage of their existence.

77   Thin Barrels

A London correspondent, the fortunate owner of a pair of Boss guns, came to me the other day in mild concern. The guns, which dated from about 1900, were in a perfect state of preservation, but an eminent gunmaker, who had checked them over preparatory to the opening of the season, had shaken his head over the thinness of the barrel walls, which gauged only 25 mils (that is, ·025 in., or 25-thousandths of an inch) in the thinnest part, usually about 6 in. or 7 in. from the muzzle. There was even a spot where they were only 24 mils. The gunmaker made it clear that the barrels were well in proof, and that the guns were quite safe, but he expressed the view that they should be used only with extreme care.

My correspondent thought that this was a case for a second opinion, so he took the guns to another eminent gunmaker, who, after duly gauging the barrels, scoffed at the other's misgivings. In his view, the matter was clearly not worth another thought. Since even eminent gunmakers evidently do not always agree, I was asked to give my opinion.

Old guns frequently come under suspicion in this respect, especially if they are true cylinders, when the muzzle-ends are sometimes described as being paper-thin; and there must be many amateur gun-surgeons who, after chopping 4 or 5 in. off their long barrels, and thereby getting rid of the thick-walled choke, are shocked to find how thin are their newly exposed muzzles. Perhaps the majority of shooters, never having calipered their barrels, imagine that, apart from the choke constriction, the thickness of barrel walls diminishes progressively from breech to muzzle. They may indeed do so, but this is not the practice in best English guns, such as those in question.

The practical requirements in respect of wall thickness vary from breech to muzzle in a shotgun barrel. At the breech end, the barrel must be thick enough to resist the maximum pressure to which it will be exposed, and if it can do that, there are no overriding requirements. This means that it must be thick enough to resist the proof pressure without bulging or, in other words, without exceeding its elastic limit; and since the proof pressure is 60 to 80 per cent more than the maximum working or 'service' pressure, it follows that, provided the service pressure is not exceeded, there will be a minimum factor of safety of 1·6 to 1·8 on the elastic limit of the material under practical working conditions. It is, in fact, considered to be good gunmaking practice to work to a minimum factor of safety of 2 on the elastic limit at any point along the barrel length.

But pressure in a gun barrel falls rapidly from breech to muzzle, and at any point beyond about the halfway mark the normal working pressure is so low that wall thickness is increasingly influenced by other considerations, as may be clearly seen from a simple example.

Consider an ordinary 12-bore gun firing a standard game cartridge. The pressure, at, say, 20 in. from the breech may be safely taken not to exceed 0·4 tons per sq. in.; and if the elastic limit of the steel is conservatively assumed to be 20 tons, we can quickly work out that a wall thickness of 15 mils (·015 in.) would be sufficient to resist this pressure with a factor of safety of 2. Indeed, Greener, for experimental purposes, made a 12-bore barrel that was only about 10 mils thick (the thickness of a common visiting card) from 17 in. to 25 in. from the breech, which he said was not in any way bulged or injured by repeated firing of the usual charge. It remained intact until it was 'ripped up with an ordinary penknife without any trouble'. So much for what is required to withstand normal pressures.

Other requirements

But in deciding the minimum thickness of his barrel walls the practical gunmaker has to have regard for the other considerations I mentioned. There are several. The barrel must be thick enough to resist abnormal pressures, as well as dents and other mechanical damage from without. It must be stiff enough to resist undue flexure when shooting; and there must be a margin to cover loss of metal through pitting, lapping and repeated blueing. Then there are manufacturing contingencies to be provided for. The particular billet of steel from which the barrel was forged may not develop the specified characteristics for one or other of several reasons. The barrel may be scored along the rib groove in the course of assembly; and the thinner the barrel the greater the difficulty in securing uniform proportionate wall thickness around the circumference. Journée records that of all the finished shotguns of normal dimensions submitted to the relatively feeble proof pressure of 620 kg. (just under 4 tons) a certain proportion burst; and this notwithstanding that the Belgian and French makers chiefly concerned appear to work to higher figures of minimum wall thickness than our best gunmakers do.

So, it comes down to this – that the question is one for the judgment of the individual gunmaker. The better kind, using high-grade steel, such as the 3 per cent chrome-nickel steel (En. 21) favoured in this country, and being anxious to make lively, well-balanced guns, will want to remove all surplus metal from the forward part of his barrels. The maker of the cheaper kind, possibly (but not necessarily) using tubes made from a lower grade of metal, and being more concerned with passing proof than with such refinements as balance, will have every inducement to work to larger dimensions.

I have from time to time measured the minimum wall thickness of English and Continental barrels, and have gained the impression that the best English makers work to 30 mils, but that, in the course of finishing, there may be some slight reduction, so that new guns are frequently sent out with 28 mils. Best guns that have seen considerable service, though preserved in first-class condition, may come down a point or two on that, perhaps on account of their having been reblued a number of times. A fine London gun I have just measured, the bores of which still gauge their pristine ·729 in., has a minimum wall thickness of 26 mils. The barrels have been reblued twice, but I should doubt if this involved the loss of more than a mil of substance.

My verdict, therefore, in the original case, was that neither of the two gun-makers consulted could be held to be wrong: both were operating in the field of personal judgment and legitimate opinion. But I believe that the second one consulted – the scoffer – would have the bulk of the best English trade behind him. Still, if my correspondent is unhappy with his Boss guns, and wishes to get rid of them at any sacrifice, I think I know of someone who might be prepared to offer them a good home.

78 The Leading of Barrels

In view of the many newcomers to shooting who buy new guns, it is not surprising that I receive a steady trickle of letters from correspondents in trouble with leading – that is to say, the formation of deposits of lead in the barrel, derived from the shot charge. These deposits, which appear as dull, longitudinal streaks when the bore is examined against the sky, are objectionable on several counts.

In the days before the rustless cartridge, leading was formed over corrosive deposits, which thus escaped ordinary cleaning, and were likely to attack the steel and lay the foundation for subsequent pitting from under cover. Apart from this, bad leading implies the existence of conditions detrimental to the efficiency of the gun, as I hope to show. The subject accordingly merits some attention.

There are several factors involved in leading – the state of the bore surface, pressure, velocity and the composition of the shot. If a gun prone to leading is examined, it will be found that the trouble occurs chiefly in front of the chamber and in the constriction of the choke. In a true cylinder or skeet gun, any leading other than that in front of the chamber will almost certainly be found towards the muzzle. Again, a gun that leads badly when new will become less troublesome with use, and in time the leading may cease. On the other hand, a gun which does not normally suffer from leading may do so if the load or cartridge is changed; and in these observations we may find the clues to most of what goes on.

Since leading is essentially the rubbing off of streaks of soft metal against the surface of a harder one, it will be obvious that the nature of that surface is a prime factor in determining how much of the soft metal will be rubbed away. In new guns, the surface of the bore, despite the mirror-like appearance it may present to the eye, is actually covered with minute scratches left behind by the final finishing process. Usually these scratches are made by a revolving tool or 'lap', so that they run around the bore, and therefore at right angles to the direction of movement of the shot, which they thus abrade most effectively, and so encourage leading. In time, by the ordinary processes of wear and cleaning, these circular scratches get worn away, when leading may be much reduced, or even cease. A few makers, chiefly French, avoid this trouble by finally polishing the bores lengthwise instead of circularly.

Pressure is another potent source of leading. Owing to what I call the Pascal effect, whereby a charge of shot behaves in somewhat the same way as a liquid, the powerful thrust of the powder gases on the rear of the charge is partly translated into a side-thrust against the barrel wall. So we would expect to find, and do find, that leading is worse where gas pressure is highest – just in front of the chamber. It tends to get bad again at the choke because there the pellets are once more subjected to a high pressure, because of their being squeezed.

Velocity, too, comes into the picture, since it is actually a combination of pressure and velocity that provokes leading: However well polished the bore may be, and however moderate the pressure (as it is towards the muzzle of a true cylinder or skeet barrel) there is always likely to be some leading when the shot charge reaches velocities much exceeding 1100 ft per sec. A standard game cartridge loaded with No. 6 shot actually attains about 1270 ft per sec. at the muzzle: a really high-velocity one may exceed 1400.

As for the composition of the shot, it is a curious fact that hard modern shot, alloyed with upwards of 2 per cent of antimony, gives more trouble with leading than did the old soft shot. This observation has been supported by decisive experiments.

An incidental factor is the nature of the deposit left in the bore by the previous shots. This comprises powder residue and wad lubricant, as well as any previous leading. Generally, the cleaner the powder the less leading, which black powder was especially inclined to promote. On the other hand, lubricant left behind by greased wads diminishes the trouble; but existing leading attracts more leading.

The effect on performance

Leading, and the conditions of which it is a symptom, are of considerable significance to performance. In an ordinary game charge of medium shot, nearly half the pellets rub the bore, and if a gun which is leading badly is fired into water and the pellets recovered, it will be found that these outside pellets have been badly worn away, perhaps to the extent of a third of their diameter, or more. As I have mentioned before, some of the metal thus lost goes out of the barrel as lead dust; and the rest is deposited as leading. Mr R. W. S. Griffiths, the tireless experimenter of the old Schultze Company, fired a large number of shots up a disused factory chimney, and collected the lead dust that came back. He estimated that about $4\frac{1}{2}$ per cent of a charge of $1\frac{1}{8}$ oz of hard shot was lost in this manner. Together with the leading loss, this might well amount to a sixteenth of an ounce.

But perhaps worse than this loss of charge weight is the loss of efficiency in the outside pellets affected. The loss of their original round shape will cause them to fly inaccurately, and to strike the target at a reduced speed, so that pattern density, pattern quality and average pellet energy will all suffer. Clearly leading is a bad thing and a bad sign.

Preventive measures

Since one of the main causes of leading is the imperfect surface of the bore in new guns, and the fact of its having been formed by rotative polishing, one of the best preventives is polishing lengthwise – a process which, as I have said, comes about through wear and tear in old, well-cared-for guns. In new guns, it can be accelerated by the use of proprietary polishing compounds, though these need using with care and restraint. I myself prefer the burnishing action of a steel-wire turk's head. I know that these things are an abomination to some fastidious shooters because of their alleged tendency to scratch the bore, but since the spines lie flat in the barrel, and present only their rounded surfaces to the metal, I do not see how they can scratch. They should be well oiled when used for burnishing.

Chromium plating is claimed to reduce leading, and may well do so, but plating *can* exaggerate minute surface irregularities, and I have known chromed barrels to lead very badly.

The plating of shot with a harder metal such as copper or nickel would appear to be a sound approach to the reduction of leading. The idea is an old one, and a plating process was patented by an Englishman named Pitt in 1878. But the practical value of plating as a preventive of leading (as opposed to the cold welding of pellets together) is suspect because of the extreme thinness of the coating applied.

The modern answer

In his 1902 edition, Journée points out that leading can be completely prevented by enclosing the shot charge in a sleeve of paper or foil which travels out with the pellets and prevents any contact between them and the bore. He remarks that the sleeve must be split lengthwise – otherwise there may be some balling of the charge. Also it should be greased for lubrication.

This admirable device was rediscovered by Winchester in recent years, and furnished the basis for their celebrated Mark 5 cartridge, with its split, protective, polyethylene sleeve, subsequently developed, by Remington I believe, into the modern plastic wad, comprising gas seal, collapsible cushion and protective shot-cup. This kind of wad seems destined to supersede all others, and to make leading a thing of the past.

As for the removal of leading, I use one of the densely bristled, Payne-Gallwey brushes made of hard brass wire, dipped if necessary in turpentine. Abrasive compounds should only be used as a last resort, and then with the utmost care.

79 Safe Angles and Ricochets

I have been asked for my opinion on the angles at which sportsmen may safely fire in relation to others, having regard for the danger of ricocheting pellets. This is a subject which most writers on shooting avoid, or skim lightly over, perhaps because the accounts of remarkable ricochets resemble some of the bomb-blast stories of the last war in severely taxing credulity.

Most writers accordingly take the practical course of merely suggesting what are the safe arcs of fire in various circumstances, which is what most advice on this subject must boil down to if it is to be of service in the field. Unfortunately, however, such advice, as commonly presented, reveals substantial differences of opinion, even among those whose considerable and undeniable experience might have been expected to produce a measure of unanimity.

In the circumstances, I think it would be most helpful if, before considering ricochets as such, or offering any personal opinions, I summarized the views of some of our leading authorities on what constitute safe angles of fire.

I turn first, and most hopefully, to the Badminton Library volume, *Shooting – Field and Covert*, by Lord Walsingham and Sir Ralph Payne-Gallwey. Lord Walsingham was, of course, one of the great shots of the late Victorian and Edwardian eras. In addition to being a first-class performer, he was a man of vast practical experience, especially with driven game, at which he must have fired many thousands of cartridges in an average season. Shooting so much in company, one feels that he ought to have formed firm and authoritative opinions on where the dividing line lay between safe and unsafe shooting. So ought Sir Ralph, for although, as a shot, he was not in the same class as his distinguished co-author, he, too, was a man of great experience, as well as being of a more enquiring and analytical turn of mind.

For all that, the views they express are sketchy and barely acceptable. They are comprised in the diagram the essentials of which I have faithfully copied here. It is included without caption or other explanation in the chapter on partridge shooting, and may fairly be taken to relate primarily to such shooting, in which the birds commonly come low over the guns. Yet, as will be seen, the safe angle between the gun and his next-in-line is reduced to as little as 15 degrees. I have done much partridge driving in my time, and have no idea what indiscretions I may have committed in the heat of action; but, having just done a mock-up of the situation in the field, and measured angles with a prismatic compass, I must say that 15 degrees seems to me to be cutting things pretty fine. There is too small a margin for inadvertent transgressions.

I find support for my views in those of Major Hugh Pollard, an outstanding authority of the inter-war period. In the Lonsdale Library volume, *Shooting by Moor, Field and Shore*, he gives diagrams showing 35 degrees as the minimum safe angle between line of fire and neighbouring gun in the case of ground game, and 30 degrees in the case of aerial targets. That seems to me more reasonable.

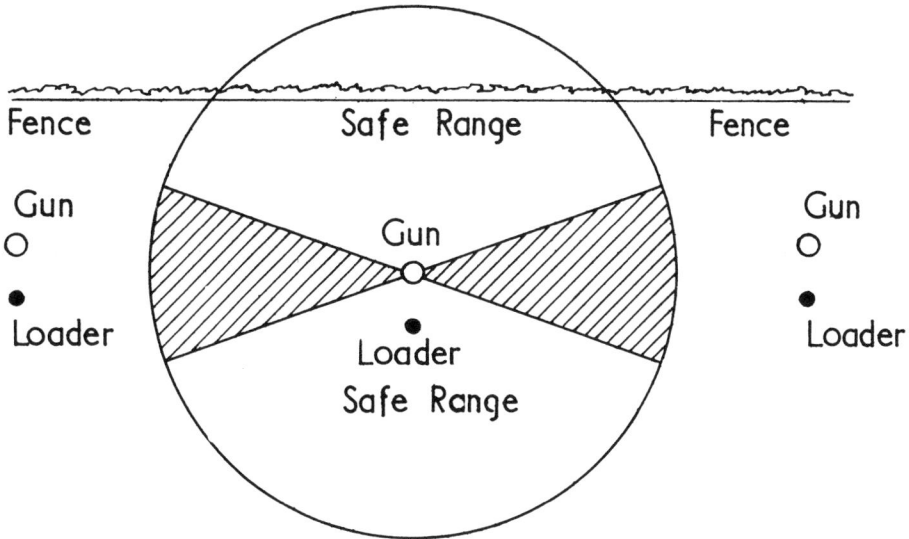

CUTTING IT FINE   Lord Walsingham's and Sir R. Payne-Gallwey's conception of safe shooting angles at a partridge drive. Only 15 degrees separate the line of fire from neighbouring gun or loader.

In a book devoted entirely to safety in the shooting field, one would expect the author to be more detailed and perhaps more cautious; and in his admirable small volume on *Gun Safety*, Major Roderick Willett fulfils these expectations. For the normal partridge-driving or covert-side situation shown in the previous illustration, he adopts a minimum safety angle of 45 degrees for ground game, though he concedes that shooting within the danger areas thus marked out is permissible for high-flying birds. In other words, it is not the angle projected on the ground that matters, but the angle between the actual line of fire and that joining the gun with his neighbour.

I must confess that Major Willett's 45 degrees, when actually measured on the ground, seems somewhat in excess of reasonable requirements, and it is certainly a limit that is often transgressed. But it must be remembered that rules laid down and normally observed in cold blood are always subject to some degree of transgression when excitement is running high, and it is well that they should make some allowance for the fact. Also, it is when shooting at ground game that the greatest danger from ricochets is likely to occur — at least, if the ground is at all stony.

Ricochets

This brings me to ricochets as such; and it would be convenient now to anticipate my broad conclusion by saying that, in my opinion, *there is no such thing as a perfectly safe angle at which to fire in relation to a neighbouring gun.* This is because pellets can and do come straight back to the shooter in certain circumstances – a fact of which I have unexceptionable evidence received at first hand. They can even rebound from birds. In this context, therefore, safety is relative: the bigger the angle the safer the shot, *generally speaking.* But the qualification is necessary, because a man who delayed shooting until the bird concerned had attained what appeared to be a safe angle in relation to a neighbouring gun might thereby take it against a background of trees, from which pellets might ricochet dangerously; whereas if he had taken it earlier the background could have been clear sky.

In his *Tir des Fusils de Chasse*, General Journée has much to say about ricochets. He lays down some general laws, and gives tabular and other information about angles and velocities. He emphasises particularly the dangers of firing solid lead ball in woodland – much practised, incidentally, by Continental shooters expecting wild boar – and testifies to the possibility of ordinary pellets coming straight back to the shooter. I will not attempt to summarize this information, because the last-mentioned possibility covers all lesser risks. I will only say that Journée, in the light of his own experience, both direct and vicarious, gives the impression that accidents caused by ricocheting pellets are both numerous and serious. The fact that an ordinary shooter like myself has intimate knowledge of several cases (involving two lost eyes) fully supports this impression, and reinforces the need for care. Perhaps I can best conclude with one or two examples from my own experience.

At a partridge drive in Hampshire, a single bird came straight towards one of the shooters. He, and he alone, fired at it against a background of clear sky. Immediately, he experienced what he described as a 'violent blow in the mouth'. A pellet had rebounded *from the bird*, and chipped the corner off one of his front teeth.

A shooter fired at a wounded duck on the water. The charge ricocheted from the surface and wounded a person on the opposite side of the pond.

A shooter fired at a rabbit going away across a stony field. A pellet came straight back and deeply penetrated the thigh of someone standing alongside the shooter. (In this case, there was a happy ending, for the victim had been suffering from sciatica, and the pellet struck his sciatic nerve. When he recovered from the immediate effects of his wound, he found that his sciatica was cured!)

To sum up, therefore, there is no angle of fire that is absolutely safe from ricochets. They thus constitute an all-pervading risk in shooting, and one that is worthy of clearer recognition and more studious avoidance than it normally gets.

80   Chamber Contamination

Complaints, it seems, are getting around concerning the alleged contamination of shotgun chambers by plastic cartridges. There are reports of the formation of a resistant deposit on the chamber walls, and also of rusting.

The large manufacturers, both here and abroad, are well aware of the trouble, but they do not yet appear to have arrived at an agreed diagnosis, still less a cure.

The evidence in my possession does not enable me to give a well balanced account of the symptoms. All I can say with certainty is that when large numbers of plastic cartridges are fired, and the chambers of the gun are not regularly cleaned, a deposit accumulates on that part of the chamber wall which is in contact with the exposed plastic tube. This is not associated with cartridges of any particular brand or brands.

The evidence I have of rusting is less, both in bulk and consistency, and comes to me in correspondence and press extracts from America. Eley tell me that they have had no complaints of this particular trouble; and in the U.S.A., where it is well established, there seems to be some doubt as to whether or not it takes place independently of any deposit. The point here is that the deposit might escape recognition in repeaters, and only the rusting attract attention. There is also one report of a red deposit, stated *not* to be rust, in the neighbourhood of the metal heads of plastic cartridges.

I have no information on the chemical or physical nature of the deposit first referred to, though it is stated to require vigorous work with a wire brush for its removal.

Paper cartridges are generally exonerated; though some investigators belonging to the technical staff of the *American Rifleman* report having found significant amounts of moisture (presumably condensed moisture) in the chambers of the guns after firing a number of both paper and plastic cartridges under hot and humid conditions.

Some theories advanced

A number of theories have been put forward to account for these observations, none of them commanding instant respect. It has, for example, been pointed out that water vapour is a normal product of propellant combustion, and might in certain circumstances cause the rusting. So, it is rather feebly suggested, might perspiration from the shooter's hands if he made a practice of holding his cartridges, as some do, while waiting their turn at the trap. The practice of some shooters of blowing down their barrels after firing has been similarly blamed. The fact that there is no corresponding rusting when paper cartridges are used is accounted for by the suggestion that the wax or other water-resisting coating or impregnation of the paper case acts as an inhibitor.

As for the deposit, one suggestion is that it is an accumulation of minute quantities of plastic material worn away from the cases. Another is that it is an accumulation of miscellaneous sorts of dust attracted to plastic cases by static electricity, and compressed against the chamber wall – usually oily –– by the gas pressure generated on firing.

So far as I am aware, chemical action has not been invoked to account for either the deposit or the rusting – except, of course, so far as all rusting is a chemical process. In the early days of plastic cartridges, some of the materials used were under suspicion of forming hydrochloric acid under the influence of heat. This would dissolve any chromium plating in the barrel in double-quick time, and thereafter attack the barrel substance; but the modern polyethylene material seems to be tacitly regarded as above suspicion in this context.

The red deposit, stated not to be rust, found in the region of the cartridge head, might still be rust. Cartridge heads are nowadays made from steel, brass plated, and if the plating is not thick enough fully to cover the under-lying metal, microscopic rust nodules could form, and be conveyed by pressure to the chamber walls, where they could accumulate.

Conclusions

As things stand at present, readers must form their own conclusions on the evidence submitted. For my own part, I lean towards the remarkable electrical properties of the plastic case as affording the most likely clue, both to the deposit and to the rusting.

Most people will have noticed the surprising quantities of static electricity produced by synthetic fabrics. I have a suit of terylene pyjamas which not only crackles in dry weather, and sticks oddly to my arms and legs, but which also glows with patches of violet light in the dark, in consequence of surface discharges. Polyethylene cartridge cases have a similar capacity for generating 'static'; and although Eley realise the significance of this, and add an in-hibitor to the material, it is not very successful, as a simple but striking experiment will show. Take an ordinary Grand Prix case and, holding it by the head, flick it a few times with a silk handkerchief. If everything is dry, the case will then be found to be sufficiently strongly electrified to pick up scraps of paper, tobacco ash, carpet fluff and the like. If, instead of flicking the case

A POSSIBLE CAUSE OF CHAMBER CONTAMINATION   Experiment demonstrating the
electrostatic properties of plastic cartridge cases.

with a silk handkerchief, it is merely shaken up with others in an old pocket
or cartridge bag, it will be found on examination with a pocket magnifier to
have a considerable amount of dust and fluff sticking to it in tiny particles.
In the ordinary way, these particles will be conveyed into the chamber
of the gun, where they will stick to the walls and undergo consolidation
under the repeated and heavy pressure of firing. If a sufficient number of
cartridges is fired, *and if the chamber is never cleaned*, the formation of a
deposit would seem to be inevitable.

But how about the rusting? For this, it is only necessary to assume that the
deposit is capable of absorbing or occluding moisture from the air. We would
then have the situation familiar to those shooters who have left guns in
fabric-lined cases for any length of time, particularly in damp situations,
when it is often found that the fabric has set up vicious corrosion at places
where it is in close contact with the metal.

It ought not to be too difficult to prove or disprove this theory. The deposit
should be amenable to physical analysis, both to ascertain its nature and
whether or not it is hygroscopic; and in a manufacturer's testing department,
where the deposit has been observed after firing so many cartridges, it should
be possible to carry out a control experiment by running through a similar
number after they have been electrically discharged.

It will be noted that this theory covers some others, involving moisture
from the shooter's breath when blowing through the barrels, or condensed
from propellant gases sucked back into the chamber by the ejection of the
spent case. Associated with this last thought is the possibility that *corrugated*

plastic cases (e.g. Remington, Federal) do not totally obturate the powder gases.

But the dominant thought in the shooter's mind is, or should be, that chambers, along with the rest of the bore, need care and cleaning, using one of the chamber brushes made for the purpose. In the last resort, the onus of preserving his gun rests now, as always, on the man who uses it.

MISCELLANEOUS

'At the end of the work you may judge the workman.'
(Yorkshire proverb)

81 *Plomb Disco*

I have dealt elsewhere with several aspects of short-range shooting, of which the average sportsman does more than he recognises or is prepared to admit. This is true, whatever kind of shooting we consider, short of flight shooting at educated wildfowl. Driven game, not excluding allegedly 'high' pheasants; pheasants, woodcock and ground game hunted with spaniels; pigeon shot over decoys or coming in to roost; duck shot at flight-ponds, or over decoys, or by tapping-in to inland streams and pools – all are more often, and I would say far more often, shot at distances between 20 and 30 yds than they are at any more extended range.

By accepting an open-boring as being best for the right barrel of his 12-bore, the average man of experience in this country pays implicit tribute to the foregoing facts, and to the need to make the most of his chances for general satisfaction. He more expressly recognises the responsibility resting on him to produce game in the best possible condition for the table. The exceptions are men who genuinely need a heavily choked gun in order to be able to cope with their class of sport, and a whole tribe of modern shooters, chiefly young and inexperienced, who wrongly imagine that merit in a gun and load is determined by the density of the patterns they are capable of making, and the greatest distance at which they can possibly kill. These are the shooters who allow an occasional glorious fluke at extended range to distort their judgment, and to blind them to the frequent loss of easier chances.

Easily made

If we take a broader look around, we cannot fail to be impressed by the strange preoccupation of the Americans with heavy choke, dense patterns and long-range potential, and by the contrasting concern of Continental shooters for filling the game bag to the best advantage in given circumstances. This concern is reflected by the availability on the other side of the Channel of several means for extending the spread of patterns beyond the capacity of an ordinary improved cylinder to do so, whereby the shooter is better equipped to cope successfully with shots up to about 25 yds, and to avoid the mangling of game. These means include the *canon rayé*, or rifled barrel of very slow twist, and various kinds of spreader cartridges. Notable among the latter are those, such as the F.N. *Dispersante* loaded with square, or rather cubic, shot, and others loaded with the so-called *plomb disco*, which, as their name implies, are not round pellets, but flattened discs of lead.

These last in particular have attracted me, because, although they are not available in this country, they can readily be made from ordinary shot. Any home-loader who can command the necessary mechanical resources can fit himself out with a simple device of twin rollers, adjustable for distance, by which ordinary shot can be mangled to a predetermined thickness, and in quantities sufficient for normal requirements.

For experimental purposes, I have recently been making *plomb disco* by a cruder method. The device I have used for this purpose is shown in my sketch. It comprises a loop of 1-in. by $\frac{1}{8}$-in. steel strip, with one end projecting beyond the other, and a perforated metal slide for accommodating the pellets.

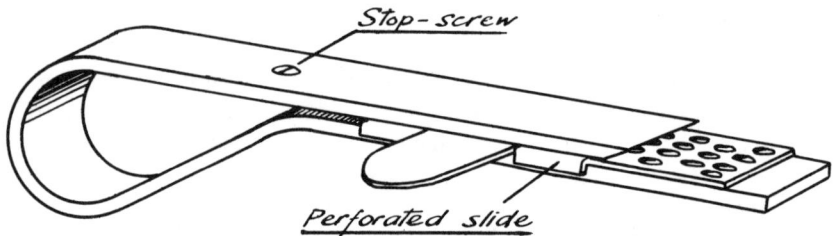

A simple device for making small experimental quantities of plomb disco. Twenty pellets can easily be made at each operation.

The slide is of the same thickness as the finished shot. It has a projection on one side to facilitate handling, and the sides are turned down so that it runs truly between the ends of the loop.

To use this device, the slide is pushed to the right. Pellets are then spooned over the perforations, so that all are filled. The slide is then reversed until all the pellets are withdrawn between the steel strips, which are then squeezed in a powerful vice, or struck on an anvil with a hammer or rubber mallet. I find that with a single blow of a light rubber mallet I can easily flatten a dozen pellets of No. 6 from their normal diameter of approximately $\frac{1}{10}$-in. down to *plomb disco* of 0·040 in., so that, for this particular operation, the holes in the slide need to be drilled with not less than a $\frac{5}{32}$-in. drill. When the pellets have been flattened, the slide is, of course, once more pushed out to the right, and turned over, when they should fall out. Even with this simple device, it is possible to make enough *plomb disco* for a pocketful of cartridges in a single session.

Limited experiments

To assess the properties and usefulness of these flattened pellets fairly it would be necessary to take two or three sizes of shot and to flatten them in varying degrees, finally testing them all for pattern. But I had to restrict my experimenting to a single case – that of No. 6 shot flattened to 0·040 in., or 40 per cent of its original diameter.

The diagram is a typical pattern obtained by firing 1 oz (270 pellets) of this flattened shot from an improved cylinder barrel at 20 yds. The spread is about 40 in., as compared with the normal figure of 26 in. for this boring and distance. The margin for error is thus increased by some 50 per cent.

The number of pellets in a 30-in. circle is 120, or 45 per cent, which is below the 130 I adopted as a minimum for medium game in *Shotguns and Cartridges*. But better results would be obtained against such game with No. 7 shot at 340 to the oz. If the percentage pellets in the 30-in. circle were maintained at the above figure, there would have been about 150 in the 30-in. circle, corresponding to something slightly better than nominal performance with ordinary No. 6 shot at 40 yds, and sufficient for game as small as woodcock.

It must always be borne in mind when contemplating this short-range shooting that, given the necessary spread, there is every justification for using the smaller sizes of shot. Thus, ordinary No. 7 has a striking energy of well over 2 ft/lb. at 20 yds; No. 8 has over 1½; and even No. 9 exceeds 1·0. These energies will not be fully realised by *plomb disco* because of its inferior ranging power; but since medium game requires no more than 1·0, there is much scope for No. 8 and no justification for using anything larger than No. 7 for the class of work under consideration.

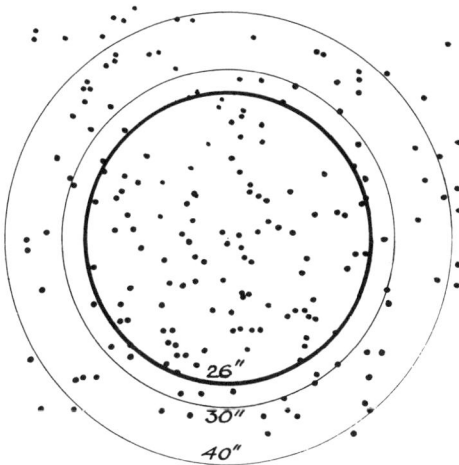

PLOMB DISCO PATTERN Pattern made by 1 oz. No. 6 (·102/·040) plomb disco from a 12-bore I.C. barrel at 20 yards. The heavy (26-inch) circle indicates the spread with ordinary No. 6 shot. No. 7 or No. 8, similarly flattened, would be more effective against small to medium game at this distance.

A necessary warning

A few incidental points need covering for the benefit of home-loaders contemplating making and using *plomb disco*.

The first is a warning. *This shot cannot be used in an ordinary loading machine because the shot stacks, and the bushings will not throw accurate weights. All charges must accordingly be weighed.* For the same reason, a slightly longer wadding column may be necessary to avoid slack loading.

As for the utility of these short range loads, I deliberately tested them in some of my familiar woodcock country, when it became at once obvious, on measuring out distances with a tape, that 20 yds is farther than most of the chances I have had at these birds over the years. It would cover many a driven pheasant coming over well-grown hardwoods, or hunted by spaniels from rough cover; and a large proportion of the pigeon coming into roost can be taken at no greater range, but with much greater prospect of success.

It needs to be remembered that the normal shooter in this country using a double-barrelled, double-triggered gun, is free to use a normal cartridge in his left barrel, so that he is not restricted to short-range work by the *plomb disco* or other spreader cartridge in his right. Also, that these cartridges have another useful function in enabling the user of a heavily choked gun to enjoy the advantages of a more open boring on suitable occasions.

82 Telescopic Sights

It would appear from the enquiries I receive that not all prospective users of these sights are familiar with the ABC of the subject. It might be useful, therefore, to run over it briefly.

I am asked what the symbols 4 X, 6 X, etc., signify in the specifications. They signify magnifying power – more exactly, linear magnifying power. So, an object one foot long seen through a 4 X 'scope would appear to be 4 ft long. Through a 6 X 'scope it would appear 6 ft long, and so on. Several points arise on this elementary fact.

First, some 'scopes are described as being of more than one power, for example, 4–8 X. These are the pancratic 'scopes, with variable magnification, capable in the case of the example of being adjusted to give anything between 4 and 8 magnification.

Secondly, how can the magnifying power be ascertained if it is not stated or known? This question presumably arises on 'scope-sighted rifles offered second-hand. The easiest way of checking the magnification of a sight is to prop the rifle on some kind of steady rest with the telescope pointing at a brick wall. If the wall is then observed with both eyes open, the right one looking through the 'scope and the left one unaided, the magnified image can be made to overlap the other. The number of unmagnified brick courses covered by one seen through the telescope can then be counted. This number is the magnification.

Choice of power

As might be expected, my enquiries reveal a tendency on the part of beginners to lean towards maximum magnification. This is usually a great mistake on several counts. For a given size of objective lens (which is the lens at the forward end of the tube) the brightness of the target diminishes in proportion to the magnification. So, too, does the extent of the field of view. On the other hand, the shooter's muscular tremors or wobblings are magnified by the sight and are decidedly more disconcerting at the higher powers. All these points need elaboration.

Manufacturers' specifications of telescopic sights usually include a figure under the heading 'exit pupil'. This figure is the diameter (usually in millimetres) of the spot of light seen when standing back from the sight and looking at the eye lens. It should desirably be at least as big as the pupil of the user's eye under the worst lighting conditions. If it is less than that, the eye will be proportionately starved of light, and the target of brightness. To avoid this, it is usually taken that the exit pupil should be not less than 7 mm. in diameter.

Now, the diameter of the exit pupil is the clear diameter of the object lens divided by the magnification. So, if we have a cheap little 'scope sight with an object lens of only 15 mm. diameter, and an eyepiece giving a power of 4, the diameter of the exit pupil cannot exceed 15 mm. divided by 4, which is only $3\frac{3}{4}$ mm. This will limit the utility of the sight under poor lighting conditions.

Field of view

The loss of field of view with high magnification is also a practical handicap. If the field is small, it is proportionately difficult to pick up the target quickly – and targets do not always wait to be picked up! The effect of magnification on field of view can be seen by taking a practical example from a manufacturer's catalogue. In it, a good quality pancratic or variable-power 'scope is listed as having a field of 42 ft with a power of 3 diminishing to 18·3 ft with a power of 9. (The field of view, incidentally, is usually expressed in English-language catalogues as so many feet at 100 yds. A figure of 30 ft at 100 yds is about the minimum for picking up a target promptly.)

On the point about muscular tremors, I need only add that telescopic sights aid the *eye*: they do nothing to improve the steadiness of aim, and the newcomer to a 'scope sight must not expect it. On the contrary, he must be prepared to see his lack of steadiness magnified along with the target, and in the same proportion.

To reduce the foregoing considerations to practical recommendations, I would say that, owing to their short range, ·22 rifles for use against small game and vermin need nothing more than 2·5 or 3-power; stalking rifles are probably best suited with 4-power; and small-bore high-velocity rifles intended for long-range shooting at vermin can justifiably go up to 6 or more, according to circumstances. In all cases, exit pupils of not less than 7 mm. should be regarded as desirable; and as, with the higher powers, this implies a large object lens and proportionate cost, it is no good looking for 'scope sights that are cheap, high-powered and satisfactory on all counts.

Parallax

In an article in the *Shooting Times* of 16 March 1968, on 'Zeroing a Stalking Rifle' I recommended, as a convenient practical procedure, adjusting the sights so that the bullet hit the mark at the first point of intersection of sight-line and trajectory, say at 25 yds for the 150 grain 30-'06 bullet. This would assure that it also hit the mark at the second point of intersection at 225 yds – provided, of course, that the ammunition conformed to the published ballistics.

But the Scottish correspondent, writing from under the Kilpatrick Hills, correctly observed that this might expose the operation to parallactic error. The point is not universally understood, but is really quite simple, and is well worth going into.

Fundamentally, a telescopic sight is a very simple contrivance. It can be considered as comprising two lenses only. The front one, the object lens, throws what opticians call a real image of the target towards the eye end of the tube. This real image corresponds to the bright spot of light thrown by a burning glass, which is really a real image of the sun's disc; or it corresponds to the picture thrown on a photographic film by a camera lens. At the exact focal point where this real image of the target is thrown, the telescopic sight has a reticle; and the function of the eye lens is simply to magnify the image and the reticle together.

Provided the image and the reticle lie in exactly the same plane, the eye can be moved from one side of the eye lens to the other, without causing any shift of the reticle in relation to the target. But if this condition is not fulfilled – if, for example, the image lies slightly nearer to the eye than it does to the reticle, any movement of the eye to one side or other of the centre of the eye lens will cause the reticle to shift its position in relation to the target, even though the rifle has been held in exactly the same position throughout. Any such shift constitutes a parallactic error, or, less correctly, a parallax error.

In practice, some parallactic error is always likely when aligning a 'scope sight on a nearby object. This is because the sight is adjusted at the factory so that the image of the target coincides with the reticle for distances of about 100 yds or more. If the target is brought progressively nearer, the image is thrown farther and farther back, and increasingly behind the reticle. So, at 25 yds, according to my correspondent, there is a risk of material error in the sighting-in method I described.

This, as I have already indicated, is a perfectly proper point, and in certain circumstances would need to be covered by re-focusing the objective. But for a game-shooting rifle it is hardly valid. It must be recognised that no parallactic error can occur so long as the eye remains opposite the centre of the eye lens, where one intuitively locates it. And even if one deliberately displaces the eye from the centre to the edge of the field of view, the resulting parallactic error barely exceeds an inch at 25 yds, according to a rough check I have just made.

So, the method I described for sighting-in a rifle at the first intersection is still to be recommended, though, out of respect for my correspondent's point, I would add a word of caution as to the desirability of taking care not to displace the aiming eye from the centre of the eye lens in the process.

83 Paying the Price

A man usually has to pay for his pleasures, and he is often lucky if he can compound the debt in money terms.

The pleasures associated with guns and shooting are no exception; but it needs recognising that they may establish internal debts that can only be satisfied by accommodation. Let me try to make myself clear.

These pleasures have many roots. To some the greatest is the indulgence of the hunting instinct, here seen in one of its most innocent forms, as being concerned *au fond* with the procurement of food. They constitute, perhaps, the pure, original strain of shooters, to whom the pursuit, outwitting and taking of game transcend all associated interests. Closely allied to them are those who find their utmost satisfaction in dog work – not in isolation, but as part of the business of hunting with the gun.

To others, the greatest attraction of shooting is the opportunity it affords of cultivating and exercising skill; and related to these are those who get their best reward in exercising their skill competitively. Because of the opportunity it affords of competing on level terms, shooters of this kind are as happy shooting inanimate targets as they are living game – maybe happier, for they win prizes and acclaim.

Then we have a miscellaneous group. It includes all amateur ballisticians who delight in unravelling the problems arising out of the performance of guns, and in carrying out tests and experiments. Home-loaders are to be found here, especially the more advanced kind; gun-tinkerers, too, including the formidable few who rank as serious amateur gunsmiths. The élite of this tribe will even make a 150-lb punt gun, and carry it triumphantly through proof.

Farther away from the field of action, we find a scholarly lot, devoted to the study and collection of antique and other guns, and even odd fraternities such as cartridge collectors. But I would deliberately exclude from the honourable order of gun-lovers those who collect costly guns for the mere satisfaction of their acquisitive instincts. Also the barbarians, whose shooting is perhaps no more than a social adjunct to their commercial activities, whose guns may occasionally be seen bearing the marks of shameful abuse and neglect. In contrast, I would give a high place to those who, barred by age, failing health or worldly circumstance from active shooting, nevertheless treasure fine guns for what they represent in beauty and skilled craftmanship.

Room, too, must be found for all those who shoot for the sake of the intangibles – the open air, the good fellowship of other sportsmen, the healthful exercise, the freedom from the competitive intrigue of business or professional life, and the scenes and places into which shooting introduces its devotees. There must be several others whom I have overlooked.

But my purpose in this review is not to catalogue the pleasures to be derived from guns and shooting, but to emphasise the multiplicity of interests involved, and the fact that few shooters, if any, find the whole of their pleasure in pursuing only one of them. Many, if not most, pursue several, with varying degrees of enthusiasm. A few may even pursue the lot!

That being recognised, I can make my point, which is that these varied interests are by no means entirely compatible, and that the pursuit of one may prejudice another.

Perhaps the simplest case and certainly one of the most familiar, is that of the man who is primarily devoted to shooting as one of the hunting sports, but who loves guns for their own sake, and owns more than he strictly needs. These he feels impelled to use, and he does use them – to the detriment of his performance. They may all be game guns; they may even have been adjusted individually so as to be of the same fit; but for all that, subtle differences in weight, balance, trigger pulls and handling qualities will prevent him from attaining that perfect accord with his weapon which is the prerogative of the one-gun man. Unless he is unusually adaptable, this less-than-perfect accord will be duly reflected in a somewhat lower standard of performance than he is otherwise capable of attaining. It is the price he has to pay for the pleasure of using his several guns.

'The indulgence of the hunting instinct is here seen in one of its most innocent forms, as being concerned, *au fond*, with the procurement of food.'

Hypochondria

A worse case is that of the devotee of shooting with keen side-interests in guns, which impels him to be constantly experimenting. He experiments, maybe, with stocks of different fitting, and with different loads, borings and sizes of shot. He may try changing his basic technique, going from the Stanbury or natural posture to the Churchill forward stance; and in the process he may come to accept a stock of unusual dimensions. If he possesses the means to be constantly changing his guns and having recourse to high-class shooting schools and gun fitters, he may develop into a gun-hypochondriac, who is not prepared to face with equanimity the fluctuating fortunes of shooting afield, or to recognise the statistical imperative of occasional off-days. No – he must fly to a new pill.

This pursuit of the ideal gun, the ideal load and ideal technique, like other ideal pursuits, may well be a source of arduous pleasure; but it is one that will assuredly go to the debit of the kills-to-cartridge account.

I will not multiply instances: those I have given will suggest many others. Their lesson is that the pleasure of diversifying one's shooting interests may have to be paid for, not only in money terms, but in some loss of potential performance. That being so, the need for some accommodation should be recognised and cheerfully met.

The only shooter who is likely to avoid the necessity is the one-gun man who is wholly devoted to shooting afield. But there is an important proviso: his gun must be free from any inherent vices capable of preventing him from developing the proficiency that should accrue from his exclusive familiarity with it. That it should also be suited to the kind of sport he pursues goes without saying.

84   Time and Change

The ninety-fifth anniversary of the *Shooting Times* provokes a retrospect. My memory may not go back as far as 1882, but it goes vividly back to the world of that period, which lasted with little change until the First World War, in which I was old enough to serve.

It was an era of exaggerated social inequality and of wealth too unequally distributed. No doubt the balance needed some redressing, though the process of redressing it does not seem to have yielded commensurate returns in raising the general level of happiness and content. But in those days we had not fallen under the domination of those modern inventions whose specious gifts have betrayed our civilisation and added immeasurably to the stress and disquiet of our lives. Away from the old industrial areas, the countryside was still largely unspoiled. There were no motor cars worthy of mention – no motor roads, not even any tarmac. Our country towns and villages were not then being battered and stunned by torrents of meaningless traffic, and everywhere, in the fields and on the roads, the horse was king. For all the lack of modern conveniences, life in a modest middle-class household was easier, more gracious and more enjoyable than anything we have since known.

Of course, it was the Golden Age of shooting ... or was it? Perhaps we may be permitted some doubts. Looking back, we are inclined to be dazzled by the accounts of the enormous bags of pheasants, partridges, and grouse made at the fashionable shoots of the period, and to lament the breaking up of the old estates that made them possible. But we have to remember that there was an exclusiveness about all this which was as regrettable in its way as is the undue pressure on shooting from which we nowadays suffer. If, as we are assured and believe, sport is the grand cement of the rural population, it is surely well that all keen to participate should have some opportunity of doing so. It is the strength of hunting that all can take part, whether mounted or not.

But Major M., who was wounded in the Boer War, though still a 'strong runner', and who lived in the middle of a great estate where shooting was carried on on the largest possible scale, could get no shooting of his own, for all that he was very keen. All the Naboth's vineyards within reach had long

Man with dog and gun – 'The heir to a saner generation and a manifestation of constancy in a world of bewildering change'.

since been mopped up by the great landed proprietor, and Major M. was lucky to get an invitation to a single 'cocks only' day at the back-end of the season. Nowadays, although the glory of the great estate is no more, the Major's son, who is as keen on shooting as was his father, does much better. There is a nice, well-run little syndicate of friends to which he belongs; and, of course, his motor car enables him to accept invitations at a distance, which would have been out of the question in his father's day.

There were other aspects of shooting in the great days, the disappearance of which we need not regret. They were clearly indicated by that bright star of the *fin de siècle* shooting world, the Marquis of Ripon, when he wrote, 'Sometimes when I am sitting in a tent, taking part in a lengthy luncheon of many courses, served by a host of retainers, my memory carries back to a time many years ago when we worked harder for our sport, and when, seated under a hedge, our midday meal consisted of a sandwich, cut by ourselves at the breakfast table in the morning, which we washed down by a pull from a flask; and I am inclined to think that those were better and healthier days.' Richard Akehurst, in his admirable *Game Guns and Rifles*, has reminded us that the Earl of Malmesbury reckoned to have to walk a mile for every head of game he bagged. I used to do that, or rather more, during some of the most truly enjoyable shooting days I have ever known, when I was a Crown Licensee in the New Forest. Even Francis Joseph, the last Austrian Emperor, who must have enjoyed opportunities never surpassed for shooting on the grand scale, is on record as preferring above all things to go out alone with his dog, as a simple rough shooter.

Nor need we shed any purely sentimental tears about the passing of that great estate. Its noble proprietor was a good man, a good landlord and a good employer, who brought order and prosperity to a large agricultural region. His passing, and that of what he represented, was much to be deplored for several practical reasons. But the estate itself, historically speaking, was but a thing of yesterday. Its founder was a Whig lawyer, and as he added manor to manor and field to field, more than one good Tory squire went down before him.

Plus ça change

Narrowing my theme, I come to the implements of shooting. Here I recall Alice and the Red Queen. You will remember that when they had come to a breathless halt after Alice had been dragged by the hand at high speed across the country, she found to her astonishment that they were still standing on the same spot. 'Of course,' snapped the Red Queen, 'you'd have to run a lot faster than that to get away from it!'

Since 1882, we have had notable improvements in the quality and consistency of our smokeless powder. We have had the great boon of the non-corrosive cap, doubly welcome for its late arrival. We have enjoyed marked improvements in the standardisation of cartridge dimensions and in the accuracy of their manufacture; and we have witnessed the advent of the plastic cartridge with its skirted plastic wad and protective shot-cup.

We have, in short, marked important gains, not only in ammunition but in guns; for although the hammerless double-barrelled gun was well established in the early 1880s, and in some of the forms still most highly favoured, we have since had reliable ejectors added, and some surplus barrel length and weight taken away.

But looking around us, we may well be excused for thinking of Alice in the situation I recalled. The modern sportsman enjoys a somewhat lighter gun than his counterpart of 1882, and has rather less trouble in maintaining it in prime order. Under wet conditions he is freed from the trouble of swollen cartridges. What else? Nothing significant to the average man that I can think of. It is doubtful if we can nowadays make patterns even as good as those made by our ancestors with their paper cartridges, wool felt wads, rolled turnovers and black shot. For the final and conclusive evidence of the progress we have made, we must look to the records of sport afield, and to our own experience.

Looking back over the past nine-and-a-half decades – perhaps the most troubled and revolutionary period in the history of the world – I find it extraordinarily pleasant to contemplate the shooting man, with his dog and gun, pursuing a manly and beneficial sport in the open air, and in surroundings as far removed as possible from those created by our over-urbanised civilisation. In him, I see the heir to a saner generation, and one of the all-too-few manifestations of constancy in a world of bewildering change.

Index

eumatic principles 89–92
eyes:
  focusing of 64
  master 215
  optional illusions 210–11

flinching:
  basic causes of 59–60
  cures for 61
  effect of 59
focusing of eyes 64

gun trade specialists 97
gunmakers, records of 94–8
guns:
  accuracy of 77–8
  appraisal of 30–1, 83–4
  AYA 111, 112, 223
  come last 71–4
  degenerative changes in 247
  elegance in 92–4
  fallible 28–9
  fatigue in old 245–6
  hammer 128–32
  'hard shooting' 31
  imported 69
  life of 247–8
  magnum 72–3, 76
  Mauser 620 149
  nostalgia for 98–100
  personal choice in 99–100
  pump 107–9
  strengths and weaknesses today
    101–4
  Westley Richards 'Heronshaw'
    110, 112
  wildfowling 74–7
  2-inch 12-bore 113–15
  28-bore 71
  30-inch barrel 81–3
  .410 118

habits, formation of 65–6
hammer guns, revival of 128–32

imported guns 69

latent skills 33–5
leading 251–3
  effect of chromium plating on 253
lever 84
life of guns 247–8
loading, methods of 45–7
loads, low shooting caused by heavy
  244
low shooting:
  causes and cures 243–4

magnum guns 72–3, 76
master eye 215
moment of inertia 85
momentum v. energy 234
muscular sense 85
muzzle flash 169–71, 175

New Forest, a day recalled 22–3
Nock, Henry 127–8, 172–3, 220
nostalgia in firearms 98–100

Oberfell and Thompson 193, 199
optical illusions 210–11

patterns:
  appearance v. efficiency 142–4
  determination of best 137–9
  effect of velocity on 140
  extra dense 139–40
  holes in 136, 143–4
  improved cylinder 143
  plomb disco 265
  results of experiments 135–7, 147
penetration:
  affected by velocity 163, 164
  requisite energy 162
performance:
  delusory 30
  effect of atmospheric conditions
    49, 183–4
    charge elevation 32
  lapses in 30
pitting, conflicting theories on 150–3